COUNSEL

Most High

MW01041679

COUNSEL OF THE

Most High

Karen Henein

COUNSEL OF THE MOST HIGH
Copyright © 2007 Karen Henein

All rights reserved. No part of this publication may be reproduced, stored in a retrieval system, or transmitted in any form or by any means—electronic, mechanical, photocopying, recording, or any other—except for brief quotations in printed reviews, without the prior written consent of the copyright owner or publisher. Any unauthorized publication is an infringement of the copyright law.

Unless otherwise indicated, Scripture has been taken from the HOLY BIBLE, NEW INTERNATIONAL VERSION®. Copyright © 1973, 1978, 1984 by International Bible Society. Used by permission of Zondervan Publishing House. All rights reserved.

Verses marked LB are taken from The Living Bible, copyright © 1971 by Tyndale House Publishers, Wheaton, Illinois, 60189. Used by permission.

Some words from Scripture have been italicized for emphasis by the author.

A few names have been changed to protect the privacy of the individual being referred to.

Counsel of the Most High: Receiving God's Guidance for Life's Decisions/Karen Henein—1st ed.
Includes bibliographical references.

ISBN # 1-894928-99-7

Printed in the United States of America

Dedication

To God Most High
and to the three loves of my life:
Sam, Darrin, Samantha

Contents

Chapter

1. Seeking Direction...1
2. Believing that God Does Guide Us.................................15
3. Pursuing a Relationship with God 29
4. Desiring the Right Path..45
5. Seeking Counsel through Prayer...................................61
6. The Intersections of Life..77
7. The Counsel of the Word..85
8. The Counsel of the Spirit 105
9. The Counsel of Others..141
10. Physical Signs and Circumstances 159
11. The Counsel of Collected Wisdom..............................185
12. What Would Jesus Do? 197
13. Extraordinary Counsel...203
14. Waiting for Counsel..225
15. Correcting Counsel: Being Restored to the Right Path....241
16. Acting on the Counsel of God......................................253
17. A Life of Highest Purposes..259

       Appendix A...267
       Appendix B 269
       Appendix C 273
       Bibliography...275
       Endnotes 289

Thank You Notes

I would like to acknowledge and to thank all of the family members and friends who encouraged, supported, counseled, and prayed for me during the months I was writing this book.

I would like to express special thanks to my husband Sam and to my good friends, Shirley Hutchison and Faithe Holder, who painstakingly read through, proofed and critiqued various drafts of this book. Their assistance, their eye for detail and their honest comments were invaluable. I would also, of course, like to thank my professional editor, Larissa Bartos, for her excellent work.

I would like to thank all of the friends and family members who gave permission to include stories that involved some aspect of their lives.

Finally, I would like to thank my husband Sam, my son Darrin, and my daughter Samantha for patiently bearing with me while I was absorbed in the process of researching, writing and publishing this book. Their words of good cheer helped me to go the distance.

1.

Seeking Direction

For this great God is our God forever and ever.
He will be our guide until we die.
Psalm 48:14 (LB)

The Joy of Having Direction in Life

It is easy to lose one's way in the streets of old Tokyo. In most cities, buildings are numbered consecutively. Buildings in old Tokyo, however, are numbered according to when they were built. A building numbered 22 can be located beside a building numbered 93 and across from a building numbered 158.

I wandered down a street in Tokyo one summer, trying to find a museum, knowing only its street number. As I walked, I had no idea if I was heading in the right direction. The sequence of the street numbering made no sense and offered no clues. First, I wandered one way down the street, then back in the opposite direction. It was frustrating, confusing, and tiring! I suppose that the local people know enough to ask for cross streets and landmarks. I did not have those guideposts. Being lost and wandering around without a proper sense of direction made that day feel pointless and wasted.

Some years later, I had the opportunity to drive in a new car with the latest Global Positioning System (GPS) technology. I entered a street address into the GPS system and immediately began receiving *precise directions* to my destination. I was told exactly how many miles to drive in a particular direction. I could see my progress on the computerized map on the console. I was told when to turn left and when to turn right. I could see what cross streets and landmarks to look for. When I deliberately strayed from my route to look for a gas station, the system told me that I was off course. It also told me how to get back to the appropriate route. It was amazing! Not a second was wasted. It felt wonderful *to head straight for the goal* and to arrive, unfrazzled, in a timely fashion!

Have you ever felt like you were wandering without a clear destination …without a map or a compass…without the certainty that you were on the right road? In those seasons of your life, have you felt lethargic, easily discouraged, insecure, confused, and not particularly motivated? In those seasons, did life feel flat and without much purpose?

In other seasons of your life, have you known what it feels like to get up in the morning, energetic, excited, enthused—ready to roll up your sleeves and tackle a project? *Having some direction in life makes a lot of difference.*

I have always been intrigued by stories of Biblical characters who received clear direction in their lives. Acts 9:11, for example, records the story of God speaking to a Christian named Ananias. Ananias was told to go to a street named Straight, to find the house of a man named Judas and to ask there for Paul. How I wish that God would speak that clearly to me every day!

We are not meant to wander aimlessly through life without clear purpose or direction. We are not meant to feel frustrated, confused, and tired, as I was that summer day on the streets of old Tokyo. While we cannot avoid having *occasional* days that feel wasted and futile, *most of the time* we are not meant to feel as if time is pointlessly passing by, day after day. On the contrary, God made us to live our lives with a strong sense of where we are going.

Just like the GPS system does not show the whole map from start to finish, we do not necessarily get to see our whole "life map" right away. Whether we are seeing *where our very next footsteps* will fall or *to the farthest horizon*, we are meant to have some sense of where we are on the map of our lives. We are meant to know whether we should be going straight ahead with confidence—turning left or right toward a new destination—or seeking to find our way back to the desired best route.

God created each one of us to be special. Each one of us is significant and has a unique contribution to make to this world. God has a plan and various purposes for *each* person that will utilize the best that is within them. This plan and these purposes will fit into God's bigger plans and purposes for the whole generation in which the individual lives. Just as only God could design the complex universe that we live in (where the sun, moon, and stars obey His laws, the tides know the line where they must ordinarily stop, and the autumn leaves know when to fall), only God could design the purposes for which He created more than six billion people on this present earth. Only God knows how all of those purposes fit into His overall plan. Some people will seek those purposes and choose to fulfill them. Others will disregard God's very existence and miss their most promising path.

This book is about how we can seek God's counsel to find *His specific plan and highest purposes* for our individual lives. This book is also about how we can seek God's counsel and direction regarding our more minor *everyday choices*…how we can know what we are meant to accomplish *this* hour and *this* day. A single footstep may seem insignificant…but over time our footsteps take us somewhere.

Because God has given each person a free will, we all have the option of planning and designing our own life. We can try to find our own way. We can choose our own daily footsteps. We can set our own goals and choose our own destination. The Bible tells us, however, that if anyone tries to find their life, they will lose it.[1] Only if a person is willing to lose the right to control their own life by submitting to the plan and purposes God has for them will they truly find their life. The path to true fulfillment and eternal significance for each person is the path that God designed for them before they were even born.[2]

Communicating with God

In this modern, hi-tech world, we are used to a high level of communication. We are blessed with cell phones, e-mail, and instant messaging, which enable us to communicate right away with friends, family, and business colleagues. I have a sister who lives in Afghanistan and I constantly marvel at how easily I can e-mail her. As soon as I press the "send" button, my message has traveled half way around the world. I have a son and a daughter who live in residence at university. I can "instant message" on my computer with them and receive their immediate responses. My son, my daughter, and my husband never leave the house without their cell phones, so they are one speed-dial digit away from me.

Wouldn't it be wonderful if we could communicate with God in these ways? If we could "instant message" with Him...if He was on our cell phone speed-dial system...if we could e-mail Him about the decisions that we face and ask for His advice? Although we cannot, in fact, phone Him, e-mail Him, or "MSN" with Him, I believe that we *can* communicate with God far more easily than we have supposed. *We can ask Him what He has to say about any issue in our lives.*

We can ask Him what we should study in school, whom we should date, whom we should marry, when we should have children, what career we should pursue, where we should live, how we can bless those around us, what we should invest in, what we should give away. We can also ask Him about the more minor details of the present day. We can listen for His

---

[1]   Matthew 10:39
[2]   Psalm 139:13-16; Jeremiah 1:5

answers and receive them when they come. God has invited us to come boldly and with confidence to His throne. He has promised to receive us with mercy and with grace.[3] This book will explain how each one of us can approach God with boldness and with confidence. This book will examine how to *seek* and to *receive* the counsel of the Most High.

My Personal Search for God's Counsel

In my personal journey, I have been fascinated by the ways in which God has provided guidance and direction since I became a Christian in my late teens. I heard a sermon when I was nineteen years old about God's guidance. That day, I wrote down a checklist of the items to consider whenever I needed to discern God's counsel. I kept that piece of paper *for years* until it became so worn and ragged that I had to throw it away!

I have searched out hundreds of Bible verses that shed light on how God guides us. Over the years, I have spoken on this topic in various venues within Canada and beyond. I have exchanged stories about God's guidance over countless cups of coffee with Christian friends. I have learned lessons from my own life (including my mistakes!) as I have sought, over three decades of Christian growth, to find and to fulfill God's *daily purposes* and His *highest overall purposes* for my life. I have earnestly sought God's counsel regarding my education, career, marriage, motherhood, ministry, and innumerable everyday decisions. I have developed my own checklist of issues to consider regarding God's will. You can find this list at Appendix B.

I am not a preacher or a teacher. I am a fellow traveler with stories to tell—stories from the Bible, stories from history, stories about well-known people, stories from family and friends, stories from my own personal journey.

Practicing as a trial lawyer for twenty years heightened my desire to seek God's counsel, not just for my own life, but also

---

3   Hebrews 4:16

to enable me to wisely help those who came to me for counsel. I felt the weight of my responsibility to hurting people who were caught up in tragedy, loss, or conflict.

I once had a case involving a widow whose husband had died in a burning car. He had been pinned under the wreckage of the fiery vehicle and had remained conscious to the horrific end of his life, pleading with emergency personnel to pass on his final words to his family. In another matter, I tried to offer compassionate counsel to a beautiful woman who had fallen out of a motorboat after it had made a sharp turn. Her body had come into contact with the high-powered engine propeller and she had lost the use of one arm and suffered significant scarring on her face. On another occasion, I had the task of cross-examining a man whose face had been badly disfigured after he had received high-voltage electrocution.

One sad case after another crossed my desk over the years—a family had died of carbon monoxide poisoning in their sleep because of a malfunctioning furnace; a young man had suffered serious burns to most of his body after he had gone back into a house on fire to rescue his younger brother; the breadwinner of a large family had died when an ambulance went to the wrong address; a three year old boy suffered permanent brain damage when a doctor misdiagnosed his condition; another little boy has spent years in bed, also severely brain-damaged, after a near-drowning.

I sought the counsel of the Most High as I tried to discern what was the most just, fair, reasonable and decent way to resolve each case that crossed my desk. Sometimes the victim of alleged negligence was my client. Sometimes the victim was on the other side of the case, alleging that my client had caused the accident or the circumstances that had brought them in harm's way. Sometimes the client was a corporation or the government, caught up in complex conflict with individuals, companies, or insurers. Feeling inadequate because of the limitations of my own human wisdom, I constantly asked for God's help in my role as counselor to others. They depended on me for wise counsel and for resolution of the matter at hand. I, in turn, depended on the counsel of the Most High.

I wanted to learn everything that I could about seeking and receiving God's counsel, so that I could find direction in my own life, but also wisdom regarding the decisions I made that so profoundly affected other lives. I took the pursuit of truth and justice very seriously. Only God could tell me what truth and justice looked like in each case. God could also tell me the best way to help people move forward with their hurting lives and their broken circumstances.

I have often felt the same need for God's counsel in my decades of motherhood. With my own limited understanding and knowledge, I did not always know what was best for my son and my daughter. I constantly needed God's guidance and counsel regarding how to raise my children. Most of us need direction for more than just our own lives. We need direction for the many decisions we make that affect others.

Being in Step with God

Thankfully, we can be in step with God. We can receive ongoing direction for our lives and direction regarding how we can best help others. Sometimes the directions will be in the form of general principles to live by. Other times the directions will be as clear and precise as the directions that a GPS can offer. Each one of us can lead a very deliberate, purpose-filled life that achieves meaning and significance. Our lives can please God and bless the lives of those around us, just as God intended.

We can be like the apostle Paul, who said: "Therefore I do not run like a man running aimlessly; I do not fight like a man beating the air."[4] Paul strode forward with great purpose in every step. He knew when to travel to a particular destination and when to leave each place. Paul knew the race that he was meant to run and he ran to win. He ran with all his might, all

---

[4]   1 Corinthians 9:26

his heart, and all his soul. He had clear direction, and with that clarity came passion, focus, courage, and unquenchable spirit.

We are meant to have passion and purpose, direction and drive, energy and enthusiasm most of the time. We are meant to ignite, influence, inspire, and impact our world. We are meant to richly bless and serve others. *We can live such a life if we learn how to seek the counsel of God.* Each one of us can find out why God created us and the purposes for which He has sustained us to this point in our lives.

If you seek God's best plan, my friend, you will not come to the end of your life discovering that you have been climbing a ladder that is leaning up against the proverbial wrong wall. You will not find yourself struggling to get up on a Monday morning, wondering why you are going to a job that you dislike that has no point beyond paying off the mortgage. You will not lie on your deathbed feeling like your life has not mattered or counted. You will not look back on your days regretting that so many of them seemed wasted, futile and joyless. The point of this book is not to make you look backward, but to propel you forward, seeking the purposes that remain ahead of you. It does not matter how old you are. Stories in this book will demonstrate that some individuals have fulfilled their most significant purposes even in their sixties, seventies, or eighties.

If your present life does feel pointless, it is not too late to discover new purpose and to make the most of your remaining days. If you are willing to call God the Most High, and are willing to ask for His guidance and counsel, you will find yourself enjoying satisfying work, surrounded by people that you can love and bless. You will live a life of high adventure. With more than five decades, ninety countries, and six continents behind me, I can attest to that adventure! With God as your counselor, you will run the right race, my friend. You will run with conviction. You will matter. You will count. Whether you become a postman or the President, a baker or a banker, a homemaker or a social worker, a highly paid executive or a volunteer, a powerful voice or a listening ear, you will achieve all that God designed you for. You will play your part in making this world a better place.

The most wonderful part of all of this is that you do not have to be rich, have a certain IQ, be physically attractive or socially popular to achieve this kind of blessed, focused and deliberate life. You do not have to be of a certain race or citizenship. You do not have to have a stellar education. You do not have to be a certain age. You can be rich or poor, black or white, short or tall, male or female, young or old, employed or unemployed. You do not have to pass an exam or win a lottery. All you have to do, no matter who you are or where you are from or what you think of yourself, is seek to know God and His direction for your life. This book is intended to help you in that pursuit. No race barrier, glass ceiling, rejection letter or pink slip can stop you from leading a purposeful life if you sincerely desire to know Him and His plan for your life.

No One is "Too Ordinary" for God's Purposes

Perhaps your reaction to this is that you are "too ordinary," and that God could not possibly have special purposes for your life. My friend, God specializes in using humble, ordinary people. The disciples that Jesus chose were ordinary men. God still polishes "ordinary" people for His highest purposes.

I once met a Christian man in Liberia, a country in West Africa. This man owned a small autobody shop made of cinderblock and rusted corrugated metal. He worked hard to earn a modest living and cared about living each day of his life for God. I was present one day when a mutual friend asked him if he could join us for an activity later that week. This humble African man graciously declined. When pressed for a reason, this man disclosed that he would be flying to Washington D.C. He had been invited to a Presidential Prayer Breakfast being held in the White House! He had previously met some senior American government officials when they had visited Liberia. They had been impressed with the depth and sincerity of his faith and had subsequently chosen him to represent his African nation at the President's Prayer Breakfast. This conversation with this humble auto mechanic on the other side of the world showed me afresh that God loves to take "ordinary" men and women places that they never imagined they would go.

One of my favorite speakers is a fellow Canadian, Henry Blackaby, a pastor and well-known author. I recently heard him speak at a small luncheon. He told his guests over and over what an "ordinary" man he is, how he was born and raised in a small town in the country, and how he once pastored small churches. One of his chief desires in life has been to find *God's purposes* for his life and to live out those purposes.

As a result, this "ordinary" man has lived an extraordinary life. He has been summoned to give counsel to a President and Vice President in the Oval Office. Numerous CEOs of Fortune 500 companies, Christian leaders, and senior UN officials have also sought his godly advice.[a] Henry Blackaby is an example of an "ordinary" person whose life ceased to be ordinary the moment he sought God's purposes.

There is nothing "ordinary" about God's purposes in *any* of our lives. In God's plan, *all of us have places to go and people to meet.*

Our Lives are not Random

This emerging generation of teenagers and young adults have popularized the expression "That's so random." They meet someone they have not seen for a while and say "That's so random." Many do not see those kinds of encounters as divine appointments, or a part of God's intended purpose for that day. Many do not see that their lives are meant to have a plan and a purpose and that, in fact, nothing is "random."

A number of young adults I have met have no idea what they are going to do with their lives. They have no direction. They are just passing time in their school courses, their jobs, or their travels. Many are truly drifting, with no desire even to find a destination. (Some will continue to drift through mid-life and beyond!)

Please don't misunderstand me. I believe that all young people need some unpressured time to find out what they are going to do with their lives. Educational experience, experimenting with different college majors, backpacking, and temporary jobs are some ways to validly spend time while looking for answers to the big questions of life. What amazes me is that so many are not even looking for answers. So many are not searching for purpose or direction. They have bought into secular philosophies that teach that life has no ultimate meaning. It is enough for these young people to live in the "random" pleasure of the moment, assuming that when the sun rises the next day there will be a fresh set of random new experiences. Direction is of no relevance to them. This is not the path to significance in life, nor is it the path to deep and lasting fulfillment.

I can identify with these young adults, because I was once drifting, too. After one year of university (that I had not found particularly meaningful), I spent a year backpacking around Europe with my sister. Along the way, I read many secular philosophers and authors whose worldviews suggested that life was random, with no defined purpose or meaning. I remember enjoying a best-selling novel from that era that described young hippies drifting around places like Spain and Morocco. For a while, I liked the freedom of just drifting around with no pressure to go anywhere—no pressure to do or to be anything in particular.

Several experiences that year shook me out of my drifting state. One of them was the near suicide of a beautiful young woman. My sister and I were spending some time working on a farm in Norway, and one afternoon, we heard screams coming from the bedroom of the farmer's lovely wife Marit. We ran into her room and saw her bed linens covered in blood. Marit had slashed her left arm. One of the other young people working with us tried to tourniquet the arm, and while someone else called for an ambulance, I tried my best to calm Marit down. She had been thrashing wildly around, resisting help. I told her to stay still, that we would try to save her, and that she was needed by her young children. She responded that everyone had told her that she was a terrible mother. We told her that her husband needed her. She laughed, disclosing that she had found out he was having an affair. We tried to suggest other reasons why she should cooperate to save her own life, but she had a ready answer to refute those reasons. Then she suddenly lay very still. I will never forget the moment she looked into my eyes and calmly asked me: "What are *you* living for?"

I had no answer.

That question was to haunt me over the coming months. I realized that I had no real purpose for my life as I was living it at that time—no purpose beyond each day's fleeting pleasures. I could give Marit no compelling reason for living because I had not yet found one. Something felt so empty deep within.

As I continued to backpack around Europe that year, I began to search for *real purpose,* for the *meaning of my existence* and for a *deliberate reason to live.* I started on a path that led to God…to recognizing Him as the Most High…to seeking His plan and His highest purposes for my life…to wanting to know what He has to say about all the decisions and choices of my life. I have come to trust His wisdom and His love.

The Life-long Search for Direction

This search to *know God* and to *know His purposes* is not just a search for young adults. I am now middle-aged and am surrounded by men and women who, like me, are *continuing* to search for purpose and direction in their mid-life years. I have made many mid-life changes and daily continue to seek the help and guidance of God. I have finished years of education, enjoyed more than two decades of marriage, practiced law for twenty years, raised two wonderful children, and built a home, but I am still on a journey. I have weathered many difficult and painful circumstances that I would never have chosen to be part of my life. I have survived my mistakes and my mis-steps. There are destinations yet to reach, challenges to meet, and obstacles to overcome.

I left my law practice a few years ago. There are new purposes at this stage of my life. I seek the guidance and counsel of God *today* as earnestly as I did a few decades ago. I have learned that, when I stop listening for God's counsel, I can quickly become lost or find myself drifting again. I have been writing this book for myself as much as for any of my readers—I still want and need to hear God's guiding voice as I navigate the ever-changing landscape of my life.

Direction: By Default, Design or Divine Counsel

The Bible says that we reap what we sow.[5] Way leads to way. The path we are on (either deliberately or by default) leads somewhere. We will either *aimlessly* wander, drifting from one experience to the next, believing everything that happens is just random, or we can *deliberately* choose to seek out a set of clear purposes. That deliberate path can be what *we*, in our limited human wisdom, think is best, or it can be what *God* tells us is best. These are all choices that each one of us can make. Our daily choices in this regard are like seeds being sown that will bear some kind of fruit further down the road.

People seek direction in their lives in many ways. Many avidly read horoscopes. Some, even as prominent as the late Princess Diana, put their faith in psychics and New Age mystics.[b] Some read the latest self-help book or choose to follow the latest trend. Some try to mimic what has worked for

---

[5]   Galatians 6:7

someone else, negating the fact that God has made them to be special and unique. The match-making business in North America is now worth over 1.2 billion dollars. People in such vast numbers trust computerized matching services to select the person with whom they will live for the rest of their lives (or not). Countless people try to find direction in every possible way *except* seeking God and His counsel.

Yet, for many others, there does seem to be a renewed spiritual hunger in the world today, a hunger to know God. Christian books are soaring on bestseller's lists and selling millions of copies. The Bible continues to be the greatest bestseller of all time. *The Passion of the Christ* has become one of the most-viewed movies of all time, having already grossed one billion dollars. One television pastor I admire broadcasts to over 100 million viewers each Sunday. Many are questioning: "Is there a God? Can I know Him? Does life have a purpose? What are God's purposes for *my* life? Why did He create *me*?"

If you are one of these, this book will help you to understand how you can *know* God, how you *can* communicate with Him, and the many ways in which *you can receive His counsel*. Whether you are looking for answers to the "big" issues in life (what you should study, what career you should pursue, whom you should marry, where you should live, what goals and purposes will make you want to get out of bed in the morning), or whether you want guidance for the countless smaller decisions that we all make every day, this book will help you to seek and to find the counsel of the Most High.

I cry out to God Most High, to God, who fulfills his purpose for me.
Psalm 57:2

2.

Believing that God Does Guide Us

I will instruct you and teach you in the way you should go;
I will counsel you and watch over you.
Psalm 32:8

He who belongs to God hears what God says.
John 8:47a

God has a voice. He is, in fact, the supreme Voice in the universe.

Some years ago, my husband and I lived as tenants on the second floor of a beautiful old home near a world-renowned university. Robert, the tenant who lived on the first floor below us, was a brilliant professor in the field of astrophysics. He was a frequent speaker, at scientific conferences all over the world, on the evidence that he was researching about how the universe had come into being. Robert was not a Christian.

One evening, we invited Robert to join us and some of our church friends for a potluck dinner. Our friends asked him about his career and Robert tried to explain to them, in layman's terms, the complex theory that he was developing.

Robert said that scientists had discovered the presence of sound waves in the universe and that the beginning of the universe had something to do with these powerful sound waves. One of our friends piped up, "You mean sound waves like the voice of God in Genesis?" (Our friend was referring to where it states, in the first chapter of the Bible, "And God *said* "Let there be light."⁶) The professor was momentarily taken aback and paused to give the question some thought. Then he responded that the sound waves he was investigating *could* be considered analogous to a very powerful voice. These powerful sound waves are apparently still echoing out in space. God's voice has been present from the beginning of the universe. He is still speaking to anyone with ears to hear.ᶜ

God wants to counsel and to guide us. We will not likely receive God's counsel, however, unless we are first convinced that He *wants* to guide us and *has promised* to guide us. We must be convinced that God has plans and purposes for our lives. The Bible is full of stories and promises regarding guidance. Before I go on, in following chapters, to tell modern day stories and to share practical principles regarding how to hear God's voice in your life, let us look at some Biblical examples of God's guidance.

It does not matter how well you get to know me as you read this book. What really matters is how well you get to know God and His ways! If this book was just about how I have observed, perceived, imagined, or understood God, then it would be of quite limited worth. This is not, after all, a "self-help" book. It is a "God-help" book, so the focus must be on what God has done and can do.

This chapter will lay a Biblical foundation for what I will say later about how God still communicates with individuals in modern times. We will not yet focus in detail on the *methods* of God's guidance, but rather, this chapter will instead focus more

⁶   Genesis 1:3

on the *fact* of God's guidance in Biblical history and on the *general promises* God makes about providing guidance.

Abraham

God told Abraham to leave his people and to travel to a land that God would show Him[7]. God must have spoken to Abraham very clearly for him to leave his family, his home and his familiar surroundings to head off into the unknown. This was a radical move in his life. When Abraham started out, he did not know where he was going to end up. I have been to the deserts of the Middle East and cannot fathom the kind of courage and faith it would have taken to set off on the back of a camel towards the far horizon, not even knowing where tomorrow's water would be found. Abraham must have been certain that God *had* spoken to him and that He would *continue* to speak to him.

God did continue to speak to Abraham. For example, Genesis 24 tells the story of how Abraham found a wife for his son Isaac. Abraham told his servant to return to Abraham's homeland and that God would send an angel ahead of him to help him find a wife for Isaac. Abraham clearly believed that God would guide his servant to the right wife for Isaac, for Abraham had come to trust in the God who had led him through the trackless desert.

The servant traveled to Abraham's homeland, also believing that God would, indeed, guide him. The servant prayed: "…help me to accomplish the purpose of my journey. See, here I am, standing beside this spring, and the girls of the village are coming out to draw water. This is my request: When I ask one of them for a drink and she says, 'Yes, certainly, and I will water your camels too!'—let her be the one you have appointed as Isaac's wife. *That is how I will know.*"[8]

---

[7]   Genesis 12:1
[8]   Genesis 24:12-14 (LB)

After the servant found Rebecca, in the *exact manner* that he had requested, he recounted the story to Rebecca's brother Laban. The servant declared that God had led him *"along just the right path"*[9] to find the right bride.

In response, Laban and Rebecca's father replied: "Take her and go! Yes, let her be the wife of your master's son, as Jehovah has directed."[10] They believed that God had, in fact, guided Abraham and his servant just as the servant had recounted. They believed it to the point that they were able to let go of the beautiful and beloved Rebecca to send her on her own journey across the desert. She willingly left all that was familiar to her.

All of the key characters in this story were absolutely convinced that God was a God who wanted to guide them and was capable of guiding them specifically. God had prepared a wife for Isaac and had lovingly revealed who she was to Abraham's servant. This was literally "a marriage made in heaven." I am awestruck at the servant's testimony that God led him *"along just the right path."* How much I desire to be led along "just the right path". If you are taking time to read this book, I trust that this is the desire of your heart, too! God can lead you along "just the right path" to find your mate, your career, your home, your ministry, and your life purposes.

Moses

God also clearly told Moses what to do to fulfill God's highest purposes in his life. He gave Moses detailed directions as to how He was going to use eighty-year-old Moses to deliver His people from the hand of Pharaoh. The Israelites were slaves in the land of Egypt, under the merciless rule of Pharaoh. God continually told Moses ahead of time what He was going to do, what Moses should then do and how Pharaoh was going to respond. Everything God told Moses came true, as Moses

---

[9] Genesis 24:48 (LB)
[10] Genesis 24:51 (LB)

obeyed God's directions, one step at a time.[11] Pharaoh eventually let the people of God leave Egypt, just as God had planned and promised from the outset.

God's divine guidance is further demonstrated in the way that God then led Moses and the Israelites out of Egypt and eventually into the Promised Land. As the Israelites crossed the desert, God led them by a pillar of cloud by day and a pillar of fire by night.[12] According to Exodus 13:22, the cloud and the fire were never out of sight.

As the Israelites continued their long and difficult journey, Moses continued to fully believe that God *would* and *could* guide them. In Exodus 33:12b-13, Moses spoke with God: "You say you are my friend, and that I have found favor before you; please, if this is really so, *guide me clearly* along the way you want me to travel…"(LB) The Lord replied, "I myself will go with you…" (v. 14 LB) Moses had such an intimate relationship with God that we are told, in Exodus 33:11, that the Lord spoke with Moses "as a man speaks with his friend."

It is interesting that God was also leading the Israelites individually at that time, not just Moses. In Exodus 33:7 we are told that "*anyone* inquiring of the Lord would go to the tent of meeting outside the camp." It was in this same tent that Moses himself often met with God to seek His ongoing instructions.

When it came time to distribute the Promised Land in lots for each tribe and clan, Moses asked God for instructions as to how the land should be divided[13]. Whenever I read the Old Testament, I marvel at how *specific* and *precise* God's instructions to His people were, whether He was dividing land, detailing what clothes His priests should wear or giving the "blueprint" for the building of His temple. *God loves detail.*

---

[11] This incredible story is told in Exodus chapters 3-13
[12] Exodus 13:21
[13] Numbers 27:5

Samuel

God first spoke to Samuel when he was still a boy. At first, Samuel thought he was hearing the voice of the priest Eli. Eli told Samuel that it must be the Lord trying to speak with Samuel. So Samuel responded when the voice spoke to him again: "Speak, for your servant is listening."[14] Samuel continued to listen to the voice of God throughout his lifetime. For example, God revealed to Samuel which man to anoint as the first king over Israel.[15] When that first King (Saul) was disobedient, God then told Samuel that David was to be anointed as King.

I want to cultivate the attitude of Samuel: *Speak, Lord, for your servant is listening.* In following chapters, we will discuss the many ways in which God *does* speak and all of the practical ways that we can listen.

King David

King David was also a firm believer in a God of intimate counsel. Over and over in the Psalms, David either asks for or acknowledges God's guidance. In the following selection of verses, we can see David's strong conviction and assurance that God is indeed a God of guidance and counsel.

In Psalm 5:8, David prayed: "Lord, *lead me* as you promised you would;…Tell me clearly what to do, which way to turn" (LB). In Psalm 25:4-5a, David again prayed: "*Show me* the path where I should go, O Lord; point out the right road for me to walk. Lead me, teach me" (LB). David also affirmed that God "*guides* the humble in what is right and *teaches them his way*…He will instruct him in the way chosen for him" (Psalm 25:9, 12b).

In Psalm 23, David described the Lord as his Shepherd. He wrote that "He *leads* me beside quiet waters…He *guides* me in

---

14   1 Samuel 3:10
15   1 Samuel 9:16

paths of righteousness." David was familiar with the role of a shepherd as he had been a shepherd in his youth. David knew that a shepherd's task was to lead and guide his sheep, using his rod and staff to keep the sheep on the right path. The shepherd was expected to keep his sheep away from danger, correcting their course if they strayed.

In Psalm 32:8, David recorded how God had assured him: "I will instruct you and teach you in the way you should go; I will counsel you and watch over you." In Psalm 73:23-24, David recorded: "Yet I am always with you; you hold me by my right hand. You guide me with your counsel..." This is not a picture of a God who occasionally or randomly guides, but of a God who is willing to *continually* counsel us to our last breath.

In Psalm 139:9-10, David wrote: "If I rise on the wings of the dawn, if I settle on the far side of the sea, even there your hand will guide me, your right hand will hold me fast". This is a picture of the God who lovingly journeyed with David everywhere he went. Over and over again, I have personally learned that we can travel even to the far ends of the earth, and yet, God will be there, too. This is wonderful news for those who long to continually be in God's exquisite presence. (It is also an inevitable truth discovered by those who are trying to run away from God, naively thinking that they can outdistance Him or hide from Him in some remote place!)

David was a leader who regularly "inquired of the Lord." There are many examples of him doing this. Here is one: "In the course of time, David inquired of the Lord, 'Shall I go up to one of the towns of Judah?' he asked. The Lord said, 'Go up.' David asked 'Where shall I go?' 'To Hebron,' the Lord answered."[16] We do not know exactly how God spoke with David, whether by audible voice, inner impression, the counsel of others such as priests, the Urim and Thummin (see chapter 10), or by some combination of various means. All we know is

---

[16] 2 Samuel 2:1

that God's response always seemed crystal clear to David whenever David "inquired" of Him. This book will examine whether or not we can have that same level of intimacy with God.

David believed that God did more than just daily guide him. He believed that God had an *overall* purpose and a plan for his life. In Psalm 57:2, David wrote: "I cry out to God Most High, to God, *who fulfills his purpose for me.*" In Psalm 138:8, David again confidently stated: "The Lord *will fulfill* his purpose for me." To David, God was not only a Shepherd, guiding David along the changing path of his life, but also a God who *designed* a particular path *in advance* of leading David along that path. David knew that his life was not random, chance, or without meaning. That was precisely why he was so diligent in "inquiring" of the Lord.

King Solomon

King Solomon shared his father David's deep belief that God had a plan and a purpose for him. In Proverbs 3:5-6, King Solomon advised: "Trust in the Lord with all your heart and lean not on your own understanding; in all your ways acknowledge him, and he will make your paths straight." In Proverbs 4:11, God assured King Solomon: "I *guide* you in the way of wisdom and *lead* you along straight paths." In Proverbs 16:4, Solomon recognized that: "The Lord *works out everything* for his own ends." (This is a precursor to what Paul later said in Romans 8:28: "And we know that in all things God works for the good of those who love him, who have been called according to *his purpose.*")

In Proverbs 16:9, Solomon wrote: "In his heart a man plans his course, but *the Lord determines his steps.*" Like his father, King Solomon knew that life is not random. Solomon knew that he could be guided along the path and the purpose planned for him if he trusted and acknowledged God.

The Prophets

Many of the Old Testament prophets described God's plans, purposes and guidance. In Isaiah 14:24, God told the prophet: "Surely as I have planned, so it will be, and as I have purposed, so it will stand." In Isaiah 28:26, the prophet wrote: "His God instructs him and teaches him the right way."

I have always especially loved Isaiah 30:19-21: "...How gracious he will be when you cry for help! As soon as he hears, he will answer you. Although the Lord gives you the bread of adversity and the water of affliction, your teachers will be hidden no more; with your own eyes, you will see them. *Whether you turn to the right or to the left, your ears will hear a voice behind you, saying: 'This is the way; walk in it.'"* This same theme is echoed in Isaiah 48:17b: "I am the Lord your God, who *teaches* you what is best for you, who *directs* you in the way you should go." Do you not long, as I do, to hear that voice behind you saying "This is the way; walk in it"?

In Isaiah 50:4b, Isaiah wrote: "Morning by morning he wakens me and opens my understanding to his will"(LB). Isaiah expected God's counsel on a daily basis.

The prophet Jeremiah saw God in this same light. In Jeremiah 29:11, he recorded: *"For I know the plans I have for you,"* declares the Lord, *"plans to prosper you and not to harm you, plans to give you hope and a future."* God promised to fulfill those good plans if His people would turn to Him and seek His face. We will discuss throughout this book how God is a God of love, a God who wants the best for us, and a God who wants to help us and not harm us if we seek Him and His will. Believe that God has wonderful plans to prosper you, to give you hope and a future!

Confidence of Old Testament Characters in a Guiding God

It is remarkable that all of these characters in the Old Testament *knew* that God had spoken to them. The Bible states that God spoke to Abraham, Isaac, Jacob, Joshua, Moses,

David, and many others. It does not say that these people thought that *possibly* God *might* have spoken to them. These are not portraits of men who wandered, wavered, and dithered. These men were bold and confident in God's guidance, so much so that Abraham was willing to move to a totally foreign land, an aging Moses was willing to confront a very powerful Pharaoh, and David was willing to go into battle, sometimes with the odds against him. None of these men doubted that God was guiding them and speaking to them. They were willing to risk their very lives on the accuracy and certainty of the counsel that they had received.

Jesus

The New Testament reaffirms God's desire to guide His people. There is, however, a new twist. In John 14:6, Jesus describes *Himself* as "the way and the truth and the life." Jesus said, in the next sentence, that no one can come to the Father except through Him. The New Testament boldly proclaims that Jesus is "the way." He is not described as "one option" or "an alternative path" or "one possibility." He is called "the way." This is the critical core of the New Testament. No honest seeker of God's way can ignore this radical statement that Jesus is "the way."

In boldly asserting that He Himself is "the way and the truth and the life," Jesus said that He was speaking on behalf of God the Father. In John 14:10b, He said: "the words I say to you are not just my own." Some have tried to define Jesus as simply a good teacher. But Jesus does not let you see Him as merely this. He describes Himself as *the Son of God*.[17] His followers recognized Him as the Son of God.[18] This forces every reader of the Bible, and every seeker of the Christian faith, to decide whether or not it is true. Each one of us must *dare to believe this* or dare *not* to believe it. We cannot escape making a choice. If

---

[17]   Matthew 16:16-17; John 10:36-38; John 5:19-27; John 14:13-14
[18]   Matthew 16:16-17; John 3:35-36

we try to escape, then the decision will be made—in the negative— by default.

In *Mere Christianity*, Oxford professor and author C.S. Lewis brilliantly argued that a man who was *merely human* who made the kind of claims that Jesus did would not have been a great moral teacher. He would either be a lunatic (Lewis delightfully compares him to a man who claims to be a poached egg) or else he would be the Devil himself. C.S. Lewis asserted that we can call Jesus a fool or a demon, or we can worship Him as God, but we cannot let Him merely be a wise human teacher. By claiming to be the Son of God and "the way, the truth and the life," Jesus did not leave that option open to us.

C.S. Lewis presented us all with this challenge, described as the great trilemma: each of us must make a decision about Jesus and who He is—Lord, liar or lunatic. I totally concur with Lewis' logic: either Jesus is, in fact, "the way," or He was the greatest con artist or megalomaniac who ever lived.[d]

If you have not made up your mind on this issue, my friend, then I invite you to give it thought as you read through this book. Refusing to make a decision will actually *be* a decision to reject Jesus as the Son of God.

One of my favorite stories about Jesus is the story of how He spoke with His weary and discouraged disciples after they had been up all night fishing. In the morning, Jesus asked them if they had caught any fish. When Peter and the others responded in the negative, Jesus *counseled them* to throw their net on the other side of the boat. John 21:6 records that, when they listened to Jesus, they could not haul the net in because of the large number of fish.

I want to know where to throw my net in! I want to discover how my net can overflow, too! I do not want to waste another minute of my life trying to follow my own limited wisdom, fishing all night *on the wrong side of the boat*. Jesus did not come to spoil our fun in life. He came that we might have life and have it to the full! [19]

If we are sincerely seeking the counsel and guidance of God, then we must come to terms with His Son Jesus and who He claimed to be. We cannot disregard Jesus and expect to receive the counsel of God. God's revelation to mankind did not end with the Old Testament. In fact, God's revelation to mankind did not end with the life, death and resurrection of Jesus. God's revelation to mankind continues with the Holy Spirit.

The Holy Spirit

Jesus taught and counseled His followers face-to-face while He lived here on this earth. Just before His death, Jesus promised, in John 14:16-17: "I will ask the Father, and he will give you *another Counselor* to be with you forever—the Spirit of truth." Jesus was referring to the Holy Spirit. In John 16:13, Jesus further promises: "When he, the Spirit of truth, comes, *he will guide you into all truth*. He will not speak on his own; he will speak only what he hears, and he will tell you what is yet to come." We will spend a whole chapter talking about how we are meant to receive counsel through the Holy Spirit speaking to us. This is one of the most exciting dimensions of the Christian life.

Paul

Paul, one of the greatest leaders of the early Christian church, believed that God has a specific will or plan for each person and that He wants to communicate His purposes to us. In the first chapter of Ephesians, Paul discusses how God has made known to us "the mystery of his will" which "he purposed in Christ." Paul went on to say that: "In him we were also chosen, having been predestined according to *the plan* of him who

---

[19] John 10:10

works out everything in conformity with *the purpose* of *his will..."*

In Romans 12:2, Paul stated: "Do not conform any longer to the pattern of this world, but be transformed by the renewing of your mind. Then you will be able to test and approve what God's will is—*his good, pleasing and perfect will."* In Colossians 1:9, Paul said: "For this reason, since the day we heard about you, we have not stopped praying for you and asking God to fill you with *the knowledge of his will* through all spiritual wisdom and understanding."

In Hebrews 12:1, Paul refers to "the race marked out for us." Paul, referring to his own race, said in 1 Corinthians 9:26, "I do not run like a man running aimlessly..." Paul had very clear aim in his life. How much energy and focus there is when we run with clear aim! Throughout Paul's letters, the theme recurs that God does have a will, a plan and various purposes for *each* Christian, and He wants to communicate those to us.

All of us have a race to run. God does not just call the great and the mighty, prophets, priests, or kings. As we discussed in the last chapter, He calls ordinary men and women. Jesus called fishermen as His disciples. He reached out to prostitutes, the handicapped, the marginalized, and young children.

Paul was not talking to an elite few. He was talking to *everyone* who was willing to read his letters, both then and now. He was talking to the rich and the poor, the weak and the strong, the educated and the uneducated. He was talking to Jews and to Gentiles, men and women.

Being Convinced

We will return to some of these verses in more detail later. At this point, I hope that you *are* convinced that the God who has revealed Himself in the Bible *is* a God of guidance and counsel. In following chapters, I will give examples of how God has led people through recent centuries and of how He still leads and guides people *today*. This book is being written for those who are *willing to believe* that God does have plans and purposes for their lives and that He longs to reveal those purposes.

My friend, God cares about the little details and the big details of your life. He cares about every step you take. He wants you to know where to cast your net so that it can be overflowing with fish. The Lord will be your Shepherd if you are willing to let Him be. He wants to reveal the best path and the highest purposes for each of our lives. He wants to show us, one step at a time, one day at a time, how to follow that path. My prayer is that God will fill each one of us with the knowledge of His will through all spiritual wisdom and understanding.

God's voice is still the commanding and supreme Voice in the universe. The world's most brilliant scientists are only beginning to understand the sound waves that have permeated the universe from the beginning of time. Detectable waves continue to echo through the universe. God's voice has been speaking from the creation of the world.

God is *still speaking* to anyone with ears to hear.

I will praise the Lord, who counsels me.
Psalm 16:7

Whether you turn to the right or to the left, your ears will hear a voice behind you, saying: "This is the way; walk in it."
Isaiah 30:21

Settle this point then, first of all, and let no suggestion of doubt turn you from a steadfast faith in regard to it, that divine guidance has been promised and that, if you seek it, you are sure to receive it.
Hannah Whitall Smith[e]

3.

Pursuing a Relationship with God

...anyone who does not take his cross and follow me is not worthy of me...whoever loses his life for my sake will find it.
Matthew 10:38-39

When I was a child, I loved cracking open my fortune cookie after a Chinese dinner. I would unfold the little white paper with anticipation, eager to discover what was going to happen with my life. As a teenager, I read the horoscope section of my teen magazines, hoping to get a glimpse into my future. With equal eagerness, I once had my palm read and was told that I would have six children. (Thankfully that was not accurate—I do not have that much energy!) I briefly flirted with crystal ball reading. I wanted it to be *that fast, that cheap* and *that easy* to find the best path for my life, but these methods of seeking direction in my life were futile. I was on a counterfeit spiritual search that brought no clarity of direction or purpose.

Only God knows our destiny. All of us actually have two potential destinies—a destiny that conforms to God's plan for our life and a destiny of our own choosing that, by design or default, is a rejection of God's plan. Once we believe that God does indeed have a *plan,* a *purpose,* and a *path* for our individual lives, we can ask Him to reveal that plan to us. As we pray for this, however, the *basis* on which we approach God is of utmost importance.

God will not reveal His specific plan for an individual life to the merely curious, nor to those who want to check out what the plan is before they decide whether to take it or leave it. God is not a cosmic fortune cookie, ready to reveal the secrets of the future to those who might laugh at the fortune or who would readily discard it if the fortune were not suitable. Seeking the counsel of God is not a flippant exercise. I learned this the hard way. In my early search to know God and His will I was half-hearted, easily distracted, not fully committed to God, and still intrigued by other philosophies. I was seeking God's will while I was still reading fortune cookies, horoscopes, and crystal balls. If you are reading this book out of mere curiosity, hoping to find some "quick fix" for your life by "checking out" God's will to see if it suits you, you will find either disappointment or challenge.

We must have a *relationship* with God before He will give us detailed guidance and counsel in our personal lives. This relationship begins like any other: seeking to know *about* God, and then seeking to actually *know* Him. Unlike other relationships, however, we cannot truly come to know Him unless we are prepared to *submit* and *surrender* to Him on His terms. His terms are non-negotiable. God is not our equal.

Let us look more closely at some of the Psalms. In Psalm 5:8, David cried out: "Lead me, O Lord…" He was making this request of a God that he was *bowing down* to. In Psalm 16:7, David wrote: "I will praise the Lord, who counsels me…" God had the lordship of David's life and was the object of David's adoration and praise. In Psalm 25:4-5, David again requested: "Show me your ways, O Lord, teach me your paths; guide me in your truth and teach me, for you are God my Savior…" Later, in verse 12, David said: "Who, then, is the man who fears the Lord? He will instruct him in the way chosen for him." David was seeking guidance from a God he clearly acknowledged as His Lord, His God, and His Savior. We must similarly approach God with respect and reverence.

Seriously Seeking God

Before we can find God's will for our lives or His counsel for our daily decisions, we first have to *find God*. We need to find out who God is and what He has to say about Himself. The seeker of God's *counsel* must first be a serious seeker of God *Himself*. God promises that if we seriously seek Him we will find Him.[20]

God has revealed to mankind who He is in the Bible. The Bible is full of many general truths about God: His character, His desire to have a relationship with each person, and the requirements of such a relationship. The Bible has been written in such a way, however, that only the *serious seeker* of God will be able to completely understand it.

If the Bible was completely straightforward, easy to read, and easy to understand, then everyone (even the cynic, the skeptic, the flippant, and the merely curious) would understand it clearly the first time they read it. Anyone who has read (or attempted to read) the Bible from cover to cover knows that this is not the case. The Bible has been written in such a fashion that only those who are *really seeking* and those who *deeply believe it contains great treasure* will fully find the great truths in it. The Bible is not one long chronological story or point-by-point essay that can be readily understood by anyone with the skill to read. It is instead a mixture of history, stories, dialogue, words of wisdom, poetry, parables, and prophecies that jump between the past, present, and future. We cannot fully understand one part without understanding its context and how it fits into the whole. What the Bible says, for example, about money in one verse has to be balanced and interpreted in light of what the Bible says in many other places.

---

[20]   Deuteronomy 4:29

At first glance, the Bible can be very confusing and seemingly contradictory.

Is God a second-rate author? Was the Bible written in such a fashion because God is not as logical and articulate as the great writers of history? Absolutely not. Even the most cursory look at nature reveals a God of flawless creativity, perfect logic, exquisite detail, and master design. We have already discussed how God loves to be exact, specific, and precise. Surely the God who designed the animals of the African Savannah and the colorful fish of the tropical seas could put together a simple, easy-to-read, step-by-step manual. We can only assume that God intentionally designed the Bible so that it would not be an easy book to read. The Bible seems designed to thwart the *scoffer* and to reward the honest *seeker*.

Just as the most beautiful gems are hidden deep in layers of rock, so some of the greatest "gems" in the Bible are "hidden" in layers of history, genealogy, stories, parables, and prophecies. In Isaiah 45:3a, God promised: "I will give you the treasures of darkness, *riches stored in secret places*, so that you may know that I am the Lord." Daniel said: "He gives wisdom to the wise and knowledge to the discerning. He reveals *deep and hidden* things; He knows what lies in darkness..."[21] This is echoed in Colossians 2:2-3, where Paul wrote: "My purpose is that they... may have the full riches of complete understanding, in order that they may know the mystery of God, namely, Christ, in whom are *hidden* all the *treasures of wisdom and knowledge*."

The great truths and purposes of God are hidden treasures that must be found. The truths of the Bible must be sought out with diligence, perseverance, and patience if they are to be fully and completely understood. Deuteronomy 4:29 tells us that if "you seek the Lord your God, you will find him if you look for him with all your heart and with all your soul."

---

[21]   Daniel 2:21-22

Searching for God, His truth, and His counsel is not an exercise for the half-hearted.

The Bible can also be compared to a puzzle. If we look at one puzzle piece, we do not have much insight into what the final scene will look like. That one piece might not provide any clue at all. The more pieces we look at, however, the more clearly we can see the whole picture. We will not see the whole puzzle unless we are prepared to do the work of fitting the pieces together, one at a time. Only then does the picture emerge, slowly but surely. We do not have to be smart and we do not have to be educated to put the puzzle together—we just have to be willing to work on the puzzle, one piece at a time. We come to know about God (who He is, His desire to have a relationship with us, and the requirements of such a relationship) one piece of the puzzle at a time.

The Bible is not meant to be casually read over the course of a weekend or on a long flight somewhere in the same way that most other books can be read and digested. I am a fast reader and could read almost any book in the course of a holiday on the beach, but could not begin to imagine reading the Bible cover to cover so casually and so quickly. I have read it a few dozen times and am still finding more and more "hidden gems" with each reading. I am increasingly convinced that the work of searching for the treasure is well worth it. But make no mistake—it is work. As Christians, we must first work at understanding God's *general* purposes for *all* men and women. It will take further committed work to discover God's *specific* and *unique* purposes for our own personal lives.

If you are not a Christian, the best place to start unlocking the mysteries of the Bible is to read the four Gospels (Matthew, Mark, Luke and John) at the start of the New Testament. These explain how you can come to know God through His Son Jesus Christ. We will talk more about this in a moment. Once you understand this first and most important piece of the puzzle, the process of fitting together the rest of the pieces becomes much easier. You do not need money or intelligence. You do not need to come to God with "enough" good deeds. God will lovingly help you to put the puzzle together if you are seriously seeking Him.

Seeking to *Know* God

At the initial stage of our spiritual journey, each of us first learns *about* God. We learn *about* God (the Father), *about* Jesus (His Son), and *about* the Holy Spirit (who comes to indwell us after we have entered into a relationship with God). God, however, does not just want us to know *about* Him. He wants us to *know* Him.

Let me illustrate by some well-worn but effective examples. In high school, you might have had a crush on a member of the opposite sex. You then set out to find out everything you could *about* them. You wanted to know where they lived, how old they were, what classes they were in, what sports they played, and what else interested them. For a while, you might have been too shy to talk to this person. You learned a lot *about* them, but you still did not *know* them. Before you could *know* this person, you had to enter into a relationship with them.

Similarly, I might read a lot *about* a particular public figure that I admire. I can read all kinds of books *about* them. It would not be fair to say, however, that I *know* them. So it is with God. At a certain point in our spiritual journey, we must cross the line that separates knowing *about* Him to actually personally *knowing* Him.

It is when we enter into a real *relationship* with God that we begin to understand what He is saying in the Bible. Jesus talked about those who "see" or "hear" the words of God with their physical senses but remain spiritually "blind" and "deaf" to them.[22] The secrets and mysteries of the Bible need to be revealed by the *Spirit*. They are revealed, as a gradual process,

---

[22] See, for example, Jesus' words in Matthew 13:11-16

to those who are open to the truth and sincerely seeking to *know God.*[23]

According to 1 Corinthians 2:14, spiritual matters can only be truly grasped by those who have the help of the Spirit (who indwells those in *relationship* with God): "The man without the Spirit does not accept the things that come from the Spirit of God, for they are foolishness to him, and he cannot understand them, because they are *spiritually discerned.*" In John 8:47 Jesus says something similar: "He who belongs to God hears what God says. The reason that you do not hear is that you do not belong to God." When Jesus appeared at Emmaus to His followers and disciples after His death, "He opened their minds so that they would understand the Scriptures."[24]

Knowing God is crucial to receiving full knowledge of His general purposes for all mankind and knowledge of His specific plan for our individual lives. God reveals very little to the cynic, the mocker, or the skeptic who has no interest in getting to know Him. Cynics may be served a few appetizers, but they do not receive the full meal. Mockers might not see anything at all. In Proverbs 14:6, King Solomon observed: "The mocker seeks wisdom [but] finds none."

When Jesus was here on earth, He did not always readily answer all men. Jesus spoke freely with His disciples. He did not always speak to His enemies. Just before His death, King Herod "plied him with many questions, but Jesus gave him no answer."[25] Jesus was often silent in the presence of those who mocked Him. Those who mock and disparage the Bible will, not surprisingly, find it makes no sense to them. They will readily conclude that it is nonsense. They will have neither eyes to see nor ears to hear. They will remain spiritually blind and deaf. Because they do not know God, they will smugly conclude that He does not exist.

---

[23]   There are sometimes exceptions to this, such as when Christians are praying and interceding for the spiritual eyes and ears of a loved one to be opened.

[24]   Luke 24:45

[25]   Luke 23:9

In summary, God will give revelation of *Himself* first before He will give revelation of who *we* are meant to be in the scheme of things. He will first tell us who *He* is before He tells us who *we* are meant to be. If we do not care about learning who He is, and entering into relationship with Him, He will not fully reveal to us who we are in the grand scheme of the universe. He will reveal, to anyone seriously seeking to know Him, that He is the Creator and Sustainer of the Universe, the Alpha and the Omega, Lord of Lords and King of Kings. He is God Most High. He will give His intimate guidance and counsel to those who come to *know* Him as God Most High.

Submission, Surrender, and Salvation

We must be prepared to *submit* and *surrender* to God before He will guide us along the best path for our lives. We enter into *relationship* with God by such submission and surrender. If we are like an untrained puppy who has to be leashed and whose master must pull and tug to lead it anywhere, this process of guidance will not work. Nor can we be like an unbroken wild horse, which refuses bit and bridle. God leaves the rebellious and the self-worshippers to their own devices. We must be prepared to *submit to God* and to *surrender the course of our lives* to Him before He will be like a shepherd to us. Sheep are not led by leashes or reins. They willingly follow their shepherd, trusting that he is taking them to safe pasture. This surrender to God is part of entering into right relationship with Him.

The book of Proverbs talks about the fear of the Lord being the beginning of wisdom and understanding in our lives.[26] We cannot hope to fully obtain true wisdom, discernment, knowledge of God, or understanding of truth until we acknowledge that God is Lord. We must believe and accept that God is sovereign and supreme. We must submit and surrender to His sovereignty in our life.

---

[26]   Proverbs 1:7

In Proverbs 3:5, Solomon said that if we *trust in the Lord with all our heart* and lean not on our own understanding, if *in all our ways we acknowledge Him*, He will direct our path. God reveals His plans and purposes to those who trust Him, submit to His lordship with their whole heart and acknowledge Him in every aspect of their lives.

This submission and surrender is not an onerous thing. We come to God, through His son Jesus, because God *loves* us. Jesus also loved us enough that He was willing to die for us as a sacrifice for our sins. Jesus endured much pain, suffering, and humiliation during His last hours. *This is the measure of His love for us.* We are submitting and surrendering to *love*. God does not want to hurt us or punish us if we seek Him. He wants to express His unfathomable love to us. As we discussed in the last chapter, if we seek Him and His ways, *His plans for us are to bless and prosper us, to give us hope and a future.*[27] God wants to forgive, restore, help, heal, bless, prosper, sustain, and guide us in the context of a loving relationship.

We must be prepared, however, to submit and surrender to God on *His* terms, *not our own*. In the New Testament, God lays out His general plan for all men and women—His plan for how they can come into relationship and right standing with Him. In a nutshell, God has revealed to us that He sent His son Jesus into this world to die for our sins because of His love for us.[28] The old covenant, by which God's people in the Old Testament came into relationship with Him (by sacrificing animals to seek God's forgiveness for sins), was replaced by something even better. God revealed a new plan to reconcile sinful men and women to Himself. Jesus was the *final* and *most awesome* sacrifice for the sins of all mankind.

If we are prepared to confess that we are sinners (the greatest sins being our rebellion from God and our arrogant enthronement of "self"), prepared to turn from all known wrongdoing and prepared to accept that Jesus died on the

---

27 Jeremiah 29:11
28 John 3:16

cross for our sins, then we can enter into a personal relationship with God. We can have the privilege of being in relationship with God the Father, Jesus the resurrected Son, and the indwelling Holy Spirit. God's full counsel and revelation will come only to those prepared to submit and surrender on these terms. Colossians 2:3, already quoted above, tells us that *in Christ* "are hidden all the treasures of wisdom and knowledge." Jesus Christ cannot be left out of the relationship with God. Neither can the Holy Spirit. They are both integral to receiving the counsel of the Most High. God has revealed Himself to be a triune God.

Jesus Himself said: "I am the light of the world. Whoever follows me will never walk in darkness, but will have the light of life."[29] It is not enough to know *about* Jesus. One must *follow* Him, *submitted and surrendered*, before one can truly walk on a well-lit path. Jesus later said (in John 14:6): "I am the way and the truth and the life..." Jesus also said in Matthew 10:38: "...anyone who does not take his cross and follow me is not worthy of me...whoever loses his life for my sake will find it." We must submit and surrender our lives to God through accepting His Son Jesus and welcoming His Spirit in our innermost beings, before we will truly find our life and find our real destiny.

The Choice is Ours

As we discussed in the last chapter, each one of us is faced with a choice. We can choose a path of our own making. We can rely on "self." We can "lean on our own understanding," against the advice of King Solomon, thinking that *we* know it all. We can hope that the path of our choosing leads to certain destinations, but we all learn soon enough that nothing is certain in this life and that all paths have unexpected twists and turns. We all encounter the uncertainty and insecurity of life when events such as 9/11, the Asian tsunami, or the threat

---

[29]   John 8:12

of the flu pandemic hit the world with frightening force, affecting us all in some way.

We can spend our lives reading fortune cookies, checking out horoscopes at the back of magazines, and consulting psychics on the Internet. We can trust in the gurus of finance who forecast the economy or the weathermen who tell us whether it will rain a few days hence. We can be lazy. We can be cheap. We can be too easily pressed for time. *We can want it to be that easy to chart our course.* We can place our bets. We can take our chances. We can be "free" and decide that we do not even want a plan. We can choose to believe that life is just random, chaotic, and meaningless. All of us have the choice to live our lives in any fashion that we choose *on our own terms.*

Or we can submit and surrender to God *on His terms.* The rest of this book is for those prepared to do that. This book will make no sense or be of little use to anyone unprepared to seek God on *His* terms. If we are not prepared to accept the truths, principles, and requirements that God has already *generally* revealed to all mankind, then we cannot expect any more *specific* revelations for our personal lives. We can not pay God to reveal the future the way we would pay a fortune teller—we must pay with our lives. Jesus said in Matthew 16:24-26 (re-emphasizing what he already said in Matthew 10:38 referred to above): "If anyone would come after me, he must deny himself and take up his cross and *follow me.* For whoever wants to save his life will lose it, but whoever loses his life for me will find it. What good will it be for a man if he gains the whole world, yet forfeits his soul?"

Jesus was calling for nothing less than complete submission and surrender. We must give the whole of our lives over to Him to find life. We cannot *find* our lives first and then decide if we want to follow God. Only when we have submitted and surrendered to God will our eyes truly see and our ears truly hear the fullness of what God has in store for us.

If you do not yet have a personal relationship with God through His Son Jesus, and would like to make the choice to enter into such a relationship, I invite you to turn to Appendix A for your opportunity to begin this relationship. You will never understand the entire puzzle of Biblical revelation and truth (about life generally and your own life specifically) until this crucial first piece is put into place.

The Choice that Changed My Life

This choice, whether to live life on my own terms or to surrender to God on His terms, became real to me at the age of nineteen. I had been backpacking around Europe for almost a year, searching for answers to many of the questions I had about life. I had devoured books by the world's greatest novelists, poets and philosophers. I had spent days in some of the world's greatest art galleries and museums. I had engaged in countless conversations with people of different ages, religions, backgrounds, cultures, and walks of life. I had spent long train rides and bus rides deep in introspective thought. I had occasionally prayed.

I spent New Year's Eve that year in a small town in Greece, having a few drinks with my sister and some American friends. I left the bar on my own and became lost trying to find my hotel. I wandered down a dark street, feeling increasingly uncomfortable as I sensed a few drunken men following me down the deserted road. Instead of leading to my hotel, the road ended at a construction site. I was scared and felt more alone than at any other time of my life. I remember kneeling down and praying, asking God to help me find my way. Of course, what I wanted was to find my way safely back to my hotel that night. But in a much deeper sense, I felt at the "end" of letting "self" direct my path. I was as lost spiritually as I was physically. Living life on my own terms had brought me to this literal and symbolic "dead end." That night I decided to turn my life around. I was tired of pride, self-centered pleasure, and intellectual vanity. I cried out to God to help me find the way to Him.

I had reached a point of submission and surrender. I was willing to live life on God's terms. I wanted to begin finding *His* way. It was the beginning of finding the right path for my life, a path that has led me to much joy, adventure, fulfillment, passion, and purpose. It is also a path that has led me straight into the arms of a loving God. I have submitted and surrendered to the only *unfailing* love to be found in this universe. More than three decades have passed since that night in Greece, but I can state that God's love has indeed been *unfailing* through all of life's ups and downs.

Many Knees Have Bowed

Countless others have made this same choice throughout history, to submit and surrender to God on His terms. Rulers of powerful nations have tried to stamp out Christianity. The Romans fed Christians to the lions. Bibles have been burned and banned over the centuries. Churches have been locked or destroyed. And yet, there are about two billion Christians in the world today, two thousand years after Jesus came to this earth. The poor, the weak, the disadvantaged and the outcasts still come to Jesus, but so do Presidents, the CEOs of Fortune 500 companies, Ivy League scholars, astronauts, scientists, professors, bankers, doctors, lawyers, authors, Olympic athletes, and artists.

What is so surprising about "successful" men and women becoming Christians is that Christianity offers no special advantages to the rich, the powerful or the strong. The secular world is full of advantages for the wealthy, the beautiful, and the gifted. Christianity, in contrast, puts everyone on a level playing field. In fact, if there is any "disadvantaged" group in Christianity, it is the rich and the strong. The Bible says that from everyone who has been given much, much is required.[30] The Bible also says that it is harder for the rich to enter the Kingdom of God. Jesus said that while it is possible for the rich

---

[30] Luke 12: 48

to find God, it is like a camel going through the eye of a needle![31] Why would anyone rich and powerful (and in their right mind) come to Christ unless they had really encountered His reality?

Yet, I have seen extremely wealthy and influential men and women publicly weeping as they have become Christians. I have seen the beautiful and the brilliant literally fall down on their knees. What have they found? That God's love is the only unfailing love in this universe...that what God offers is far beyond price...that when they give to God all that they are and have, He gives back all that He is and has....that nothing they have can even begin to compare with Him.

Conclusion

The whole key to what will be described in the following chapters is this: we must choose to enter into a real, vital, and genuine *relationship* with God the Father, Jesus the Son, and the person of the Holy Spirit. God is "triune" in His nature and we cannot accept one part of His being and reject the other parts. Our relationship with God must be an intimate and nurtured relationship for us to be able to receive the counsel of God.

This makes sense. Our ability to receive counsel and direction in this life from fellow human beings has direct correlation to the degree of intimacy that we have with the person from whom we are seeking counsel. We can approach a stranger in the street and ask for directions to the nearest hospital. We would not ask that same stranger for counsel on how to save our troubled marriage. We can ask a casual acquaintance for advice about where we should vacation, but we would not likely ask for their counsel on how to deal with unforgiveness or jealousy in our hearts. We seek and receive the deepest counsel about the deepest issues from those with whom we are most intimate.

---

[31] Luke 18:24-25

And so it is with our relationship with God. Our ability to receive daily counsel from Him will depend on how intimate our relationship with Him is. All intimate relationships require work, investment and "upkeep." We will explore this relationship in later chapters, which deal with subjects such as prayer, studying the Word, and seeking the Spirit.

Your reaction to this might be that you have heard that salvation in Christ is a "free gift" that we do not have to "work" to "earn." I wholeheartedly agree. Salvation in Christ, conferring on us forgiveness for all our sins, is indeed a free gift, and we can do nothing to earn it. Our salvation is not earned by "works," but received by faith.

Receiving the free gift of salvation, however, does not mean that the rest of the Christian journey is a free ride. One of the key points of this chapter is that we must enter into true relationship with God if we are to hear His voice. All relationships take hard work. They take work in their early formative stages and they still require work decades down the road. Ask a husband or wife. Ask a parent. We must never confuse the "free gift" of our salvation, which we have done nothing to earn, with the disciplines of the Christian life. As we will explore in later chapters, communicating with God through such means as prayer and reading the Bible are called "disciplines" for a reason. They require discipline, commitment, and work! The good news is that these disciplines lead to an incredibly rewarding relationship with God that is worth every ounce of effort put into developing that relationship!

I invite you to pursue, deepen, and invest in an intimate relationship with God. God holds open His loving arms to all who would run into their embrace. He offers love, acceptance, forgiveness, blessing, and provision to those who would come to Him through accepting what His Son did for them on the cross. And to those who come, He also promises the trustworthy counsel of the Most High. Jesus calls out to us,

"Follow me!" This book is for those who want to make that choice.

For God so loved the world that he gave his one and only Son, that whoever believes in him shall not perish but have eternal life....Whoever lives by the truth comes into the light...
John 3:16, 21

Now listen, you who say, "Today or tomorrow we will go to this or that city, spend a year there, carry on business and make money...You do not even know what will happen tomorrow...Instead, you ought to say, "If it is the Lord's will, we will live and do this or that.
James 4:13-16

Come near to God and he will come near to you.
James 4:8a

...I am the Light of the world. So if you follow me, you won't be stumbling through the darkness, for living light will flood your path.
John 8:12 (LB)

4.

Desiring the Right Path

...be wise and keep your heart on the right path...
Proverbs 23:19

Some years ago, my husband and I committed to spending five weeks on a medical mission trip to Ferkessadougou in the Ivory Coast, West Africa. My husband is a medical doctor and loves doing volunteer medical work in the Third World. Ferkessadougou is in the same corner of the world as Timbuktu—it is not an easy place to get to! First, I had to convince my law firm to let me take five weeks off of work. We had to find reasonable airfare that we could afford for the whole family. When we showed up at the airport, our two young children in tow, we found out that our reservations were not on the airline computer and that the flight was supposedly full. We miraculously managed to get seats at least as far as Brussels.

Our plane was the last plane to arrive at the Brussels airport that morning before an air traffic controllers' strike was announced. We survived the bedlam at the airport (even the "up" escalator wasn't working, which was not a minor inconvenience with the mountain of luggage, including medical supplies, which we had with us!). We managed to get on a bus to Germany. The airline counter at the German airport had not, however, been advised that we had been re-routed there! We eventually got on a flight to Abidjan (capital of the Ivory Coast). Quite surprisingly, someone was in Abidjan to meet us, although we had been significantly delayed and had not been able to contact anyone. They were able to find accommodations for us overnight before we flew up to Ferkessadougou.

We would never have completed a journey like this unless we had a *strong desire* to do so. We had more than desire in this instance. We believed that this was the exact path that God wanted us to be on. Our desire to see this through, combined with our sense of mission, helped us to put one foot in front of the other until we finished our journey, overcoming every obstacle in our path. My husband and I were both convinced that this was *the right path* for that summer of our lives, and we set our faces like flint to stay on that path. Of course, God helped us each step of the way, but we also had to have *strong desire* and *determination* to see this journey through to its end.

Some years later, I was asked to be the keynote speaker at an executive outreach in Guayaquil, Ecuador. It was an awesome opportunity to speak to a few hundred very wealthy and influential Latin American women about my Christian faith. There seemed to be no obstacles when I first committed to this. In the few months between the date that I made my commitment and the date that I was expected to leave, however, some *major* obstacles occurred. My husband was diagnosed with a large and dangerous aneurysm in the aorta just above his heart. His cardiac surgeon advised him that the aneurysm was so large, and the aortic wall stretched so thin, that the aneurysm would likely suddenly burst and cause sudden death at some point soon. Open heart surgery was booked for early that fall, with my husband's recovery expected to take some weeks. After much talk and prayer, my husband and I decided that I should still press on with my preparations for the executive outreach in November.

Yet further obstacles appeared, including my daughter badly dislocating her knee (requiring crutches and physiotherapy) and my son requiring wisdom tooth surgery. I had three family members undergoing general anesthesia in the OR in the weeks leading up to my departure! With God's help, I still managed to get to Ecuador! Once again, I would never have kept my feet on this path unless I had had a *strong desire* to keep this commitment. I was convinced that this was part of *the right path* for that season of my life and I was determined to press on. My wonderful family so generously supported me!

Where there is a Will there is a Way

In elementary school, I loved reading about the explorers who circumnavigated the globe…discovered the source of the Nile…first set foot in North America…crossed America to the Pacific…and opened up the interior of Africa. You can imagine the obstacles that men like Christopher Columbus, Captain Cook, and Dr. Livingstone faced! Their desire to go where they went outweighed the difficulties they encountered getting there. You have probably heard of the old expression "where there is a will there is a way."

We have already discussed how submitting to God, on His terms, is a necessary step in the process of receiving God's counsel. It is a gate that must be walked through. Our initial submission and surrender to God must be undergirded, however, with genuine ongoing *desire* to know God and His ways. The Christian life is a journey full of its own difficulties and obstacles. No one promises an easy path. In fact, the Bible instead warns that there will be storms, difficulties, temptations, trials, and persecutions. We must *desire* this path—*desire* to find it, *desire* to stay on it and *desire* to find it again if we get lost along the way. We will never *stay on* the right path for our lives if we are not prepared to tackle obstacles and weather storms.

Right Paths and Wrong Paths in Scripture

The Bible clearly talks about "right paths" and "wrong paths" for each of our lives. Consider these verses from Psalms and Proverbs:

> You have made known to me *the path of life.* (Psalm 16:11a)

> Show me *your ways,* O Lord, teach me *your paths.* (Psalm 25:4)

> Teach me *your way,* O Lord; lead me in a *straight path...* (Psalm 27:11)

> Because I consider all your precepts right, I hate every *wrong path.* (Psalm 119:128)

> In all your ways acknowledge him, and he will make your *paths straight.* (Proverbs 3:6)

> I guide you in the way of wisdom and lead you along *straight paths.* (Proverbs 4:11)

> Do not set foot on *the path of the wicked* or walk in *the way of evil men.* Avoid it, do not travel on it; turn from it and go on your way. (Proverbs 4:14-15)

> Make *level paths* for your feet and take only *ways that are firm.* Do not swerve to the right or the left; keep your foot from evil. (Proverbs 4:26-27)

> The *highway of the upright* avoids evil; he who guards his way guards his life. (Proverbs 16:17)

Listen, my son, and be wise, and keep your heart on the *right path*. (Proverbs 23:19)

One of the "wrong paths" most often referred to in Proverbs is the path of sexual immorality. Proverbs 7:25-27 warns about the sexually immoral woman and cautions: "Do not let your heart turn to her ways or *stray into her paths*. Many are the victims she has brought down...Her house is *a highway to the grave*, leading down to the chambers of death." Finding the right path and avoiding the wrong paths is not a light matter. There are destructive dangers and serious snares on the wrong paths.

A study of these and other similar verses teaches us that in life there are right paths and wrong paths, straight paths and crooked paths, good paths and evil paths. We will come to many crossroads in our lives. Many times we will face the choice of whether to keep going straight or whether to take a detour around an apparent roadblock. Many times we will have to decide whether to turn right or left or even to turn back.

From the outset, there is a guiding principle that will make many of the decisions quite clear. The guiding principle from Scripture is quite simply this: to choose, then to stay on or to get back on, the "good" path and the "right" path. Its corollary is to avoid (or to get off of) the "evil" path, the "crooked" path, the "wrong" path. If we always choose to do what we believe is "good" and "right" (instead of what we believe to be "bad" or "wrong"), we will not likely miss God's best plan for our lives.

We make choices every moment of every day. We choose to act in love (or not). We choose to have faith or fear. We choose to have hope or despair. We choose to say something kind or something hurtful. We choose to tell the truth or to lie. We choose to build someone up or to tear them down. We choose to get out of bed or to sleep in. We choose to eat a healthy meal or a not-so-healthy meal. We choose to press on or to quit. To be diligent or lazy. To be moral or immoral. To forgive or not forgive. A thousand times a day we choose the right path or the wrong path, the path of good or the path of evil, the path that keeps us going straight to a worthy destination, or the crooked path that leads us to snares, traps, distractions and even destruction—the path of "life" or the path of "death."

A Matter of Desire

Let me reinforce this basic truth: if we hope to find the right path in our lives, hour by hour, day by day, over the course of our lifetime, we must have a *strong desire* to find that *right path*. If our desires are to be selfish, to get ahead at any cost, to succeed using any means, and to please only ourselves, then we will not find the right path. If our desires are to do what is good at all times, what pleases God, and what is consistent with what we know about His truths and principles, then we are likely to *find* and to *stay on* (or to *get back on*) the right path.

We will not find the right path by randomly stumbling around, hoping to find it by chance or luck. We will not find the right path by wandering all over the world, thinking that merely accumulating miles will lead us there. We will not find the right path simply because we may be rich or powerful, intelligent or charming. We will not find the right path because we join a special club or have the coolest friends. Having wealth, pedigree, status, education, celebrity or popularity will not provide us with a fast-track to the right path. *We will only find the right path if we deeply desire it.* Having found it, we must deeply desire to *stay on it* (or to get back on it). Our desire to stay on that right path must be greater than the force of the storms we will encounter. Our desire must be stronger than the enemies who will come against us and bigger than the obstacles that will appear to block our path. We will not "go the distance" without sincere and deep desire.

If I do not *desire* to lose ten pounds, what are my chances of losing them? If I do not *desire* to visit a particular place, what are my chances of getting there? If I do not *desire* a college education, what are my chances of receiving one? If I do not want to volunteer deep in the African bush, what are my chances of finding myself there? If I do not *desire* to be a good person, what are my chances of being a good person? If I do not *desire* to follow the ways of God, what are my chances of finding them? If I do not *desire* to know the counsel of God, what are my chances of receiving it and following it?

God's Love

What motivates us to find and to stay on the right path? There may be many motivations, but the one that will do the most to keep us on that path is a *deep desire* to be in *continual right relationship* with a loving God. God created us. Everything good in our lives has ultimately come from Him. God wants to bless us. He wants the very best for our lives. He wants us to be fruitful and fulfilled. He has wonderful plans for us. He wants to walk with us and talk with us, and if we truly grasp this love, we will want with all of our hearts to stay on the path where He is walking beside us. We will come to so deeply value His presence, His comfort, His help and His guidance that we will feel lost and alone the moment we stray from the path where He walks. Our recognition of God's *exquisite love* for us and the love we feel for Him in return will become the prime reasons for deeply and sincerely desiring to walk on the right path.

If we walk the right path because of a sense of duty or to please someone else (like a parent or spouse) or to impress the world, we will have trouble staying on it. The journey must be a journey of love or we will not likely stay the course. With wrong motivation, we will not survive the rough parts of the road. We need our hand firmly placed in the comforting hand of a loving God when the going gets rough.

If we really believe that God loves us, then we will also be able to readily believe that He *always* has our *best interests* at heart (even when circumstances appear otherwise). If we really believe that God loves us, we will want to know what He has planned for us. If we really believe that God loves us, we will *know* that the right path is a path that will ultimately bless us, prosper us and not harm us.

Proverbs 8:32b promises: "Blessed are those who keep my ways." Similarly, Deuteronomy 5:33 promises: "Walk in all the way that the Lord your God has commanded you, so that you may *live* and *prosper* and prolong your days..." In 1 Kings 2:3, we read: "Observe what the Lord God requires: Walk in his ways...and keep his laws and requirements...*so that you may prosper in all that you do and wherever you go*..." Jeremiah 29:11 assures us: "'I know the plans I have for you,' declares the Lord, *'plans to prosper you and not to harm you, plans to give you hope and a future.'*" Is there anyone who does not desire blessing, prosperity, hope, and a future? Are you prepared to overcome the obstacles and weather the storms if you know your path will ultimately lead to the *wonderful provisions* of *a loving God*?

We will desire the right path more and more as we realize that this is what keeps us in close relationship with God. Jesus said in Matthew 12:50: "Whoever does the will of my Father in heaven is my brother and sister and mother." We are in kinship with the living God when we sincerely seek to be in the very centre of His will. We can walk in step with Him, drawing on His strength, peace, wisdom, love, and constant help.

When we do not seek or follow God's will for our lives, then we forfeit true relationship with Him. Jesus said in Matthew 7:21: "Not everyone who says to me, 'Lord, Lord,' will enter the kingdom of heaven, but only he who does the will of my Father..." This is a sobering verse. It is not enough to know *about* God or to *claim* to know Him. We must also seek to know His will and then to obey it with His empowerment. We must cherish and cling to the right path.

No one stays on the right path every moment of his or her life. We all make some poor choices. We all yield to some temptations and wrong desires. We all know what it feels like to choose bitterness, selfishness, unforgiveness, unhealthy habits, laziness, or cruel words.

The Bible warns us that we will reap what we sow.[32] When we begin to reap unhappiness and destruction in our lives, we have yet another choice to make. Will we *keep on* making wrong choices and choosing the wrong path, or will we desire to get back on the right track? It is never too late to desire the right path. It is never too late to *get back on* the right track. God's grace and mercy are always waiting for us back on the right path. But we will never be able to leave behind wrong choices, wrong habits, wrong attitudes, and wrong relationships unless we desire to leave them behind.

In the last chapter we talked about submitting and surrendering to God. An attitude of submission and surrender to God can only be maintained over a lifetime if we *want* it. We must *want* God to reign in our lives more than we want "self" to reign. We must *want* to return to Him and to His love. He is always ready to love us, forgive us, and restore us. I know this well because I have had to seek that forgiveness and restoration many times in my life. It does not matter, my friend, how old you are or what mess you think you have made of your life. It is not too late to find the path that God wants you to be on. Even now there is hope and a better future waiting for you!

If you find yourself straying off the right path over and over again, going off on paths that you know are wrong, then ask yourself whether you really believe that God loves you and that He wants the best for you. If you do not deeply believe that, my friend, you will likely have trouble desiring and successfully staying on the right path. You must *settle in your mind*, once and for all, *that God loves you and has a wonderful plan*

---

[32] Galatians 6:7

for you. You must *settle in your mind* that God's plans and purposes for you, although they will sometimes be costly, are plans that ultimately lead to blessing and significance. There will indeed be storms to buffet you, and you might sometimes be bruised and battered along the way, but *God loves you and has a wonderful plan for you.* There is no point in reading further until you have this settled in your mind, once and for all.

You might have suffered so much pain and abuse in your life that you will need some counseling to help you reach the place where you can settle this in your mind. I pray that each person reading this will reach a place where they can joyfully believe that God loves them and that He wants the best outcome for their life.

Way Leads to Way

Way does indeed lead to way. If we choose to be on a certain path today, then we will wake up tomorrow morning still on that path unless we make a conscious change.

I remember going through a period in my early twenties when, although I considered myself a committed Christian, I was mostly hanging out with friends who were not Christians. The majority of the men I met and socialized with were not Christians. This was the pool of men who asked me out on dates. I was discomforted by the fact that I was not meeting any Christian men. I wanted to marry someone who shared my faith and my values. I used to complain about the lack of Christian men to anyone who would listen. The years were passing and I bemoaned the fact that I was not married when so many of my friends were getting married. I was constantly trying to find "dates" to escort me to the weddings of my friends.

Silly as it may sound, it took me some time to recognize that I was not likely to meet a Christian mate unless I primarily *desired* to socialize with Christian friends and to fellowship in Christian settings. (Of course, all of us should still enjoy the friendships of neighbors and colleagues who are not Christians, but these should not be our marriage prospects.) My excuse was that I was deeply involved in my university studies and then in launching my career. Most of my classmates, and later my colleagues, were not professing Christians. But I enjoyed their company.

I had to reach a place where I decided *deliberately* and *consciously* to start going to church more regularly and to attend a weeknight program at our church called "College and Careers." I had to come to a point where I *deeply desired* more Christian fellowship. Once I made that choice and *was on that path*, I began to make many close Christian friends. Around that same time, my future husband reached the same realization, developed the same desire, and began to make the same choices. It is only when we were both on that path that we met each other, began dating and eventually married. What amazes me, even now as I look back, was that it took me so many years to realize that I was on the wrong track socially if I hoped to date Christian men.

The path we are on determines the friends we will make, the people we will date and marry, the opportunities that will come our way, and the people who are available to give us advice. Way leads to way. *What we desire most* will determine what path we find ourselves on.

The Right Path Can Be Dark and Difficult

As we have already seen, the right path is not always the easiest path or the most popular path. Matthew 7:13-14 tells us this: "Enter through the narrow gate. For wide is the gate and broad is the road that leads to destruction, and many enter through it. But small is the gate and narrow the road that leads to life and only a few find it." The good news is that the right path is usually not too crowded. You will not get stuck in traffic gridlock!

Psalm 23 talks about God being David's Shepherd and leading him to green pastures and still waters. We all love to memorize verses like that. But Psalm 23 also talks, just a few verses later, about David being led through the "valley of the shadow of death." We must *stay on* the right path even if it is dark and difficult in places, even if it is lonely. It is inevitable that we will all encounter tough times, painful places, forceful storms, and unsolicited enemies. This does not necessarily mean that we have stumbled off the right path. These difficulties might come precisely because we are on the right path. The challenge is to press on, desiring to be on the right path no matter what.

More Examples from Life

I have had many goals and desires in my life, some good, some not so good, some more God-centered than others. Now, as I start my fifties, I have finally created for myself a very simple mission statement that sums up my greatest and deepest desire at this stage of my life. For the rest of my life, I desire to know God, to know His will, and to seek the empowerment of His Spirit to fulfill it. I pray that my desire remains stronger than any obstacles I face, for I know that this "right path" will have its dark, difficult and lonely hours! But there will also be wonderful blessings and rewards, fruitfulness and fulfillment. I want to reach my highest potential, to run my race to the finish line, to bear good fruit even into old age, and to enjoy my life to the fullest in the centre of God's will! God's best path for my life will take me there.

I have surrounded myself with friends of similar mindset. My husband and I enjoyed a dinner party a while ago with a wonderful Christian couple that we have known for years. This husband and wife are deeply committed to God and have always desired God's best path for their lives. The husband built a very successful career in the technology sector, rising to a senior executive level. He made an excellent income. As the years progressed, however, both he and his wife realized that he was traveling far too much. This, they agreed, was taking too much of a toll on their marriage and family life.

They began to pray for God to show them whether to stay on that path or to make a change. As they earnestly sought God on this, the husband learned that his company was planning to use the technology he was working on as a means to market pornography in order to help the company keep its competitive edge. At that point, it was clear that a career change had to be made. Our friend had to walk away from his job and its financial safety net. This couple had no security or certainty as to how they were going to support their young children or pay their mortgage. God even made it clear to the husband that he was going to have to walk away from some stock options he had worked so hard to earn.

God blesses those who deeply desire the "right path," even when it costs them. As this friend went through the process of leaving his company, he was unexpectedly told that he would receive a very generous "exit package." This is extremely rare when a person voluntarily leaves their employment! This financial package would provide seed money for the new business that our friend had always dreamed of starting. The "right path" is always the best path. I am so encouraged and inspired by friends such as this couple who have had the courage and commitment to always find the "right path," at whatever cost, as they journey through their lives.

I am similarly inspired and intrigued by the story of well-known author John Grisham, who has sold about 225 million novels worldwide. While practicing law for a decade, Grisham wrote his first two novels in his spare time. His work was initially rejected by many publishers. Like any other struggling young writer, he was having a hard time getting noticed.

Grisham, a committed Christian, was not willing to compromise his values and his faith to sell his books. One of his agents tried to convince Grisham to spice up his future work with more sex and profanity. Grisham refused to lower his standards. Only five thousand first edition copies of his first novel, *A Time to Kill,* were printed and they did not fly off the shelves. Grisham was once again having difficulty finding a publisher for his second novel, *The Firm,* yet he still refused to add more sex and more swearing. He was committed to keeping his feet on the right path.

God showed up in Grisham's life in a most interesting way. A copy of the manuscript of *The Firm* was stolen before a publisher had been found. One Sunday morning, Grisham was at church. He had just come back from the store, where he had bought juice and crackers for his preschool Sunday school class, when his wife told him to call his agent. Although Grisham had never submitted a manuscript of *The Firm* to any studio, a bidding war had started that morning on the West Coast over the movie rights to the novel. The stolen manuscript must have somehow ended up in Hollywood. Grisham told his agent to take the highest bid and *went back to church.* He stayed through a long sermon, the observance of communion, and a few baby dedications. Later in the early afternoon, he received word from his agent that the movie rights to *The Firm* had sold for $600,000. An equally amazing offer for the publication rights to the book followed soon after.[f]

From that point on, Grisham became a highly successful, world-renowned author. He was successful without abandoning his principles and beliefs. Although he sometimes describes salty characters and the seamy side of town, the worldly and the wayward, Grisham is an exemplary novelist in his genre. He relies on writing quality to sell his books, not on sex, profanity or violence. He uses his fiction to advocate for the homeless, promote justice, expose corruption, challenge the corporate conscience, and press for higher professional ethics.

I love this story because it is a great example of a man committed to *staying on* the right path. Grisham put one foot in front of the other, one day at a time, trying to live by the standards and values of his faith. He refused to give in to a secular formula for success. He did not succumb to the crass standards of many other authors in his genre.

It is striking that Grisham's big breakthrough happened while he was humbly and faithfully serving young children at his church on a Sunday morning. God shows up in our lives when we are doing the right thing in the right place at the right time. Who would have thought that serving juice and crackers to a Sunday school class was the path to Hollywood success and best-selling books? It appears to me that Grisham found an extraordinary path for his life because of his desire and commitment to follow a "right path" and to avoid a "wrong path."

I have also long admired Eric Liddell, the Olympic runner whose life was depicted in the movie *Chariots of Fire.* Liddell's best running event was the 100 meter race and he was chosen to represent Britain in that event at the 1924 Olympics. When Liddell learned that the qualifying heat for the 100 meter race would take place on a Sunday, he withdrew from that race. Liddell wanted to honor the Sabbath and strongly believed that he should not run on a Sunday. That was the principle and standard he lived by and he was not willing to compromise this principle and standard, even if it meant forfeiting Olympic glory.

Liddell was allowed to run instead in the 200 and 400 meter races. He agreed to do so because those events were scheduled on weekdays. Liddell was most gifted and most competitive, however, in shorter sprints. Running in these longer distance races meant that he was racing against much tougher odds. His competitors were world class champions specifically trained in these longer distance events.

God honored Liddell's commitment to do what he believed was right. The crowds roared as Liddell won Olympic gold in the 400 meter race. The cheering crowds in that Olympic stadium have long since vanished. What remains is a shining example of a man committed to staying on what he strongly believed was the right path and the best path, no matter what it might cost him. Eight decades later, the cheers and the applause of his fellow Christians have not died down!

Moving On

The middle section of this book will explore the various practical ways that God uses to guide each one of us onto (and then along) the best path for our lives. These ways will be useful only to those who truly desire God's counsel—who truly desire to be on (and to stay on) the "right path" and the "good path." As you read through the coming chapters, be mindful of how much God loves you, how eagerly He desires to know you, how willing He is to listen to you as you pour out your heart, how keenly He desires to reveal Himself to you, how willing He is to forgive and to restore you, how much He is lovingly working in people and circumstances around you to help you find the best path for your life. Settle your mind on these facts and it will not be difficult to truly desire that best path!

...I delight to do your will...
Psalm 40:8 (LB)

*I have considered my ways and have turned
my steps to your statutes.*

*I run in the path of your commands,
for you have set my heart free.*

Psalm 119: 59, 32

5.

Seeking Counsel through Prayer

If any of you lacks wisdom, he should ask God, who gives generously to all without finding fault, and it will be given to him.
James 1:5

…Pour out your hearts to him…
Psalm 62:8

One of the joys of parenthood is being able to counsel one's children. Over the years, my son and daughter have often come to me asking for guidance. When they were in elementary school, they needed advice on designing a car powered by a mousetrap, constructing a model of a medieval castle, and "burning" a buttered document in the oven so that it looked ancient. After school, both of them often sought counsel on how to handle a difficult teacher, a mean classmate, or a tiff with a friend. In their adolescent and early adult years, there have been so many things to talk about as well! My husband and I both try to be loving, involved parents, and that means being as available as much as possible whenever our son or daughter wants advice.

God is an even *more* loving Father. How much He wants to give His guidance and counsel to His children! The Bible makes many awesome promises about what God will do when we ask Him for something. In Matthew 7:7, Jesus makes this amazing invitation: *"Ask and it will be given to you; seek and you will find..."* In John 14, Jesus promised us that, if we ask for anything in His name, God the Father will do it for us. In John 15, Jesus once again promised that, if we abide in Him, we can ask for anything and our request will be granted. In James 1:5-6, James wrote: "If any of you lacks wisdom, he should ask God, who gives generously to all without finding fault, and it will be given to him." James goes on to say, "...you have not because you ask not." God is a God who loves to give. He wants us to *ask* for all that we need, including His counsel.

We can come into God's presence through the practice of prayer. It is in prayer that we have the privilege of making requests of God. In prayer, we can ask for any good thing. *We can come into the presence of the Most High God and ask for His advice about anything!* I used to marvel at the number of people who would pay me hundreds of dollars an hour for my legal counsel, but who would never take the time to ask God for His counsel! God's counsel does not cost money and it is infinitely superior! Of course, there are times when we need to seek counsel from fellow human beings, but we should not neglect to seek God's counsel, too!

Once we are prepared to submit and to surrender to God on His terms—once we desire to know Him and His plan for our lives—then we can come to Him in prayer and make our requests for His counsel. We can ask for the revelation of His plans and His purposes for our lives. We can ask Him to tell us the best path for us to follow. We can ask Him day by day (sometimes even moment by moment!) for ongoing directions. If we feel lost and confused, we can simply ask how to get back on the right path. If we are not sure whether to turn to the right or the left, we can simply ask.

This is one of the great privileges of being in *relationship* with God. He loves us. He longs to communicate with us. He cares about every step that we take. He cares more than we can possibly imagine.

We have already quoted many of King David's Psalms. Over and over, King David *asked* God to lead him, teach him, guide him, and show him the way. Many of these Psalms are really prayers to God, requests for the counsel of the Most High. In Psalm 27:7, for example, David cried out: "*Hear my voice when I call, O Lord; be merciful to me and answer me.*" In Psalm 86:7, David declared: "In the day of my trouble, *I will call to you, for you will answer me.*" In many other Psalms David bears testimony, in the past tense, of how God had indeed led him, taught him, and shepherded him. David always displayed confidence that, if his heart was right with God, God would answer him when he prayed. Each of us can have this same confidence. God may not answer us the same day that we pray (nor in the way that we might expect), but He *will* answer us.

In the books of Samuel, Kings and Chronicles, we read from time to time about how David did not know whether he should go to war at a particular time. He was an experienced military leader. He could have relied merely on his own judgment, but he knew that he should "inquire of the Lord." He did not want to go into battle unless he knew in advance whether or not God would be with him. He was a successful king because he knew how to inquire of God. One example of this can be found in 1 Samuel 23:2, where David "inquired of the Lord, saying 'Shall I go and attack these Philistines?' The Lord answered him, 'go attack the Philistines." In that chapter, David actually repeated his inquiry twice, wanting to make sure that he had heard correctly from God. God patiently confirmed that He had, indeed, told David to attack his enemy. God was with David in that battle.

Rebecca, the mother of Jacob and Esau, is an Old Testament example of a woman who had an intimate relationship with God. She felt comfortable asking Him questions about her life. When she was pregnant, she did not understand what she was feeling in her womb. In Genesis 25, we learn that Rebecca asked God: "Why is this happening to me?" Any woman who has ever been pregnant can identify with how anxious a woman can feel when her body is changing and she does not understand whether or not all that she is feeling inside is normal. "So," Genesis 25:22b tells us, "she went to inquire of the Lord." She learned that all the inner movement was because she was bearing twins who were jostling each other in her womb. God went on to tell her some details about the future of the two sons she would bear.

The realization that I could have this same kind of dialogue with God gave me great comfort during my pregnancies. My busy obstetrician often did not have much time to answer all of my questions or deal with my mom-to-be angst! However, God was willing to give me all the time in the world. I could talk to *Him* about all the mysterious physical changes I was going through.

Jesus Himself modeled the importance of prayer. He valued His relationship with God His Father. He would often take time to be alone to talk with God. Luke 5:16, for example, tells us that "Jesus *often* withdrew to lonely places and prayed." On the night before His crucifixion, He left His disciples and found a place to pray alone. He actually asked God if it was necessary for Him to have to die. At first, Jesus prayed: "Father, if you are willing, take this cup from me."[33] However, Jesus ultimately deferred to the will of His Father and continued to pray, "yet not my will, but yours be done."[34] If it was necessary for Jesus to pray about His Father's will for His life, how much more important should it be for us?

---

[33] Luke 22:42
[34] Luke 22:42

A Daily Appointment to Pray

We must all be encouraged to cultivate and maintain the habit of daily prayer. This is the way that we initiate daily dialogue with God. We will read, in the middle section of this book, the many ways in which *God speaks back* to us. He has many methods of communicating His counsel and revealing His plans to us. The main way in which *we* communicate with God is through prayer. We need to find quiet and private time each day to seek God in prayer. This is a critical Christian discipline.

In my early adult life, I prayed sporadically and not as frequently as I should have. Often some urgent need or sudden crisis prompted me to pray. One day, someone close to me challenged me to *regularly pray each day*, even if I could just afford to pray for five minutes. I accepted the challenge. The five minutes became ten minutes, then fifteen. This habit, slowly nurtured over time, eventually turned into praying for at least one hour a day. This habit is now non-negotiable. It is an anchor to my whole life that I cannot live without. If you are not already in this habit, I do not suggest that you start with an hour each day. Instead, start with five or ten minutes. Watch what God does *in response* as you maintain that habit over time!

Do I do it out of duty? No! I do it because it has become a vital part of my walk with God. Do I do it because I am super-spiritual? Absolutely not! I am an ordinary person, with ordinary weaknesses and shortcomings. I have simply realized that prayer is the encounter of an *ordinary person* with an *extraordinary God*. Do I do it to impress anyone? No, I pray alone for an hour each morning. This time of prayer is a very private time. I pray at other times of the day with family or friends or at church, but that is something different. I am talking in this section about personal prayer—of a time where I am alone with God.

I have found this hour of prayer to be energizing, empowering, enlightening, calming, stabilizing, and enriching. It is a daily time of *exquisite encounter* with God the Father, with

Jesus the Son, and with the Holy Spirit, who are all very present with me. I have learned to soak in God's love and to pour out my love, praise and gratitude to Him. All of my problems become so miniscule when I stand in awe of *who* God is and the fact that He communes with an ordinary person like me. I become aware of any sin in my life that offends God. I do not want anything to jeopardize the intimacy of my time with Him. I have learned to keep short accounts regarding my sins, my failures and my omissions.

It is wonderful, every morning, to sit in silence, solitude, and stillness. The whole world stops. All of my activities are put on hold. For one hour, there is no reason to rush...no problem to tend to...no task to accomplish. I am intensely aware of the Divine, caught up in a sense of the grandeur, majesty, power, and sovereignty of the living God. Nothing seems impossible; nothing is too difficult for Him. And so I pour out my heart: my gratitude and my praise; my mistakes, weaknesses and shortcomings; my needs and my problems; the needs and problems of those I love; my intercession for the souls of others; and my desire to serve God, to be utterly spent and used for His highest purposes.

And in that sacred hour, alone and set apart to God, I seek His counsel and His guidance. I seek to know His will, His purposes and His plans, and how I fit into them. No words can adequately describe how amazing this experience is. As I mentioned earlier, I do not come to this daily encounter out of a sense of duty or obligation, routine, or ritual. I come because my whole being craves the peace, serenity, joy, faith, trust, hope, encouragement, strength, and courage that well up in me. It is in this hour that the Spirit daily fills me afresh. It is in this hour that I can seek the counsel of the Most High and *know* that He will give it to me. He may not give me His counsel that very day (or week or month!), but I know from experience that His counsel will come.

I confess that there are some days when I am so weighed down, feeling so defeated and discouraged, that I must push myself to maintain my appointment with God. There are also occasionally times when I am angry at God or confused about something painful that has happened to me. There are occasionally times when I wonder if I really need to pray for a whole hour, because God already knows about everything that concerns me. But these occasions occur less and less often.

When I keep my appointment with God, my despair and discouragement disappear and are replaced by hope. My confusion melts away. I may not know what God is going to do about my crisis or my trial, but I finish my time of prayer confident that He will deliver and save. He will tell me what to do next. Until that becomes clear, I know that I can rest in Him. I become aware of promises such as Psalm 34:17: "Yes, the Lord hears the good man when he calls to him for help, and saves him out of all his troubles" (LB). The Spirit brings to my remembrance how God has eventually helped me to solve *every problem* over the past fifty years. He has never let me down. He has never failed or forsaken me (even when I have failed Him). Today has its fresh problems, but I know that God will counsel me about those too. He will show me how to carry on.

We are meant to have an intimate relationship with God. God describes Himself as our Father. Jesus is Lord, Savior and Redeemer, but He also calls Himself our Bridegroom, our Brother, and our Friend. The Holy Spirit is described as our Companion, our Counselor, and our Comforter. These are relationships of great intimacy. We do not need to come to God (the Father, the Son, or the Holy Spirit) with formality. We ought not to treat God as a stranger. We can pour out our hearts to Him as King David did in his Psalms—hiding nothing, freely admitting our anger, confusion, frustration, sorrow, pain, anxiety, and uncertainty. We can admit our sin and our brokenness, our fallen natures and our human weaknesses. God is never surprised if we tell Him that we are lost...that we do not know where we are going...that we do not know the answers... that we have made mistakes and messes. He wants us to tell Him if we have strayed onto the wrong path (deliberately or otherwise). Prayer is honest and transparent intimacy.

I know that I am not alone in cherishing this time of solitude and stillness in private prayer. Countless others know the richness of what I am describing. I have had many mentors in this area of prayer. Some of my "mentors" have been authors on the subject of prayer, such as Andrew Murray, Dutch Sheets, Joyce Huggett, and Stormie Omartian.

Jesus, in Matthew 6:6, counsels us to "go into your room, close the door and pray to your Father." Find a time and a place where you can be alone and undistracted. Find a place where you can relax. Begin by consciously letting go of your stress as you reflect on the fact that you are entering the presence of God. Meditate on His greatness, His power and His love. All of life's worries and cares will begin to feel much smaller. Make a deliberate decision to stop feeling anxious and overloaded as you recognize the significance of being in the presence of the Most High.

For a number of years, I spent an hour praying in my car while I commuted. While my children were young, that seemed to be the only place where I could count on a quiet, undisturbed hour. I kept the windows rolled up and the radio off. I was fortunate to be able to travel on a highway where I could immediately get into a certain lane and stay in that lane for most of that hour. I kept a safe distance from the car ahead and watched its brake lights. Then I drove on "automatic pilot." (In that hour of commuting, just for the record, I never once got in an accident or received a speeding ticket. God so lovingly protected me for more than a decade!) In the calm and silence of my car, I was able to pray. I was actually happy when there was a traffic jam or some road construction, because I knew that would give me extra time to pray! Imagine a car in the midst of "stop and go" rush hour traffic becoming a tranquil sanctuary!

I soon realized that this hour in traffic was the most important hour of my day. I treasured it. I knew, because prayer *does* move the hand of God, that I would accomplish more in that hour than in all the rest of the hours of that day. That hour blessed my law practice, all of my relationships, and every dimension of my life. In that hour, I sought God's counsel over and over in every area of my life.

I do not commute along that route for work anymore. When I now drive that route for other reasons, sometimes tears well up in my eyes as I remember specific prayers that I prayed, and how God has answered those prayers—prayers for so many things, including God's guidance as to what I should do.

In this season of my life, I have the luxury of praying in a quiet room in my home in a comfortable chair at the start of each day. I usually sip my second cup of coffee. The rest of my family has left our home for the day. The din and babble of the world is far from me. This is my time of talking *to* God. Occasionally He answers me right within that hour of prayer by impressing something deep in my spirit. Most of the time, I know that He will respond to me later (sometimes much later) in the various ways I will describe later in this book. I know that *eventually* He will help me, comfort me, strengthen me and meet my needs. Pertinent to this book, I also know that He will provide, in due course, the counsel that I request.

You may be saying to yourself that you cannot afford to pray for an hour every day. This is understandable. Life is busy and full of stress! I had that very same reaction when I first heard of people praying that long every day. I thought that a person had to be some sort of saint or monk to pray for that long. As I mentioned earlier, I suggest that you start with five or ten minutes—whatever time you think you *can* afford and *commit to*. Although it may not be immediately apparent to you, giving up this five or ten minutes will save you much time in the long run. With God's guidance, you will not make as many mistakes. You will not waste as much time. You will not spin your wheels getting nowhere. Your time of prayer will probably grow longer as you see more and more of God's answers to prayer, including the provision of His guidance and counsel. When you come to realize how much time you will save each day by receiving specific directions from God, you will "rush" to your appointed time and place of prayer.

I am fascinated by the life of a busy woman like U.S. Secretary of State Condoleezza Rice. She is often in the news, talking with this or that world leader, working on solutions to the complicated problems of the world. She is one of President Bush's most trusted advisors and one of America's most admired women. Being such a powerful woman, she is no doubt extremely busy. She apparently works 14-hour days. In a single year, she travels to dozens of countries. And yet, she is known as a woman of prayer. She is a sincere Christian woman who regularly prays for guidance, asking for God's help in making her decisions. Her Christian faith is paramount in her life. *If a woman as busy as Condoleezza Rice has time to pray about her decisions, what excuse do any of us have?* Let me challenge you, my friend: is it too much to give up five or ten minutes of your day? Where will God take your life if you are willing to faithfully do that?

Praying without Ceasing

While a daily appointment alone with God is important, that is not all there is to prayer. *God remains accessible all day.* We remain in His presence even when we go out to meet the din and the babble of the busy world; He is with us as we go out to interact with many others, to fight our battles, to tackle our problems, to roll up our sleeves, and to carry on with our work. I learned that God was with me during the days that I played with my children in the sandbox *and* on the days I fought my cases in court. He is truly accessible anytime and anywhere.

I love the letters written by a 17th century monk named Brother Lawrence. I have re-read these letters many times over the years.[8] Brother Lawrence was a simple and humble monk who worked as a cook in the kitchen of a monastery. He learned the art of having a constant dialogue with God throughout the day. Brother Lawrence wrote that he made it his business to be in God's presence *throughout the day*, not just during his *regular time* of prayer. He learned how to talk with God on his knees, but also during the busiest moments of his day. He learned how to commune with God while he chopped vegetables and stirred pots. He recognized that God is *always* intimately present with us. God can be addressed anywhere and anytime.

It is easy to rationalize that we are too busy, that our days are too full for prayer. But stop to realize that it takes just as long *to frame a prayer* to God about something as it takes to *frame a thought*. If we are going to invest time *thinking* about something, then why not invest that exact same amount of time *praying* about it? For example, I can *think*: "I don't know what to do." Or I can *pray*: "Lord, I don't know what to do. Please help me." I can *think*: "So and so makes me really angry and I don't know how to deal with her." Or I can *pray*: "Lord, you know that so and so makes me really angry and you know why. Help me to know how to deal with this."

This *invites God* into every decision, small or large, and into the moment by moment choices we make in every relationship and in every circumstance. As Brother Lawrence so clearly learned, it can become a *habit*, as second nature as breathing. Prayer can become a *substitute* for many of our thoughts. Why spend so many moments *talking to yourself* (as if you know all the answers!) when you can spend the same amount of time *talking to God* (who assuredly knows all the answers and longs to reveal them to us!).

I love to pray after I finish a conversation and am not sure what to think or feel or do: "God, what do *You* have to say about all of this? What do *You* think? What should I do?" God has been present for the whole conversation. He knows the surrounding circumstances and the pending choices. I don't have to repeat it all or explain it all or describe it all (unless it helps me to clarify the issues). I have already heard what the other people have had to say in the conversation. I already know what I have thought and said. So then I consider this: *Why not ask God what He thinks about it all?* Why not ask Him and expect that He will tell me His thoughts? Asking God what He has to say about my situation takes a matter of seconds.

We can do the same sort of thing whenever we sit down to mull over the pros and cons of a particular decision. We might have to decide whether to go with option A or option B. We can simply ask God: "Lord, what do *You* think? What is best?" We can invite God into the process by silently praying these two sentences.

Brother Lawrence wrote that we must come to see just how much we need God's help with everything. Once we realize just how helpless and powerless we are without Him, we will not want to lose touch with Him. Brother Lawrence had such ongoing intimacy with God that he could say that his hours of work did not differ from his appointed time of prayer. In the hustle and bustle of the monastery kitchen, while others vied for his attention, he was just as aware of God's intimate presence as if he were in the chapel on his knees.

Modern life is complex. It can be crushingly busy. We have too little time to stop and catch our breath. It is important to set aside specific time to pray (as we discussed above), but we will never find enough time to pray about the many choices and decisions we must make if we wait to discuss it all in our private devotional time. Even an hour is not long enough to pray through every aspect of our lives! The commitment to shut the door, shut out the world, and focus on talking to God is a critical daily discipline if we are serious about seeking God's counsel. But so is the kind of "Brother Lawrence dialogue" that assumes and believes that God is intimately involved in *every* moment of our day, *always* with us, *always* just a prayer away if we remain in right relationship with Him.

We do not always need to be in a chapel or in some quiet and private place to pray. This is really the same thing as what Paul wrote about when he urged the early Christians to "pray continually" (also translated as to "pray without ceasing").[35] Of course, we cannot pray every single second. But every moment we should be *aware* of God's presence with us. Just as we do not talk non-stop with a friend who is beside us, we do not talk non-stop with God. We talk when the moment requires it or stimulates it, whether we are with a friend or "with" God.

Former President Jimmy Carter is an impressive modern example of "Brother Lawrence-style" prayer dialogue. As Governor, and later as President, Carter often, even in the middle of a meeting, was observed to close his eyes, bow his head and pray for a matter of seconds while other people continued talking. Some observers thought the President was tired. In fact, this was part of President Carter's deeply ingrained discipline of asking God what *He* thought about various circumstances as they unfolded. President Carter was willing to risk looking tired, inattentive, and bored if that was the price he had to pay for seeking the counsel of the Most High. President Carter wanted God's help regarding the relentless stream of weighty decisions to be made.[h] *If a President, caught up in the pressures of that stressful office, could pause to invite God into his ongoing decisions, what excuse do the rest of us have?*

So I challenge you to cultivate and to maintain both habits, if they are not already well entrenched in your daily life. If they are, then I encourage you to press on! We must all set aside deliberate time to pray, time when we are not distracted, when we can be "on our knees" and alone with God. But we must also trust that He leaves that room with us and is with us wherever we go. In the moments when we would ordinarily just "talk" with ourselves we can choose to talk with God instead, turning those moments of thought and self-talk into valuable moments of prayer. Instead of just *thinking* about the countless decisions and choices we make each day, let us *pray* about those decisions and choices "on the go." Let us challenge

---

[35] 1 Thessalonians 5:17

ourselves to invite God into *even the most minor decisions* that we make! This practice unleashes the presence of God into our lives in amazing ways. It invites more of His love and His power into *all* of our circumstances.

God is equally interested in the *big picture*, the *important questions* and the *huge issues*. Of course, we can invite Him into the big decisions and the big issues too. We spend considerable time musing and mulling over these issues. Why not pray more and mull less? Ask for the counsel of the Most High! He is the only one who knows all of the answers. He is waiting for you and for me to ask Him!

Then Wait for God to Speak Back to You

When you have finished praying, anticipate that God *will* speak with you. Once you have said everything that you have to say, expect that God will tell you what is on His mind—what He thinks, what He desires, and what He knows is best. We will explore in later chapters the many ways in which God can and will speak *to* each one of us. Our part is to pray, then to watch and to wait, to believe that He will communicate with us. Listen for His voice, my friend. Believe that His answer will come. Wait as long as you have to wait. There is a time for you to talk and then there is a time for you to listen.

Nicky Gumbel, in his *Alpha* teaching, used an illustration about prayer that I love. Here is my adaptation of Gumbel's illustration. This example demonstrates what happens when we pray but do not then wait to hear what God has to say in response.

Imagine going to your doctor and telling the doctor about all of your problems, *then not waiting to hear what the doctor has to say*. Imagine telling your doctor that you have headaches, have trouble sleeping, have lost or gained weight, have a pain here or there, and then telling the doctor: "Thanks for listening. See you next month." Imagine leaving the doctor's office without his advice or response or help! What a waste of time and energy that would be, not to mention an act of utter stupidity. And yet how often do we do that with God? We tell Him our problems and our needs, our worries and concerns, our areas of fear, uncertainty and confusion. We tell Him all about it, but do we really *wait* and *watch* and *listen* for what He has to say in response? We must talk *to* God, but far more importantly, we must listen for *His response*.

Most of us make better talkers than listeners, whether in our earthly relationships with others or in our relationship with God. I seldom have trouble telling my husband and my children what I have to say on a topic. Listening to what they have to say is a skill I have had to work at developing (and I am still learning!), and so it is in our walk with God. It takes little effort to tell Him our woes in life, but it takes some work to listen to what He wants to say to us in response. Just as we need to listen to our loved ones whether we like what they say or not, whether it is pleasant or painful, we need to listen for God's response whether we like it or not, whether we find it pleasant or painful. Intimacy demands this.

Whole books have been written on the subject of prayer and I encourage you to read all of the great classics in this area, such as Andrew Murray's *With Christ in the School of Prayer*, for example. The subject is too broad to cover in this book. The point that needs to be made here is that prayer is foundational to the personal and intimate *dialogue* between you and God—both the habit of a devotional prayer time and the habit of spontaneous prayer throughout the day. Of course, there are also times that we can pray with friends, family, and fellow Christians at church.

Prayer is an indispensable part of the process of receiving God's counsel. I have committed myself to being a life-long student of this critical Christian discipline. I continue to learn so much with each passing year. Once I truly grasped that prayer is intimate dialogue with a loving and all-powerful God, I have never again been bored with prayer or weary of it. Prayer invites all of the mighty resources of God Most High into my humble circumstances, including His superior wisdom and knowledge!

Let us move on to explore the many exciting ways that God can and will speak to us, as He has spoken to countless others throughout history. God will respond to us. He will answer us. He will tell us His thoughts and His solutions. He will give us guidance and counsel. He will reveal His plans and His purposes for us. But we must learn to *listen* in the various ways we will now discuss.

Ask and it will be given to you; seek and you will find…
Matthew 7:7

…if you seek him, he will be found by you…
2 Chronicles 15:2b

6.

The Intersections

of Life

I am the light of the world.
Whoever follows me will never walk in darkness,
but will have the light of life.
John 8:12

The Road Keeps Changing

There are times in life when we are on a straight road, driving alongside routine and familiar scenery. It might get boring sometimes, but at least it is comfortable and we have a sense of knowing where we are going. Sometimes, we have to make a *minor* change, such as moving to another lane or adjusting our speed to a new speed limit. These minor changes take little thought. Every once in a while, however, we find ourselves at a new and unfamiliar intersection. We do not always have a map handy or a clear set of directions. We cannot escape the fact that we are at a major intersection and *a decision has to be made.* Do we stop...proceed forward (with confidence or with caution)... turn left or turn right? When the cars start honking around us, the pressure is on to decide!

God is there to help us—with both the *minor* lane changes and the pressure-filled decision-making process at the *major* intersections of life. God often uses more than one way of speaking to us and counseling us, especially if the issue is important, such as whether to marry someone or what career to pursue.

I have heard, over the years, that we should think of each individual piece of received guidance as either a red light (stop!), a green light (proceed through the intersection), or a yellow light (proceed with caution or wait until the guidance becomes clearer). This analogy has become somewhat cliché, but I have personally found this tool very helpful, however, as I have sought God's counsel, particularly on major and complicated decisions. I mention this analytical tool for the sake of those who have never heard of it.

With our most important issues in life, we should consider each of the methods of God's guidance outlined in the next several chapters. When we are at a major intersection of our life, we should discern whether, *overall*, the "light" is red, green or yellow. If the light is green, we need to discern whether to go straight or make a turn. On the other hand, with the countless minor changes and decisions it is often sufficient to rely on just one method of receiving God's guidance.

God's Main Methods of Speaking to Us

The main methods of guidance we will be discussing in the next six chapters are: the Word, the Spirit, the counsel of others, evolving circumstances, our personal storehouse of accumulated wisdom, and extraordinary means of guidance such as dreams or prophecies. We will also be briefly looking at "counterfeit" means of guidance that Christians must avoid, such as horoscopes, mediums, fortune-tellers, tarot cards, psychics, or any other manifestation of the occult.

The Color of the Light is Not Always Obvious

In Appendix B at the end of this book I have included a checklist that can be used, especially when making an important decision. Whenever we work through this kind of checklist, we need to prayerfully consider what God has spoken to us through the Word, the Spirit within, the counsel of others, the circumstances unfolding around us, our inner wealth of wisdom, and perhaps other means. We will not always have consistent red, yellow or green lights—that would be too easy! For example, if we seek the counsel of three or four others, that counsel might not be similar. Some counselors might advise that we proceed with a particular course of action. Others might advise against our proposed action. Others might say that the issue is still too murky and that we should wait until it is clearer.

Similarly, whenever we try to discern our inner spiritual impressions, we might receive some mixed signals, such as a strong desire and compelling faith to proceed mixed with some anxiety. That is why we must consider important decisions from all angles and see what the clear majority of the "signal lights" are telling us. If we conclude that *most* of the guidance we have received indicates that the light is red, then we should respect that. We need to avoid relying on a *single* verse of Scripture or a *single* source of encouraging counsel to proceed. At a minimum, if we have enough red or yellow lights, we should wait until we receive further insight and guidance. If *most* of the lights are clearly green, then we can proceed and not be overly concerned if *one* advisor disagrees with us or the circumstances are not yet perfect.

Sometimes it is hard to even see the color of the lights. Have you ever been driving towards the sun when it is getting low in the sky? It can be almost blinding. Similarly, if we are driving in fog or through a snowstorm, the colors of the traffic lights are often not visible. It is nerve-wracking to approach an intersection without being able to clearly see the color of the lights. We need to approach these intersections with great caution and slow speed. *We must not move through an intersection until we are sure of the color of the lights!* During the years that I handled motor vehicle accident litigation, I saw my share of tragic accidents which had occurred in intersections during blinding sunlight, fog or blowing snow. Intersections can be very dangerous places when the traffic lights are not clearly visible.

Sometimes we are just "color-blind." It has been my observation that one of the areas in which we most frequently hear God amiss (or hear what we *want* to hear) is in the area of dating and marriage. If we are really attracted to someone, it is human nature to want to pursue a relationship with that person. It is easy to read Scripture long enough until we find some kind of verse affirming our pursuit. I became adept at turning to "The Song of Solomon" or the stories of Isaac and Rebecca or Ruth to receive "confirmation" regarding dating someone I was attracted to. When we are swept off of our feet, it is tempting to shop around for favorable advice. It is possible to mistake our feelings of attraction and infatuation for the joy of the Spirit. If we are seriously asking for God's counsel in this area, we cannot be manipulative. We must be willing to proceed with brutal honesty and open hearts. We must seek the advice of those who know us best: parents, siblings and best friends—people we know will tell us the truth, even if it is not what we want to hear. *We should not predetermine the color of light we want to see!*

After my husband and I had been seriously dating for several months, we began praying about whether or not we should marry. We began seeking the counsel of others and listening to what God was saying in our daily Bible reading. In the midst of this process, a young woman approached my husband at church one evening. They had never dated and did not really know each other. One day, she confided in him, very seriously, that God had spoken to her. She felt that not only was my husband supposed to marry *her* but he was supposed to move with her to another province where she had accepted a job! I found that a little unnerving! I was glad that my husband did not believe that God was leading him in the same way. I do not judge her for a moment, though! All of us have, at some time or another, been misguided by substituting our own wishful thinking for the will of God. We need to be especially cautious, perceptive and mindful in the romantic intersections of our lives!

Similarly, we must be cautious as we pray about anything that we really desire. If we really want a new car, a nice holiday, or a prestigious job, then it is easy to hunt for a few "green lights." We know what friends to ask (usually those who also crave a new car, a nice holiday, or a prestigious job). It is easy to come to a hasty decision and to make the commitment before we really know what God has to say about it. We must desire God's counsel *more* than we desire what we are praying about. If we are not willing to hear "no," then we are wasting our time even praying about it.

Of course, we cannot go through this in-depth kind of analysis with every single decision we make! We would get nothing done if we spent too much time debating what to wear each day or what to make for supper. It is well worth going through this in-depth process, however, when we make big decisions like buying a house, moving to a new city, changing our educational or career direction, beginning or ending a significant relationship, or taking on any substantial new commitment. We rarely have to make these kinds of major decisions in a rush.

The more minor decisions can be based on what our inner impression is, combined with our years of accumulated wisdom and knowledge. We will spend a whole chapter talking about how our growing reservoir of wisdom, good judgment, and discernment can help us with the *majority* of each day's decisions that have to be made "on the go."

The weightier the decision, the more we need to combine our personal impressions and instincts with a reflection on what we have recently been reading in the Word or what advice someone else can offer. It is with the most weighty life decisions that we ought to consult the kind of checklist I have included in Appendix B. You can create your own personal checklist if you want. Your personalized checklist will help you to gather and analyze your thoughts as you ponder the counsel that you have received from various sources.

There is *no set order* to the methods God uses to guide us. He might start by highlighting a particular verse of Scripture in our hearts or He might start by putting a remarkable opportunity in the middle of our path. He might start by planting an idea through the counsel of someone close to us. Then God will use the other means of counsel to *affirm* and *confirm* what He has told us through the original means of guidance. I have found that, particularly with important decisions, God will keep giving confirmation of His direction until I have clear peace about taking that new direction. If I do not have full peace about something, I do not move forward until there is enough confirmation to give me peace about what I am doing.

The Yield Sign

There is another kind of traffic sign that we must also consider—the "Yield" sign. I once ignored a "Yield" sign during a driving test. The testing official promptly told me that I had failed the driving test! I learned the hard way that "Yield" signs are important!

We must constantly be aware of "Yield" signs in our lives. *We must continually yield our decisions to God.* It is easy to go through our days making all of our own decisions based on our wants, our preferences, our human judgment, our dreams, and our ambitions. Many people go through their entire lives ignoring all the "Yield" signs along the way. And then they wonder why their road leads to calamities and collisions. Many then blame God for these tragic events.

It is better to yield our wills to God. This is really just another way of re-emphasizing what we discussed in earlier chapters: the need to submit and to surrender our lives and to desire to be on (and to stay on) the right path. If we yield our lives to God, we will be prepared to wait until we can accurately see the colors of the lights along the way. God will provide clarity and certainty if we are sincerely seeking His will. If we make a mistake, God will help us avoid a collision. God is always ready to help the yielded spirit, even in the fog, the blinding sunlight, or the blowing snow.

Moving On

Let us begin to look in detail at the various means that God uses to counsel us. It is my hope and prayer that, by studying these means, you will be well able to make wise decisions in every area of your life for the rest of your life. I pray that you will discover God's highest purposes for your life. I pray that you will be able to hear God's voice as you have never heard it before. I especially pray for those approaching a major intersection in their lives. May God clearly show you the color of His lights!

...I pray also that the eyes of your heart may be enlightened
in order that you may know the hope to which he has called you...
and his incomparably great power for us who believe...
Ephesians 1:18-19

.....yield yourselves to the Lord...
2 Chronicles 30:8 (LB)

...Stand at the crossroads and look...
Jeremiah 6:16

7.

The Counsel
of the Word

Your word is a lamp to my feet and a light to my path.
Psalm 119:105

*The Son is the radiance of God's glory and the exact representation of
his being, sustaining all things by his powerful word.*
Hebrews 1:3

*For the word of God is living and active. Sharper than any double-
edged sword, it penetrates even to dividing soul and spirit…*
Hebrews 4:12

Have you ever walked in pitch black darkness with only a
flashlight to guide you? My family spent one summer living in
the highlands of Kenya. My husband and I were participating
in a medical mission trip there while our children were
preschoolers. The four of us were returning one night to our
African home, taking a shortcut along a very steep, narrow
path through some trees. The moon and stars were covered by
clouds and we had one flashlight to share for the four of us. Its
beam barely showed us where it was safe to take the next step.

Beyond each step, we could not see where the path was going. It was a frightening experience, especially since we knew that there had been violent robberies in that area earlier that summer. There were also wild animals, snakes, and bats! We walked very close together so that all of us could see the guiding beam of light. There were large stones in the path and little gullies that had been carved out during the recent rains. We had to be careful not to trip or turn our ankles. We were so thankful for a light to guide us, even if it only illuminated one footstep at a time.

God's Word: A Light for Our Path

Psalm 119:105 reveals one of the ways that God most often uses to guide our lives: *His Word is a lamp to our feet and a light to our path.* Later in that same Psalm[36], the psalmist requests: "Direct my footsteps according to your word."

God does not always give us grand visions of what will occur in the future. Many times, we receive only enough light to take the next step. We then have to trust that there will be further light for each new step. As the psalmist so wisely understood, life is a series of footsteps. The Bible tells us in Matthew 6 that we are to live one day at a time. Our life journey takes place one step at a time. Just as the Israelites under Moses had to continually follow the cloud by day and the pillar of fire by night, we have to follow whatever daily light we are given. We usually see only the next few steps of the journey, not the whole journey. As a result, we need God's constant daily counsel.

The Bible: *Logos* and *Rhema*

The Bible can provide daily guidance for our lives, offering both general and specific instructions. The Bible is God's Word. The Greek terms *logos* and *rhema* (as found in old Greek

---

[36] Psalm 119:133

language Biblical manuscripts) can both be translated as 'word.' *Logos* and *rhema* have different connotations, however, when we consider how God's Word applies to our lives.

On the most general level, the Bible as *logos* is full of truths and principles that show us the way to lead a wise life. The Bible contains illuminating counsel on virtually every area of life, including marriage, sex, love, parenthood, work, finances, sibling relationships, health, friendship, conversation, and emotional management. The Bible as *logos* contains *general* truths for *general* application, regardless of time or place. Most of our decisions in life can be based on these *general principles* and *timeless truths*. The more we become familiar with God's Word, the more often we can intuitively know what to do, what to say, and how to react in the majority of situations. God has already provided us with a wealth of wise advice. This is the Bible, God's Word, as *logos*.

In addition, however, God will sometimes use a *particular verse* on a *particular day* to guide a *particular* individual. This is the Word as *rhema*. Have you had the experience of reading a verse one day that seems to really speak to your immediate situation? Over the years, there have been countless times when I have been seeking counsel in a particular area and have come across a verse that almost jumped off of the page at me. Sometimes a verse has acted as confirmation of an intended course of action. Sometimes a verse has acted as a warning or rebuke, changing my mind about a course of action. Other times a verse has cleared the fog or lit up the darkness so that a fuzzy decision has become very clear.

Let me give some typical examples. I have been angry at someone and then have read the verse about not letting the sun go down on my anger.[37] I have been in conflict with my husband and have gone through periods of not speaking with him for a few days and have then read the verse "a house divided against itself will fall."[38] I have harbored unforgiveness

---

[37] Ephesians 4:26
[38] Luke 11:17

towards someone who has hurt me and have then read the verse that God will not forgive us unless we forgive those who have wronged us.[39] By paying attention to these verses, and by taking necessary steps to get in line with their truths, I have no doubt saved myself from straying onto wrong and destructive paths. Other times I have read verses that have clearly confirmed decisions regarding breaking off a dating relationship, setting travel plans, buying a home, or pursuing other opportunities.

Sometimes I have wondered, during difficult circumstances, whether I was on the right path. I have questioned whether I have made a mistake in my direction. On those occasions, I have often read verses about persevering, pressing on, or being patient, or verses about how we ought to expect trials and difficulties in our Christian walk. Those verses have made it clear to me that I was on the right path, even if it had become dark, treacherous, frustrating, or confusing. In Ephesians 6:17, Paul described the Word as "the sword of the Spirit." The Word is what can help us fight through the tough times in our lives. It is a powerful tool in spiritual battle!

Sometimes God provides a *rhema* word just to show us He is very present in the midst of our circumstances. My sister-in-law started to fall down a flight of stairs when she was pregnant. She managed to catch herself and was not injured. She was shaken up! Later, as she rode home on the bus, she sat beside a woman who was reading a Bible. On the page that was open, my sister-in-law read a verse that had been high-lighted: "To him who is able to keep you from falling..."[40] This is a wonderful example of how intimately God can speak a *rhema* word to us that perfectly fits our immediate situation.

Permit me one final example of the Word as *rhema*. Many Christians are familiar with the story of Chuck Colson, once the Special Counsel to President Nixon. Although Colson was never found guilty of a Watergate-related felony, he did go to

---

[39]   Matthew 6:15
[40]   Jude 1:24

prison for some other "dirty tricks" he was involved in during the Nixon years. Colson became a Christian after leaving the White House and was still a fairly new Christian when he served time in prison.

Battling despair in prison, he turned to the Bible for hope and encouragement. One day, he read some verses from Hebrews, which talked about how Jesus had come to earth to be like one of us. Jesus was not ashamed to be called our brother.[41] As Colson thought about those verses, he realized God was speaking a *very personal message* to him. Colson received this specific insight from the passage in Hebrews: there was a purpose for him being in prison. Just as Jesus was not ashamed to call us His brothers, Colson realized that he should not be ashamed to call each one of his fellow inmates his brothers. He knew that he was being called to love and to minister to his fellow prisoners. Inspired and guided by a few Bible verses, Colson began the well-known international prison ministry that he has devoted years of his life to.[i]

The Importance of God's Word

God will never give us guidance that is contrary to His Word. Whatever guidance we believe we are receiving through some of the other means discussed in this book, it can always be tested by His Word. All guidance must line up with the Word. We can save ourselves a lot of mistakes, confusion, and uncertainty if we become well acquainted with what God has already revealed to us in His Word.

If we want to be serious about seeking God's counsel, then we need to be serious about getting to know His Word. In Psalm 119:24, David wrote: "Your statutes are my delight; they are my counselors." In Psalm 119:133, he requested this of God: "Direct my footsteps according to your word." Getting to know God's Word is a life-long discipline. Just as we are meant to live one day at a time, we are to build our knowledge of God's

---

[41] Hebrews 2:9-11, 16-18

Word one day at a time. We will receive God's counsel, *one day at a time*, as we meditate on the Word.

During my twenty years as a trial lawyer, I never dared show up in court without reading every word in the legal briefs that my opponents had served on me. I would try to know those briefs backwards and forwards and I often had a stack of thick volumes to read through! I never wanted to be embarrassed by a Judge reprimanding me for taking a position without being aware of all the facts, documents, and legal precedents. How foolish other trial counsel had looked when they had argued a point and it was clear to everyone in the room that they were not familiar with all the evidence or the case law.

One day it dawned on me that I should seek to know God's Word with the same diligence and thoroughness. *What excuse did I have to do less?* I am praying that each reader of this book will develop a desire and a conviction to know the Word even better than they presently do. I have read through the Bible a few dozen times, and with each reading I learn something new or connect different parts of the Bible in a fresh way. I have also received much counsel from its pages.

After praying each day, we must train ourselves to be very mindful of what we are reading in our devotions in the following days. Most of us spend too much time talking *to* God about our lives and not nearly enough time listening to what *He* has to say about our lives! We should read the Bible, recognizing that not only does it contain general truths about life, but that it is one way in which God can *personally* converse with us. Those who regularly read the Bible receive, from time to time, some very specific guidance regarding where to go, who to contact, what to say, and what to do.

Those who regularly read the Bible are also regularly compelled (by what they are reading) to deal with wrong states of mind, heart, and attitude such as selfishness, resentment, unforgiveness, bitterness, immorality, and greed. What we meditate on affects our ongoing thoughts, which determine our emotions. What happens in our minds and hearts affects our words and actions. *What we meditate on eventually steers our course.*

Reading the Bible Cover to Cover

I first read the Bible cover to cover when I was nineteen years old, in the last months of my backpacking year in Europe. I have already mentioned how I committed my life to Christ one night in Greece, after I got lost in the dark. The very next day, my sister and I decided to start reading the Bible. We continued to visit the great capitals of Europe, but the sights we were seeing began to pale in comparison to the riches we were discovering in God's Word. We often spent hours discussing what we were reading in the Bible in our various hotel rooms at night. Even during the day, we were often so busy discussing what we had been reading that we paid lesser attention to the Parthenon or the Roman Forum.

This process provided invaluable counsel to me as I returned to Canada and to university. I had not really enjoyed my first year at university (before my year of backpacking). After my year away, it was much clearer what I should study and why. Reading through the Bible provided clear guidance about applying for law school. I had also learned much about changes I needed to make in the men I dated, the social life I engaged in, the kinds of books I read, the movies I attended, and many other areas of my life. I knew that I could not go back to a lifestyle of partying and drinking. Reading the whole Bible that first time significantly shaped the critical years of my early adult life.

A Deliberate Discipline

I soon learned, however, that spending time reading the Bible requires deliberate *ongoing* commitment. After reading the entire Bible that first time, I coasted spiritually for a while. During the following years at university, and then during my early years of law practice, my devotional life was poor and inconsistent. It would occasionally kick-start, from time to time, as a result of some fresh stress or crisis. Then I would spiritually coast again. After reading so much work material all day long, the last thing I wanted to do at night was read my Bible. My studies, and later my work, involved such massive amounts of reading! God sometimes humored me by speaking to me when I cracked open my dusty Bible to a random page in the midst of a crisis, but this is not the way mature Christians are meant to be guided.

Someone close to me in my early adult life suggested one day that I try the "five and five." This meant getting into the habit of praying for at least five minutes every day and then reading the Bible for five minutes. He challenged my sincerity as a committed Christian if I could not do this even on my busiest days. I realized that he was right. How could I say that my faith was important to me if I was not prepared to invest ten minutes a day nurturing and developing it? How could I say I was in a *relationship* with God if I was not willing to connect with Him for ten minutes every day?

So I committed myself to practicing the "five and five." I decided that I would get up ten minutes earlier and have a second cup of coffee while I prayed and then read the Word. (I shared in an earlier chapter about the prayer dimension of this habit.)

I began to really look forward to this time each morning. I found myself bouncing out of bed more energetically than ever before. God began to speak to me through His Word. Prayers seemed to be answered more quickly than before. God, in that infancy stage of my devotional disciplines, often immediately responded to my requests for His counsel. Looking back, I can see that He wanted to encourage me in the daily habits that I was developing of both praying *and* reading God's Word.

I would sometimes tell myself first thing in the morning that I could not really afford to spend devotional time that morning. I sometimes had an insanely busy day ahead of me!

But then I would decide to do my "five and five" anyways. I would arrive at the office a little later to discover that a long meeting had been cancelled or postponed. An offer to settle a pending three week trial would arrive just as I was on my way to the "courtroom door," freeing up a large block of time.

Other times, some verse I had read that morning shed light on a decision I had to make. I soon learned that, one way or another, God honors all of the time that we "tithe" to Him! Of course, the ten minutes of devotional time began to grow into longer times, especially when I saw how God *gave back that time* to me later in the day.

Reading the Bible Cover to Cover Again

I had just started the habit of the "five and five" in the year or two before I met my husband. During his years of medical school, internship, and residency, my husband had also let his spiritual disciplines (and thereby his spiritual life) slide. He had also just started renewing the disciplines of a committed Christian life not long before we met.

When my husband and I were still newlyweds, we took a year off from our careers to travel together. We spent that year crossing the vast continent of Africa, north to south and west to east. We wanted to spend time getting to know each other. We also wanted to make decisions about the rest of our lives: if and when to have children, whether or not to buy a home, where we would live, where we would attend church, how our careers would adjust to these decisions, what ministries we would build into our lives, and so forth. As part of this decision-making process, we decided that it would be wise to read the Bible together, out loud, cover to cover. Because this had been an enriching experience with my sister, I was excited about entering into such an intense spiritual dialogue with my husband.

As newlyweds, my husband and I wanted to develop *mutual* wisdom and *shared* understanding about what we believed the Bible said about *everything* from money to work, family, raising children, and many other dimensions of life. We wanted to develop at least a general blueprint for our lives and an agreement on what our main priorities and values would be. This turned out to be an excellent process that deepened our marriage and probably spared us much conflict. It is not easy blending two independent lives into "one" life shared as a married couple!

By the end of that year, we had general agreement on many of the major life decisions we had to make together: what shape our careers would take, the size and timing of the family we wanted to start, where we would settle, what kind of income we would aim for, and how that should be balanced with the amount of time we wanted to have for priorities beyond work. These decisions were made in the framework of what we believed God's Word had to say to us about life principles and values.

We made many changes to our lives after that year, having received much counsel from God through His Word. I had previously been working long hours as a trial lawyer. Before my married life, it was not unusual to work sixty or more hours a week. My hours forever changed after our year in Africa, to accommodate our decision to start a family. When my children were very young, I was allowed to work less than ten hours a week. I seldom had to work more than twenty-five hours a week when they were older, unless one of my cases went to trial. Prior to our marriage, my husband had been working as many as one hundred hours a week as a pediatric resident at a large downtown teaching hospital. After our year of reading the Bible together, Sam decided to switch to the more family-friendly hours of general medical practice.

We had both been living for a number of years in expensive downtown neighborhoods. We decided to buy a home on the edge of the city that would require less income to maintain. I am not suggesting that everyone has to adopt these values and priorities. This is simply how God led us.

Although Sam and I continued to pursue rewarding and fruitful careers, we had ample time to enjoy our marriage, raise our children, maintain our health, develop ministries, and nurture rich relationships with extended family, friends, and neighbors. The time we invested in that first year of marriage reading the whole Bible together and discussing it for countless hours paid rich dividends over the following years.

As my husband and I go through various mid-life changes in our careers, ministries, marriage dynamics, and family life, perhaps it is time we read the Bible together again!

Lifelong Devotional Disciplines

Spending time in prayer and Bible study does not make our lives harder—it makes them easier. What I have been describing became so meaningful and rewarding as I navigated through early adult life that, decades later, I am still practicing these disciplines. The only difference is that I now commit even more time to them. As I mentioned earlier, I try to regularly pray for at least an hour a day. I usually do that in the morning. I take a daily afternoon tea break to read the Word. Sometimes I read for five minutes, other times much longer. Some days I do not find the time to read the Bible until just before bed. I am continually amazed at how often God speaks to me in the afternoon or evening about various matters I raised with Him in my morning prayer time. This sounds like a lot of time to spend connecting with God, but somehow I always manage to find enough time to get everything else done.

I do not engage in these daily devotional disciplines out of ritual, guilt, obligation, or duty. Nor do I wish to sound super-spiritual. I have simply learned that *spending* this kind of time actually *saves* me much time. It is what helps me to keep in step with God and His agenda. I avoid needless detours and frustrating dead ends in my life. A person with clear direction and purpose will always get to a destination faster than a person who does not know where they are going. Remember my example of the GPS available in some new models of cars? The *combined disciplines* of daily prayer and Bible study provide a kind of GPS navigational system for life. These *combined disciplines* help a person learn how to aim straight for the best goal without wasting precious time and energy. I am simply an ordinary Christian who has learned the incomparable value of the counsel of God's Word.

Since the year I traveled across Africa with my husband (more than twenty years ago!), I have maintained the habit of reading through the whole Bible almost every year. I need to do this to keep my goals, values, and priorities in line. There are excellent "one year" Bibles available, which divide the Old Testament, New Testament, Psalms, and Proverbs into 365 manageable daily readings. It is reasonably possible to comfortably re-read the Bible each year. Do I get bored? Absolutely not. The more I understand the Bible, the more fascinating it becomes.

Bible Study is Part of *Knowing* God

Reading the Word is one of the main ways in which we come to *know* God. We discussed in an earlier chapter how we must *know* God before we can expect to regularly receive His counsel. The Bible tells us so much about God's love for us, His character, His wisdom, and His ways. We cannot expect to be in intimate communication with God if we are not willing to invest time getting to know Him. He will not reveal much of Himself to us unless we are interested in what He has *already revealed*. He will not give us detailed guidance about His specific will for our lives unless we have serious interest in His general will for this world and everyone in it. His specific will for us will be a part of His overall will for our generation.

Why should God tell us *who* we should marry if we are not interested in what He has generally said about marriage? Why should God speak with us about *when* we should start to have children if we do not care about what God has generally said about parenthood? Why should God reveal which job to apply for if we neglect to read His instructions about the general principles of work?

If we want to develop intimate communication with God, we must show our *sincerity* by reading His Word. Sometimes we wonder why God seems to be silent. But He is never silent. His words have traveled through history and are readily available to those of us who live in the free world. If we are not interested in what He has already said, if we do not *cherish* and *value* what He has already said, why should He say anything more to us? It has been my repeated observation in life that God speaks most often and most clearly to those who delight in what He has already said, who treasure His words and store them in their hearts.

If we store God's Word in our hearts, we will have continual inner counsel. It will permeate our thoughts, perceptions, and impressions. To most of us, God's Word is accessible and available. God's Word "is not up in heaven, so that you have to ask, 'Who will ascend into heaven to get it and proclaim it to us so that we may obey it?' Nor is it beyond the sea, so that you have to ask, 'Who will cross the sea to get it and proclaim it to us so that we may obey it?' No, *the word is very near you*; it is in your mouth and in your heart so that you may obey it."[42]

Nourishment of the Word

Jesus said that "man does not live on bread alone, but on every word that comes from the mouth of God."[43] When Jesus taught His disciples to pray, He told them to ask: "Give us today our daily bread." We must, of course, have daily food, but Jesus was talking about more than actual bread. He was talking about the bread of the Word. Jesus knew that we would live at

---

[42] Deuteronomy 30:12-14
[43] Matthew 4:4, quoting Deuteronomy 8:3

our best if each day we would immerse ourselves in the Word of God.

Jesus practiced what He preached. Jesus knew Scripture well and was able to say "It is written..." Jesus often quoted the Old Testament, treating the Scriptural passage as authority on a subject. Jesus knew that it is easy to take a wrong path if we do not know God's Word well. Once he challenged some members of the Sadducees (a Jewish sect) by asking them: "Are you not in error *because you do not know the Scriptures?*"[44]

There is a wonderful description of God's word in Isaiah 55. God makes this invitation: "Come, all you who are thirsty, come to the waters; and you who have no money, come, buy and eat! Come, buy wine and milk without money and without cost. Why spend money on what is not bread, and your labor on what does not satisfy? *Listen, listen to me,* and eat what is good, and your soul will delight in the richest of fare. *Give ear and come to me; hear me,* that your soul may live....As the rain and the snow come down from heaven, and do not return to it without watering the earth and making it bud and flourish, so that it yields seed for the sower and bread for the eater, *so is my word that goes out from my mouth*: It will not return to me empty, but will accomplish what I desire and achieve the purpose for which I sent it."[45] By immersing ourselves in God's word, our souls will delight in the richest of fare. If we savor the Word, it will never be dry and boring. It will be soul-sustaining. It will be a light in the darkness. It will *connect* us to God and keep us in *communion* with Him.

There is another wonderful description of God's Word in Psalm 119. It is a lengthy Psalm, too long to be quoted here, but I encourage you to meditate on that whole Psalm. The psalmist describes God's words as his "delight"...his "counselors"...his "hope"... more valuable to him than silver or gold. The psalmist tells God quite simply: "I trust in your word" and "I delight in your commands because I love them."

---

[44]   Mark 12:24
[45]   Isaiah 55:1-3, 10-11

King David was generally a man after God's own heart. He went astray, however, whenever he ignored God's words. At one point in his life, David committed adultery with Bathsheba and then schemed to murder her husband so that he could have Bathsheba for himself. God then sent Nathan the prophet to ask of David: "Why did you *despise the word of the Lord* by doing what is evil in his eyes?"[46] David repented of his wrongdoing. God forgave him and restored him, but did not prevent David from experiencing some of the tragic consequences of his disregard for God's words. David learned the hard way to treasure the words of God—to recognize that *knowing* and *obeying* God's words were integral to *knowing* God and *maintaining a relationship* with Him. His son King Solomon learned the same truth. In Proverbs 13:13, King Solomon wrote: "Despise God's Word and find yourself in trouble. Obey it and succeed" (LB).

Transforming Our Minds

Immersing ourselves in the Word will slowly change our way of thinking. Some might ask: "Isn't this just a form of brainwashing?" I once heard an African missionary with a keen sense of humor respond by saying, "Yes, *it is* brainwashing. *But boy did my brain need a good washing!*"

The apostle Paul wrote to the Roman Christians: "Do not conform any longer to the pattern of this world, but *be transformed by the renewing of your mind*. Then you will be able to test and approve what God's will is—his good, pleasing and perfect will."[47] We renew our minds as we saturate them with God's Word, with His perspective on life, His truths, and His wisdom. As our minds are transformed and renewed it will be much easier to see what God's will is (generally and specifically) for our lives. His thoughts and His ways will become less and less foreign to us.

---

[46] 2 Samuel 12:9a
[47] Romans 12:2

God's Word: Alive throughout History

God's Word has had an unprecedented uniqueness and place in history. The sixty-six books that make up the Bible were written over a 1,500-year time span by a sum of over forty authors (ranging from kings and political leaders to servants and fishermen). The Bible was written in various places (ranging from a dungeon to a palace, in the midst of battle to the solitude of an island) on three different continents. Many have tried to criticize it, trivialize it or simply ignore it. Many rulers have tried to burn it and to ban it, but it continues to thrive, with *billions* of copies having been printed. It has been read by more people and translated into more languages than any other book in history.ʲ Countless people love and cherish it. Countless others have intense emotions and opinions about it *without having ever read it*. It has a "living" and "active" power, just as Hebrews 4:12 describes.

If you read the biographies of the great men and women of God, it is usually quite apparent that they have had a great love of and respect for the counsel of the Word of God. George Mueller is an outstanding example. He is known for starting several orphanages in England in the 1800s, which eventually housed thousands of orphans. (Before Mueller's homes, orphans were normally sent to almshouses, where they were locked up with criminals and the mentally ill and did not receive a proper education.) Mueller is also known for never asking anyone, except God, for money to finance this work. God supplied his needs and the needs of the thousands of children he cared for in many miraculous ways.

Mueller read his Bible on a daily basis, usually spending an hour reading verses and then meditating on them as he walked the fields and gardens near his home. He had realized that prayer time was not enough—true communion with God depended on also *listening to what God had to say back to him* after he prayed. He sought God's continual guidance regarding all the decisions he made in expanding and maintaining his orphanage ministry. He knew that some of that guidance would come through his daily time in the Word.

One of my favorite examples of how God spoke to Mueller through the Word is as follows. When Mueller was praying about starting his first orphanage, he asked God if he was being unrealistic to step out in faith to feed a few dozen boys when he barely had enough money to feed his own family. God spoke to Mueller through Psalm 81:10: "Open wide your mouth and I will fill it." That *rhema* verse was enough to encourage Mueller to step out in faith to open his first orphanage. Mueller believed that God had spoken to him personally through that verse. By reading the Word one day at a time, Mueller developed detailed insight into God's blueprint for his life.

Eric Liddell, the Olympic gold medalist who refused to run an Olympic event on a Sunday, was another man who cherished the Word of God. He also developed the lifelong habit of reading the Bible each morning, searching deeply for God's guidance. He was as disciplined in his devotional life as he was in his athletic training. He was accustomed to God speaking to him through the Word. For example, after making the decision not to run in a Sunday 100-metre event, Liddell was comforted to read a verse in Romans that told him that those who trust in God will never be ashamed.[48]

Days later, just before he ran in the 400-metre race, Liddell was handed a piece of paper with this verse on it, from 1 Samuel 2:30: "Those who honor me I will honor." That very day Liddell won his Olympic gold medal, setting a new world record.

Liddell, who spent most of his life as a missionary in China, ran a magnificent race in life—far more significant than the race in which he won Olympic gold. Long after he stopped running, Liddell maintained his disciplined habit of reading the Word. Canadian missionary Dr. David Michell, who was in

---

[48]   Romans 10:11

the same Japanese internment camp in China as Eric Liddell during World War II, recalled that each morning, Liddell and a roommate studied the Bible and prayed for an hour.[k] Liddell provides encouragement to the rest of us to spend significant time in personal communion with God, talking to Him and listening to His response.

My final example, Corrie ten Boom, was a Dutch woman whose family hid Jewish refugees in their home during World War II. She is a great example of a woman who always desired to be on the right path. As Jews began to flee the Nazi regime, Corrie knew that hiding as many of them as she could in her home was the right thing to do, no matter what it cost her. She was eventually arrested by the Gestapo and spent part of the war incarcerated in Ravensbruck, a Nazi concentration camp where thousands died of malnutrition, disease and execution.

Corrie valued God's Word so much that she risked her life smuggling her Bible into Ravensbruck when she first arrived. Corrie had grown up in a Christian home where there was daily prayer and Scripture reading. Her father knew the Bible well and was always ready with a Bible verse that was appropriate to a particular situation. Corrie was a deep believer in God's promise to directly and specifically guide each Christian through various means, including the Bible.

Prisoners were "processed" by the Nazis as they arrived at Ravensbruck. The prisoners had to abandon the belongings they were carrying. They then had to strip and surrender their clothes before taking a shower, so that the guards could fully search their bodies. Arriving at the camp, Corrie had her Bible hidden in a pouch around her neck. As Corrie and her sister moved along the line, getting closer to the guards, her sister suddenly felt ill. Corrie was allowed to accompany her sister into the shower room *before* the strip search. Corrie was able to hide her Bible in the shower room. She then went back into line for the strip search.

After her strip search and shower, Corrie realized with dismay that there was a second search *after* the prisoners left the shower room. Corrie had retrieved her Bible from its hiding place and it was once again in a pouch around her neck. Corrie prayed as she watched all those ahead of her having their clothed bodies man-handled from head to toe by the Nazi guards. Although everyone around her, including her sister, was hand-searched, no one touched Corrie. She was able to pass by the guards with her Bible safely hidden in the pouch around her neck, concealed by her clothes.

This Bible proved invaluable to Corrie, her sister, and their roommates as they faced grueling months in that Nazi camp. Corrie could hear from God each and every day as she passed through her ordeal. Corrie was sustained by verses such as those in Psalm 23. Twice a day, she held Bible studies in her barracks, providing hope, peace, and light to the other women in a place filled with such cruelty, horror, sorrow, and despair. Through the Word, God gave Corrie specific messages for many of her fellow prisoners. Corrie came to understand God's purpose for her own life in those horrific circumstances: to introduce these suffering women to the Savior she knew so intimately, and to help them grow in Christian faith.

In Summary

We have so much to learn from spiritual giants like Mueller, Liddell, and Ten Boom, whose bold convictions and courageous paths through life have flowed from their desire to receive the intimate daily counsel of the Word of God.

Throughout my own adult life, the Word has been a light for my path and a lamp to my feet. Sometimes it has helped me to see clearly to the farthest horizon. Other times, like that dark night in Kenya, I have been deeply grateful to see a safe place to put my next footstep. The Word has helped me to discern the right path when I have come to a crossroads. It has helped to correct my course when I have taken a wrong turn. There is much darkness in this world. I treasure the light that helps me find solid footing.

Fix these words of mine in your hearts and minds.
Deuteronomy 11:18a

They are not just idle words for you—they are your life.
Deuteronomy 32:47a

Open my eyes to see wonderful things in your Word.
I am but a pilgrim here on earth: how I need a map—
and your commands are my chart and guide....
Your laws are both my light and my counselors.
Psalm 119:18-19, 24 (LB)

8.

The Counsel
of the Spirit

*But the Counselor, the Holy Spirit, whom the Father will send
in my name, will teach you all things...*
John 14:26

*...And this is how we know that he lives in us:
We know it by the Spirit he gave us.*
1 John 3:24b

The day that Anne received the devastating phone call, she
was thankful that she had developed a relationship with the
Holy Spirit. In the hour before the life-shattering phone call
came, Anne had read a few chapters of the Bible. This was part
of her daily routine. She had been reading through the story of
Joseph and jotting down notes for a talk that she was
preparing. But there was an inner discomfort in her spirit. She
felt an inner prompting, telling her to stop writing notes, to
stop thinking about her talk, and to really *meditate* on the story
of Joseph. She had read this story many times before. She tried
to ignore this inner impression, but it was real and it was
persistent. She put down her pen, closed her eyes and began to

think about the many experiences of Joseph. Nothing seemed to particularly stand out that day.

She was still thinking about this as she drove into town some moments later. For ten minutes, she continued to meditate on the life of Joseph. There was an *inner urgency* to her thoughts that puzzled her. She sensed that the Holy Spirit was trying to communicate something to her. Still, she had no clue what that message was.

She had just parked her car in town when her cell phone rang. The call actually interrupted her thoughts about the story of Joseph. It was her husband on the phone. He asked her if she could come meet him at the local police station. Her husband, sounding numb from shock, told her that the police were about to charge him with sexual assault. He did not yet know any of the details.

A thousand thoughts and feelings rushed through Anne as she drove to the police station. Her first instinct was to pray…to keep so occupied praying that she had no time to think the worst or to feel the fear, panic, and dread that were swirling around inside of her. She had no idea what this was all about. She had enjoyed a long and happy marriage. She loved and respected her husband, who was a committed Christian. This was incomprehensible.

She briefly spoke with her husband at the police station. He still had no idea what this was about. The police officer in charge would not allow Anne to come into the interrogation room. The door closed behind the officer and her husband, leaving Anne in the waiting room. All alone, she battled the increasing fear, shock, and disbelief. She continued to resist the temptation to panic and tried once again to focus on praying. She also resisted the temptation to imagine who the female "victim" was or the circumstances surrounding the incident being discussed behind the closed door. While she focused on praying, the inner voice of the Spirit whispered the words "Potiphar's wife." She caught her breath. An instant sensation of calming peace and of God's presence filled her.

Now she understood what part of the story of Joseph she was supposed to think about! While Joseph was working in the house of Potiphar in Egypt, Potiphar's wife developed an attraction to Joseph and she tried to seduce him. Joseph was a faithful man of God, however, and he refused her seduction. Potiphar's wife then lied to her husband, falsely accusing Joseph of trying to sexually assault her. Potiphar believed his wife's lies and promptly put his servant Joseph in prison.[49]

It was crystal clear to Anne, at that moment, that her husband was innocent. *The inner voice that had whispered to her was that real.* She no longer feared what she would hear when she was next allowed to speak to her husband. It did not matter anymore. It did not matter who the woman was. It did not matter what the details of the story were. Anne was convinced, beyond any shadow of a doubt, that a false accusation was being made against her husband. She could believe, with faith, that God would ultimately protect both her and her husband from whatever lies had been told.

As she continued to pray in the police station, the Spirit gently whispered further words to her from Isaiah 54:17: "No weapon forged against you will prevail." (This is a powerful example of the Word as *rhema*, an example of how God, *through the Holy Spirit speaking within a person*, can highlight a *particular verse* to a *particular individual* in a *particular situation*.) Anne had not been frantically trying to think of an applicable Bible verse. Instead, she had been busy praying and the verse had just come to her from somewhere deep within. This verse assured her that her husband would be exonerated.

The morning after the devastating phone call, Anne looked up the verse from Isaiah 54:17, which the Spirit had given to her in the police station. She was amazed at the words that followed: "No weapon forged against you will prevail, *and you will refute every tongue that accuses you. This is the heritage of the servants of the Lord, and this is their vindication from me,* declares

---

49   The full story is in Genesis 39

the Lord." Anne promptly shared this passage with her husband, who was encouraged by it. It was another powerful *rhema* verse.

But that is not all. The Spirit impressed upon Anne to read through the chapters in Isaiah before chapter 54. These are some of the verses that almost leapt off the page at her as she obeyed that inner impression to read more of Isaiah: "...do not fear, for I am with you; do not be dismayed, for I am your God. I will strengthen you and help you; I will uphold you with my righteous right hand"; "In faithfulness, he will bring forth justice"; "You will never be put to shame or disgraced"; "Because the Sovereign Lord helps me, I will not be disgraced. Therefore have I set my face like flint, and I know I will not be put to shame"; "Do not be afraid; you will not suffer shame. Do not fear disgrace; you will not be humiliated."[50]

In less than twenty-four hours after the devastating phone call, the Spirit (who had actually begun speaking to Anne in the hour *before* the phone call!) had unequivocally impressed upon Anne that the accusation was false, her husband had done no wrong, no weapon formed against her and her husband would prevail, justice would instead prevail, and the matter would never be made public. The Spirit had also shown her many verses that promised they would never be ashamed or disgraced.

The nightmare situation did not clear up that day, that week, or even that month. It took a few months for the police to investigate the emotional and psychological history of the female complainant and whether there was substance to her story. Ultimately, the police file was closed. Charges were never laid. The matter ended.

Throughout the months of waiting, Anne had remained comforted by the Spirit and confident in what the Spirit had revealed to her from the very outset. The work of the Spirit within her had spared her months of fear, worry, wondering if

---

[50]   Isaiah 41:14; Isaiah 42:3; Isaiah 45:17; Isaiah 50:7; Isaiah 54:4

there was truth to the allegations, potential distrust of her husband, doubt, and anger. Instead, she had felt remarkable peace, faith, and hope. The Holy Spirit had reached over to hold her hand *even before the phone call had come* and He had not let go of her hand throughout the entire episode. He had lovingly counseled her throughout circumstances that could have badly shaken her marriage, but instead had strengthened it.

The Holy Spirit

I have met many Christians who are not very well acquainted with the Holy Spirit—who He is and what role He is supposed to play in our lives. We cannot *fully* receive ongoing guidance and counsel from God without knowing the Holy Spirit. I have found that those who ask why they have trouble hearing God's voice often have limited understanding of who the Holy Spirit is.

Let us look at what the Bible has to say about the Holy Spirit. If you do not know Him as intimately as Anne, I pray that you come to know Him better as you read what God has revealed about the Spirit. After we explore some Biblical references to the Holy Spirit, and how we are meant to relate to Him, I will tell you more stories and give more powerful examples of how He guides people today.

Just before His death on the cross, Jesus told His followers that they would receive the Holy Spirit. Jesus further told them that the Spirit would become their "Counselor."[51] If we want to receive deep and continual guidance from God, then we need to become well acquainted with the Spirit! He is part of the Holy Trinity that also includes God the Father and Jesus the Son. We all need to spend quality time getting to *know* this wonderful "Counselor" Jesus talked about.

---

[51] John 14

The Holy Spirit in the Old Testament

The Holy Spirit is mentioned in the Bible from its beginning to its end! Look at the very first page of the Bible. In the second verse of the very first chapter of Genesis we read: "Now the earth was formless and empty, darkness was over the surface of the deep, and the *Spirit of God* was hovering over the waters." The Holy Spirit was present at the creation of the world.

There are numerous examples in the Old Testament of how God's greatest servants were led and empowered by the Spirit on particular occasions or for certain seasons of their lives. For example, the Holy Spirit came upon **Moses** and was then imparted to the elders of Israel. In Numbers 11:17, God said to Moses: "I will take of the Spirit that is on you and put the Spirit on them." Numbers 27:18 records that **Joshua** had the Spirit in him. When **Samson** ruled Israel, "the Spirit of the Lord came upon him in power."[52] When Samuel first anointed Saul as King, Samuel said to **Saul:** "The Spirit of the Lord will come upon you in power...and you will be changed into a different person. Once these signs are fulfilled, do whatever your hand finds to do, for God is with you."[53] Later, the same thing happened when Samuel anointed **David** as King. In 1 Samuel 16:13b, we read: "...and from that day on the Spirit of the Lord came upon David in power." David beseeched God in Psalm 51:11: "Do not cast me from your presence or take your Holy Spirit from me." David cherished the presence of the Spirit in his life.

The prophets of the Old Testament prophesied by the presence of the Spirit in them. For example, the prophet **Isaiah** stated: "...and now the Sovereign Lord has sent me, with His Spirit..."[54]

---

[52]   Judges 14:6 and Judges 14:19
[53]   1 Samuel 10:6-7
[54]   Isaiah 48:16b

It is significant to note that many of the *same people* mentioned in Chapter 2 as examples of those who were intimately led by God also received the Spirit in their lives. *Those who received the Spirit of God also received His clear counsel.* Some of them (Isaiah for example) became conduits of God's counsel to others, even whole nations.

In Old Testament times, the Spirit does not seem to have come in power to ordinary people. Not everyone expected to receive the Spirit, even if they believed in God and were devoted to Him. The Spirit primarily empowered leaders (military, political, or spiritual).

At a certain point in history, God told His people that this was going to change. **Joel**, one of the prophets in the Old Testament, prophesied about future times: "I will pour out my Spirit on *all people*. Your sons and daughters will prophesy, your old men will dream dreams, your young men will see visions. Even on my servants, both men and women, I will pour out my Spirit in those days."[55] Joel's prophecy was fulfilled, as we will see below, during and after the life of Jesus.

Jesus and the Holy Spirit

The Holy Spirit began to appear, *even in ordinary people*, around the time of the birth of Jesus. For example, Elizabeth and Zechariah (parents of John the Baptist) and John the Baptist himself were filled with the Holy Spirit. [56]

Simeon, a devout Jew who lived at the time of Jesus, experienced the Holy Spirit. It had been revealed to him by the Holy Spirit that he would not die before he had seen the Messiah. "Moved by the Spirit," Simeon went into the temple courts in Jerusalem and held the baby Jesus in his arms, declaring that this was the promised Christ.[57]

---

[55] Joel 2:28
[56] Luke 1:41; Luke 1:67; Luke 1:15
[57] Luke 2:26; see the full story at Luke 2:27-35

Jesus had been conceived by the Holy Spirit. Mary, his mother, had been told by an angel: "The Holy Spirit will come on you."[58]

Just before Jesus began His public ministry, John the Baptist told people that he himself could only baptize with water, but that Jesus "will baptize you *with the Holy Spirit and with fire*."[59] Shortly after that declaration, John baptized Jesus with water. On that occasion, the Holy Spirit descended on Jesus.[60] From that point on, Jesus was full of the Holy Spirit and began the three years of His public ministry, in which he healed, delivered, and performed a variety of other miracles.

Jesus Himself was *led* by the Spirit. For example, after Jesus was baptized, He was "led by the Spirit into the desert"[61] where He faced temptation. Luke 4:14 records that Jesus then returned to Galilee "in the power of the Spirit." It is quite remarkable to meditate on the fact that Jesus Himself, *the very Son of God*, was "led by the Spirit." This was foretold by Isaiah, who prophesied about God's future chosen servant upon whom God would put His Spirit.[62] Jesus referred to the prophet Isaiah's words when He said of Himself: "The Spirit of the Lord is on me."[63]

The Holy Spirit Promised for All Believers

During His lifetime, Jesus talked about the coming of the Spirit to *all believers*. For example, John wrote about the time that Jesus spoke at the Feast of Tabernacles. John recorded: "Jesus stood and said in a loud voice, 'If anyone is thirsty, let him come to me and drink. *Whoever believes in me*, as the Scripture has said, *streams of living water* will flow from within him.' *By this*," John explained, "*He meant the Spirit, whom those who*

---

58   Luke 1:35
59   Matthew 3:11 (also see John 1:33)
60   Matthew 3:16; Luke 3:21-22; John 1:32
61   Matthew 4:1 (also see Luke 4:1)
62   Isaiah 42:1-4
63   Luke 4:18

believed in him were later to receive. Up to that time the Spirit had not been given, since Jesus had not yet been glorified."[64] From this text, it is clear that John must have written this after the death of Jesus and after the promised coming of the Spirit.

Jesus promised, just before his death, that the Father would send His followers a Counselor who would guide them. In John 14:26, Jesus further explained: "the Counselor, the Holy Spirit, whom the Father will send in my name, will teach you all things…" In John 16:13, Jesus continued: "But when he, the Spirit of truth, comes, he will guide you into all truth. He will not speak on his own; he will speak only what he hears, and he will tell you what is yet to come. He will bring glory to me by taking from what is mine and making it known to you. All that belongs to the Father is mine. That is why I said the Spirit will take from what is mine and make it known to you."

Jesus was not just talking to His disciples and followers in *those times*. As He concluded his conversation with a prayer, Jesus told the Father, in John 17:20, that He was praying for his followers at that present time, but also "for those who *will* believe in me through their message." The promise of "the Counselor" is for *all of us who believe*.

After Jesus died, He appeared more than once to some of His disciples and followers. On one occasion, Jesus "breathed" on His disciples and said: "Receive the Holy Spirit."[65]

Luke similarly recorded in Acts 1 that, after His death, Jesus appeared to His followers. "On one occasion," Luke further recorded, "while he [Jesus] was eating with them, he gave them this command: 'Do not leave Jerusalem, but wait for the gift my Father promised, which you have heard me speak about. For John baptized with water, but in a few days *you will be baptized with the Holy Spirit …You will receive power when the Holy Spirit comes on you…*'"[66]

---

[64] John 7:37-39
[65] John 20:22
[66] Acts 1:4-5, 8

The Coming of the Holy Spirit at Pentecost

Acts 2 tells the incredible story of how the Holy Spirit did indeed come upon many of the followers of Jesus, shortly after His death and resurrection. "When the day of Pentecost came, they were all together in one place. Suddenly a sound like the blowing of a violent wind came from heaven and filled the whole house where they were sitting. They saw what seemed to be tongues of fire that separated and came to rest on each of them. *All* of them were *filled with the Holy Spirit...*"[67]

Peter, Paul, John and Others

The Book of Acts tells many stories of various people being filled with the Spirit and of the consequent work of the Spirit in them. Let us consider a few examples.

In Acts 2:38-39, Peter addressed a crowd, telling them to repent of their sins and to be baptized in the name of Jesus. He then said: "And you will receive the gift of the Holy Spirit. *The promise is for you and your children and all who are far off—for all whom the Lord our God will call.*" I have put this last sentence in italics to emphasize that the Holy Spirit is a gift that all believers are to receive, not just those who lived in the time of Jesus and Peter.

On a later occasion, Peter and John spoke to a group of believers and then prayed. Luke recorded in Acts 4:31: "After they prayed, the place where they were meeting was shaken. And they were *all* filled with the Holy Spirit..." Similarly, in Acts 13:52 we are told that "the disciples were filled with joy and with the Holy Spirit." In other chapters, we are told that Stephen, Barnabas, and Agabus were full of the Spirit.[68]

Paul was filled with[69] the Spirit. He was *led* to certain places and on other occasions *stopped* by the Spirit from going

---

[67]   Acts 2:1-4
[68]   Acts 7:55; Acts 11:24; Acts 11:28
[69]   Acts 9:17 and 13:9

to specific places. For example, Paul and Barnabas were "sent on their way by the Holy Spirit" to Seleucia and Cyprus.[70] In Acts 16:6, Luke wrote: "Paul and his companions traveled throughout the region of Phrygia and Galatia, *having been kept by the Holy Spirit from preaching the word in the province of Asia.*" In the next verse we are told that the Spirit then prevented them from entering Bithynia. Paul was very sensitive to the leading of the Spirit.

Paul tells us that *we*, too, are to be "led by the Spirit." In Galatians 3:14, Paul encourages us that "by faith we might receive the promise of the Spirit." In Galatians 5:16, Paul tells us to "live by the Spirit." In Galatians 5:25, Paul further exhorts us: "Since we live by the Spirit, let us keep in step with the Spirit." In Ephesians 2:22, Paul tells us that we are to be a "dwelling in which God lives by his Spirit." In Ephesians 3:16-17a, Paul says: "I pray that out of his glorious riches He may strengthen you *with power through his Spirit in your inner being,* so that Christ may dwell in your hearts through faith."

In his other letters, Paul tells us that we are to seek the presence, the fruits and the gifts of the Spirit. Paul tells us in Philippians 2:13 that it is God, *through the Spirit*, who works in us to will and to act according to His good purpose. We need the Holy Spirit working in us if we are to fulfill "His good purpose" in us.

Revelation: "Listen to what the Spirit says"

As mentioned above, the Holy Spirit is referred to from the very beginning of the Bible to its very end. In the Book of Revelation, the last book of the Bible, the Spirit is prominent. In several places in the second and third chapters, there is the admonition: "*If you have ears, listen to what the Spirit says.*" This Book was written not just for its current time, but also for all future generations. Today, if we have ears to hear, we must still listen to what the Spirit says.

---

[70] Acts 13:4

The Holy Spirit Today

The Holy Spirit will be one of the main ways that God will speak to us today. We must be cautious about denying, minimizing, or discrediting the power of the Spirit. Jesus says in Matthew 12:32 that we will be forgiven of all our sins except one. Jesus said that "...anyone who speaks against the Holy Spirit will not be forgiven." This is one of the most sobering verses in the New Testament. I do not pretend to fully understand it, but I recognize that the Holy Spirit is not to be maligned or slandered. Paul similarly instructs us: "Do not put out the Spirit's fire."[71]

Instead of speaking against the Holy Spirit, we ought to seek to receive more of the Holy Spirit in our lives. The Holy Spirit indwells each one of us as soon as we become Christians. There does not need to be any outward manifestation of this initial fact. There is no need to join a particular denomination.

As we mature as Christians, we need to nurture our relationship with the Holy Spirit just as we need to nurture our relationship with God the Father and Jesus the Son. The Holy Spirit provides the *power* we need to live our Christian lives as we should. The Holy Spirit will be a major source of God's guidance and counsel to us if we allow Him to be.

If you want more of the "filling" or the "fire" or the "power" of the Holy Spirit in your life (different Bible verses describe this in various words), then begin to pray to receive *a fuller measure* of the Spirit. Perhaps you have not nurtured your relationship with the Spirit since becoming a Christian. In Appendix C of this book, I have included a prayer that you can pray to receive *more of* the Spirit.

The disciples that Jesus breathed upon to receive the Spirit in John 20:22 (after His resurrection) received the "filling of the Spirit" *again* in Acts 2. This shows that being "filled" with the Spirit is not a once in a lifetime event. I personally ask God

---

[71] 1 Thessalonians 5:19

every day in my prayers for a fresh infilling of the Spirit. I want my life to overflow with the power and the presence of the Holy Spirit. I want to become increasingly intimate with the Spirit. Every day each one of us can ask God for more of His Spirit.

In John 7:38-39, Jesus described the Holy Spirit as "streams of living water" that would flow *within us*. The stream can be a mere trickle of water or a mighty torrent. If you are not conscious of those "streams of living water" flowing within you, pray for a greater flow! This will impact your ability to hear God's voice more often and more clearly. You might not feel any difference the first day or the first week that you pray. Over time, however, you will begin to notice that the Spirit *is* leading you by the various means that we will now discuss.

The Guidance and Counsel of the Holy Spirit in *Our* Lives

How does the Holy Spirit guide us? There are many ways, but some of the most frequent ways are mentioned below.

1. Strong Impressions and Promptings

Sometimes we get a noticeable impression—a strong sense to either *do* or to *not do* something. When we try to ignore it, that strong impression deep inside does not go away. Anne's story at the beginning of the chapter is an example of this. If we resist it, we sometimes find out later why we had such a strong compulsion to perhaps phone someone or to *not* go someplace. We need to learn to listen more carefully to those persistent impressions that won't go away. Joyce Huggett calls this an "intuitive knowing" and encourages us to yield to impressions we receive from God's Spirit.[1]

Hannah Whitall Smith, in her great classic *The Christian's Secret of a Happy Life*, wrote these wise words: "If the suggestion is from Him, it will continue and strengthen; if it is not from Him, it will disappear, and we shall almost forget that we ever had it. If it continues, if every time we are brought into near communion with the Lord it seems to return, if it troubles us in our moments of prayer and disturbs all our peace...we may then feel sure it is from God, and we must yield to it..."ᵐ

(a) An Inner Warning

During the year that my sister and I were backpacking in Europe, we foolishly hitch-hiked a few times to save money. On one of those occasions, we waited for hours at the side of a road leading out of a small French village. At one point, a battered up vehicle approached us, driving very slowly but not stopping. The male driver seemed to be checking us out, but finally drove on. My sister and I agreed that the fellow looked creepy! We promised each other that, if that driver returned, we would refuse a ride from him. *Both of us had an inner warning that this man could not be trusted.*

Some time passed. We grew tired, thirsty, and hungry. We were concerned that we would not make our next destination before nightfall. Then *the same car came back.* Can you believe that, notwithstanding the inner warning that both of us felt, we accepted the driver's offer of a ride? I will not go into the details of what happened on that ride. This man's behaviour and conversation demonstrated that he was clearly emotionally unbalanced and potentially violent. At one point, he stopped the car and insisted on showing us a toolbox in his trunk full of hammers, screwdrivers and mallets. We both grew increasingly uncomfortable being alone with this man on a deserted, wooded stretch of road. We started to pray and God soon provided a way of escape for us before this man was able to harm us.

Fortunately, God never wastes an experience. We both learned not to ignore the Spirit's inner warning! We are all on a learning curve. God uses all of our mistakes to make each one of us more sensitive to the inner voice of the Spirit. It takes a lifetime of practice (and the tough lessons we learn from our mistakes), to develop the increasing ability to recognize that inner voice.

If we do pay attention to a strong warning *not* to do something or *not* to go somewhere, we may never find out why we had that impression. We must trust that it was meant to keep us from some danger, snare, negative experience, or temptation that we could not handle.

(b) A Prompting to Pray

Promptings and impressions are not always warnings to *not* do something. We must also learn to obey a strong prompting to *do* something or to *go* somewhere. Sometimes we are prompted to pray, even when we do not fully understand why. My sister-in-law was about to fall asleep one night when she noticed the unusually loud noise that the wind was making outside her home. She was prompted to pray for protection. She did pray, but then, feeling tired, wanted to fall asleep. The Spirit prompted her to *keep praying*. She continued to pray for a period of time, battling her fatigue. The winds became hurricane-force as the night progressed. The following morning, my sister-in-law went outside and surveyed the damage caused by the fierce winds. A large tree had been toppled by the winds, but the path of its fall had missed the house she lived in. Her obedient prayers had resulted in the protection of her home and her life.

Some years ago, I was suddenly awakened in the middle of the night and found myself sitting upright in bed. I felt instantly and unusually awake and alert. Receiving a strong impression to pray for someone and the battle going on in her soul, I prayed for a while for the woman who came to mind. I later learned that that woman died an hour or two after my time of prayer. Who knows how many others were prompted to pray that same hour? (It is even more sobering to think that perhaps I was the only one so prompted.) I later learned that this woman was heard crying out to God before her death. She

had not, prior to that night, professed to be a Christian. I will
not know in this life what exactly transpired in the spiritual
realm during that night, but I do know that it was the Spirit
within me who impressed me to pray in the middle of that
night.

I have felt that same prompting to pray for someone
(sometimes a person I have not seen for some time) on many
occasions over the years. Some of those times, I have not found
out why I was prompted. Other times, I have later learned the
circumstances that the person was in at the time of my prayer. I
have learned (sometimes by my mistakes) to always obey that
prompting to pray.

(c) Prompting to Go

On certain occasions, I have felt prompted to go somewhere
that I had not been planning to go, or to go earlier than I had
planned. When this has happened, I have inevitably run into
someone and have recognized the event as a "divine
appointment" or "divine encounter." The Holy Spirit can lead
us to the right place at the right time to meet someone He
wants us to meet—either for their benefit or sometimes for our
own benefit and blessing.

(d) A Prompting to Speak

Sometimes I have felt prompted to speak to someone that I
would not ordinarily have had much reason to speak with. I
love to garden and in my former home had large, lovely
gardens in the front yard. Many people, out for a walk, would
stop and compliment some aspect of the garden. I would
always thank them, but seldom engaged in deeper
conversation unless I already knew the neighbor. One day, a
young woman about half my age called out to me a comment
about how pretty my garden was. I was bending over busily
doing something. I turned to say my usual thank you, but

something in me prompted me to stand up, walk over to her and get into deeper conversation.

She turned out to be a Christian and had, over the years, been the nanny of two families in my community. Both families had recently gone through some trauma (an affair followed by divorce in one case, the tragic death of a young baby in the second case). I knew the families and their circumstances well enough to have often said a prayer for them whenever I walked past their homes.

The nanny told me that day about how the young sons in the first family had become Christians through her talking and praying with them. She took them to programs at a local church. She told me about some conversations she had had with the grieving mother in the second family. What she told me was very helpful in guiding my prayers for, and subsequent conversations with, those two families. It became clear to me in later weeks that the conversation with the young nanny had been a "divine appointment." I am glad that I listened to the inner prompting of the Spirit to engage her in conversation that day.

(e) A Prompting to Minister

Some Christians have been prompted by the Spirit to engage in world-changing ministries by something that they have seen in the news. David Wilkerson, the well-known pastor who spent years working with the teenage gangs of New York City, had started out as the pastor of a small country church. One evening, in 1958, he felt prompted during his time of prayer to look through a LIFE magazine. He noticed an article about seven boys who were on trial for a murder that had occurred in New York City. An artist's illustration of the seven boys caught Wilkerson's attention. Wilkerson was struck by the look of desperation that the artist had captured in the eyes of one of the boys. As Wilkerson looked into the eyes of that boy, he *knew* that he was to help those boys. The idea that he was to go to New York City persisted until Wilkerson obeyed that inner prompting.

Wilkerson traveled back and forth to New York City over a period of months and became involved in the world of teenage gangs: a sordid world of gang wars, stabbings and murders, prostitution, narcotic drugs, pornography, and promiscuous sex. The Holy Spirit continued to guide him, one step at a time, as he reached out to these teenagers, leading thousands of them to Christ. Wilkerson's story, told in the best-seller *The Cross and the Switchblade,*[n] is an amazing tale of God's guidance through various means, including the inner voice of the Spirit.

Similarly, Brother Andrew's emerging ministry was greatly impacted by a news broadcast that he saw on television in 1968. As he watched Russian tanks invade the country of Czechoslovakia, he wondered how this Communist occupation would affect Christians he knew in Czechoslovakia. That news broadcast was used by the Spirit to prompt Brother Andrew to take a carload of Bibles behind the Iron Curtain.

Over the next decades, Brother Andrew's organization smuggled millions of Bibles into many Communist nations. In more recent decades, his group has been taking Bibles into other nations where Christians are persecuted and where the gospel is not freely preached. In one night alone, Brother Andrew's group smuggled one million Bibles into Communist China. Brother Andrew's ministry, called Open Doors International, now operates in more than one hundred countries.[o] I encourage you to read Brother Andrew's books to learn more of the many fascinating ways that God has led Brother Andrew over the past several decades.

The Spirit often speaks to us through the Bible, as we saw in the last chapter, but He is not limited to that. He can speak to us through news media too!

(f) A Prompting to Act

Sometimes we are prompted by the Spirit to do something that we do not want to do. In my university days, I waitressed part-time to pay for my tuition and books. My first job waitressing was in a restaurant managed by a severe woman from Hong Kong who must have come straight from managing a sweatshop. Her name was Miss Wei. She treated all of the waitresses harshly.

I knew that I would only be working weekends at that job for a matter of months. I felt sorry for some of the young single moms who needed their full-time jobs. One day, I asked the manager if I could talk to her. I tried (with my immature advocacy skills) to present the main grievances of the full-time waitresses. The manager flew into a rage and fired me on the spot.

More than a year later, I was in need of another part-time job. I began to feel a strong prompting to go back to the manager of that restaurant and ask for a job again. You must understand that I was living in Toronto, a city of a few million people, so this was not the only possible job opportunity. The prompting persisted and kept growing stronger, no matter how much I tried to ignore it and evade it.

Finally, I decided to act upon that prompting and steeled my nerves to go in and speak with Miss Wei. As I walked into the restaurant, I saw her eyes widen with incredulity.

We had a very healing conversation. She was surprisingly humble and actually thanked me for confronting her on behalf of the other women on that past occasion. She admitted that she had been harsh and unreasonable. She had not been familiar with what was expected in a Canadian work environment. She had made some changes and morale had improved. She was willing to give me a job again! She could see that I had matured. I admitted to her that I had been overzealous in my advocacy on behalf of the other waitresses. We actually became good friends over that next year. She let me pick the weekend and evening shifts that best suited my university schedule. She became such a blessing in my life! She was actually quite a nice person beneath her tough exterior.

As I look back, I realize that this was not just about God supplying my financial needs. God knew something about my personality that I was not even really aware of myself. I am the kind of person who hates "loose threads," especially if they involve ending a relationship or last seeing a person under unpleasant circumstances. To this day, if I leave someone in that kind of situation, I have to resolve it (sometimes even years later) with some kind of contact, apology, discussion, or letter. Because of the lesson I learned with Miss Wei (and how wonderfully that situation turned out), I have been much quicker to obey the prompting of the Spirit to go back and tie up "loose threads" with another person, even if I don't feel like it. If the Spirit is prompting you to tie up a "loose thread" in a relationship that needs some repair, I encourage you to obey that prompting. The Spirit will go with you. While not all such attempts have a fairy-tale ending, you might be pleasantly surprised at the outcome.

(g) A Prompting to Investigate

I shared earlier about my husband's surgery to remove a dangerous aortic root aneurysm that came close to taking his life. Let me now share how the Holy Spirit was involved in this story.

In the spring of 2002, my husband Sam was spending many evenings cheering his favorite hockey team in an NHL play-off series. Occasionally, in the midst of the excitement of a hockey game, Sam noticed that his heart seemed to be skipping the occasional beat. He mentioned it to a cardiologist friend. Both my husband and this friend did not think much of it. Sam had a very healthy heart. He played a few hours of tennis a couple of times each week. He had perfect blood pressure and cholesterol levels. The minor episodes of skipped beats, occurring in the passion of a play-off series, were not worth investigating. It was probably just too much excitement and too much caffeine for a man in mid-life.

One night, while watching a hockey game, my husband felt clearly prompted to get a stethoscope and to listen to his own heart. His rational mind told him there was nothing to worry about. But the Spirit within would not let him continue watching the game until he obeyed the prompting to get out his stethoscope. (It would normally take a fire, hurricane, or earthquake to get my husband away from the TV during a play-off game!) What Sam heard, as he listened to his own heart, was not normal. After about a week of being in denial that anything was wrong, Sam finally went for further medical investigation. The angiogram and CT scan confirmed that his actual heart was healthy. Unfortunately, the medical tests also showed a large, ominous aneurysm, sitting just above his heart. It was dangerously close to bursting. As I mentioned in an earlier chapter, the surgeon told us that a sudden burst of this aneurysm (probable within six months, given the size of the aneurysm) would likely cause immediate death. Surgery was performed in time.

Most aneurysms of this nature are discovered during an autopsy, *after* the sudden death of an otherwise healthy person. Sam and I are both so thankful that he obeyed the unusual prompting of the Spirit, during the midst of that hockey game, to listen with a stethoscope to his own heart. It literally saved his life.

(h) A Prompting to Change Course

Sometimes the Spirit speaks to us over quite a period of time, repeating a message until we hear it clearly. As I mentioned earlier, I practiced law as a trial lawyer for twenty years. I believed that was what I was meant to do during that season of my life. From time to time, I would pray (especially when my practice was going through a crazy time!) that God would speak to me clearly *if* and *when* He wanted me to leave law and pursue some other kind of work.

As the final years of my practice unfolded, I began to notice something that was happening to me over and over again. On some occasions, when I had won an argument in court, the presiding Judge would say in their oral reasons: "Mrs. Henein, you have *persuaded me* that...." and they would go on to give the specific points that I had persuaded them about. On those occasions, I would leave the courtroom feeling a little sad. There was a dull ache in my heart. I was normally happy, as anyone would be, when I won a case in court. I always argued for what I believed to be a fair, just, reasonable, and right result. But whenever a Judge said that I had *persuaded* them about something, that word *"persuaded"* would make me think. If I had the gift of persuasion, if I was so talented at persuading people, was I using my gift and my talent for the highest possible purposes? I knew that I was using my gift of persuasion for *good* and *worthy* purposes, fighting as best I could for truth, justice, fairness, and for principles that I believed in. But were these the *best purposes* in *my* life? Was it possible that God wanted me to use my gift and my talent for even higher and better purposes from His point of view?

Every time someone told me that I had *persuaded* them (this also happened in meetings and in discussions with clients, colleagues, and opposing counsel), these inner questions would arise in my spirit. The word *"persuaded"* was a kind of "hot button" to my soul. When I heard that word applied to me, I knew that I had to spend time praying, reflecting, meditating, and trying to discern what God was telling me. I could sense that the Spirit was trying to speak to me.

Finally, without clear vision as to what exactly I would do next, I left the practice of law. I simply knew in my spirit that I should take that step. I knew that God was going to show me other ways He would use my gift of persuasion. I knew that I was entering a season of prayer and preparation for new pursuits. What they would be I did not know!

Over the past few years, some of God's new purposes have become clearer to me. I have realized that my main gift lies in the use of words—whether in personally counseling, mentoring, or encouraging someone, or in more public arenas such as writing, speaking, advocacy, and executive outreach. I want to persuade as many people as I can about the truth and reality of God's existence (as Father, Son, and Holy Spirit) and the principles of life (and eternal life) that He has revealed to us. I have developed great passion and purpose, enthusiasm, energy, and excitement, about *persuading* people about the truths of the Kingdom of God.

I have known other people who have had similar experiences. One friend and her husband felt clearly prompted by the Spirit to sell his business and their home, without any clear idea as to where they would be moving or what they would be doing next. The prompting and the impression were so clear to both of them that they knew they had no choice but to obey. The Spirit spoke to them through a verse about Abraham leaving his country and setting off into the unknown. It was only after they obeyed and sold their home and business that their new paths opened up. They moved half way across the country to start new careers. This friend has become a well-known Christian presence in Canadian media. Her husband has pursued his own opportunities. God has done many awesome things in their lives that they would likely have missed if they had not listened to the strong impression of the Spirit within.

Both in my own example of leaving my law practice and in the example of this couple, the leading of the Spirit was a critical ingredient in the life change. This kind of inner spiritual leading must always, of course, be ultimately tested by Scriptural principles, the counsel of others, and the unfolding of circumstances. When making such a radical change, a person should look at *all* the ways that God provides His counsel.

When we step out in faith to obey the prompting or cautioning of the Spirit, it sometimes takes the passage of time before we receive confirmation and affirmation that we have taken the right turn in our lives. If we have done the right thing, the confirmation and the affirmation will come.

2. The Presence or Absence of the Attributes of the Spirit

One of the other main ways that the Holy Spirit guides us is by the presence or absence of certain attributes of the Spirit in us. The main attribute we most commonly encounter in this regard is the attribute of *peace*. In Scripture, peace is described as one of the fruits of the Spirit (Galatians 5). *We ought not to do something unless we have full peace about it.* If you do not have peace, wait!!! Wisdom from above is always full of peace. If you feel unease, discomfort, turmoil, confusion, or anxiety about taking a particular step, recognize these as red (or at least yellow) lights.

Sometimes we need to take note of that inner peace (or lack of it) when we are in a position of having to trust someone. Some years ago, my sister and I were traveling by bus to the large city of Kuala Lumpur in Malaysia. The bus dropped us off on the outskirts of the city around sunrise. There were no taxis or other buses in sight. An older man approached us and asked us if he could drive us into the city to find a hotel. He was a total stranger to us. Normally, it flies in the face of every bit of wisdom and prudence I have to even consider such an offer, and I do not recommend that anyone reading this ever lightly follow this example. But at the time I felt a very clear peace and an inner sense that I should trust this man. My sister gestured with some sort of nod that she thought we should accept. She later told me that she had felt that same peace. My peace over-rode my recollection of the hitch-hiking experience I described earlier, which had ended in narrow escape from serious danger. We were not naïve about the risk we were taking.

This man ended up driving us for several hours around town. There was a large soccer event in the city and hotel after hotel advised us that they were fully booked. We finally found a room outside of the downtown area. This man expected no payment in return for his kindness and turned out to be trustworthy. He provided us with safety, not danger.

In other circumstances, *apparently* trustworthy people can lead us to harm. They can be wolves in sheep's clothing. On some occasions, I have felt a strong check in my spirit against trusting someone who seemed respectable. We cannot always rely solely on our five senses or our mental reasoning, but must learn to heed that inner prompting or that inner check in the spirit realm.

Our inner peace (or lack of it) is one of the strongest inner guides. In addition, we should also consider whether the prospect of taking a particular step (or not) fills us with joy...inspires us with faith...is motivated by love...draws on our courage...accords with wisdom...generates boldness...springs out of generosity...is propelled by compassion...fills us with energy...inspires hope...stirs up gratitude to God. These attributes of the Spirit working in us are good signs that we are probably on the right path and taking a right step.

On the other hand, if our decision seems prompted by worry, anger, pride, revenge, bitterness, or jealousy, then we can be pretty certain that we are not being led by the Spirit. This awareness of what is going on with our thoughts and emotions as we process a decision is part of what it means to be "led by the Spirit." We must be sensitive to our motivations. We must be cognizant of our inner world. We must note what wells up within us as we think of taking a certain step (or saying "no" to that step).

Mother Teresa, who dedicated her life to helping the poorest of the poor, once said that she knew when God was calling her to do something by the profound *joy* she felt at the prospect of taking that step. Joy was like a *magnet* that told her what path to take, even if the path looked difficult.[p]

Most of the time, we do not say or do anything until we have first thought about it, even if just for a moment. Be mindful of your inner world. Are you speaking or acting out of your hurt, your insecurity, your wounded pride, a desire to put someone down, a compulsion to get even, or a drive to get ahead of them? Or is it your desire to bless, to build up, to encourage, to bring good cheer, to instill confidence, and to support? Be honest with yourself.

Often we have to decide whether or not to say "yes" to a particular opportunity that comes our way. It may seem like a good thing to do. It has been my experience that when God wants us to do something, He usually provides the *inclination*, the *motivation* and the *inspiration*. If we feel excited, motivated and passionate about something good, then we are likely moving in the right direction. The word "enthusiasm" comes from two Greek words, *en Theos*, which mean 'inspired by God.' If we feel enthusiastic about doing something good, then it is likely that God has planted that inspiration within us.

On the other hand, if we are dragging our heels and feeling pressured into saying "yes" to something we have no desire to do, then we need to see this as a "yellow light." This is one more way we need to listen to the Spirit guiding us from within. The Spirit is always full of life, energy, and positive motivation. The Spirit ignites, inspires, impacts, and imparts. We are not meant to take on tasks out of guilt, obligation, duty, a people-pleasing mindset, or because we have trouble saying "no." When we say "yes" it should not be a half-hearted "yes," but a "yes" full of enthusiasm.

It should be pointed out that sometimes we might feel hesitation or discomfort when God is trying to push us out of our comfort zone. We usually know when this is the case, however, because God is persistent. He will use many of the other ways of guiding us to make it clear that we need to do something, notwithstanding our discomfort. This kind of discomfort is different from anxiety, foreboding, or clear awareness of a present danger. This kind of discomfort is the resistance we feel to being stretched or being told we should run a race longer than we are used to. We need to discern the difference between the discomfort of doing something *new* (maybe on the *next level*) as opposed to the discomfort of doing something out of *wrong motivation.*

We have been talking up to this point about the presence or absence of the fruit and attributes of the Spirit within our own selves. We can also be guided by observing whether these fruits and attributes are present in others we are interacting with. If you are considering becoming involved in a church, a ministry, or a Christian organization, observe whether the Spirit's fruit is readily apparent. Is God moving in that place? Can His presence be felt? Being "led by the Spirit" often includes being drawn towards where we can see Him already working and moving.

3. The Impartation of Knowledge

The Holy Spirit is capable of imparting knowledge to us. The "message of knowledge," for example, is described as one of the Spirit's gifts that Paul talks about in 1 Corinthians 12. We can tell when this is happening when we are inwardly aware of knowledge that we know has not come to us by ordinary human means. This knowledge can quite precisely guide our next steps.

Many years ago, I was asked to speak to a women's group on a weekday evening. I was home alone with my two-year-old son. I was proud that I had managed to get the two of us ready with time to spare, and I thought it would help me to keep calm if we arrived a little early. I went to get my car keys and realized that they were not where I usually kept them. I quickly looked in all the other logical places where I might have put them. After checking purses and coat pockets, counters and tables, I remembered with sudden panic that my young son loved to play with my keys. I asked him if he had played with them earlier that day. He said that he had. But, of course, he could not remember where he had put them! By this time, I was running late and starting to panic more! I prayed that God would help me find the keys. God knew where the keys were! It was just a matter of Him communicating it to me.

Without exaggeration, I had no sooner prayed than the idea popped into my head to look in my husband's sock drawer in our bedroom. Not a very rational thought—it was so absurd! But the thought was insistent, so I decided to go look there. I opened the sock drawer and there were a few dozen pairs of socks, neatly rolled up. Once again, the thought popped into my head to unroll a very specific pair. Inside the socks, I found the keys! It was one of the last places in my home I would have searched if I was relying on logic and common sense. I made it to my speaking engagement, albeit a little late and a little frazzled!

On another occasion, before my husband Sam and I were married, he had come to visit me at my apartment in the heart of the big city in which I lived. He parked his car, in broad daylight, right in front of the main entrance to my building. He returned to his car to discover that someone had smashed the back window with a brick and had stolen a thick envelope full of some medical charts and some wrapped Christmas presents (which included some special items that Sam had just purchased for me on a trip overseas). These items were all irreplaceable.

Sam came back up to my apartment. We decided to pray about our disappointment, shock, and outrage. Just as we started praying, the thought clearly popped into my mind that the items had been discarded at the rear of my apartment building. The thought came to me not as a possibility, but somehow as a certainty. I just *knew* that if we went out to look for them we would find them abandoned exactly where I pictured them in my mind. Sure enough, that is what happened. I suppose that medical records and Asian art pieces were not what the thief had hoped to find! I know that this inspiration to go look behind the building was not the product of logical thought. The "knowledge" had come to me in the midst of prayer and was so clear an image in my mind! I believe that the Spirit imparted this knowledge to me.

Permit me to tell one final story along these lines. Early in our marriage, my husband and I took a trip to the Cape Cod area, and one afternoon we used the indoor swimming pool of the hotel where we were staying. I remember noticing how beautifully my wet diamond ring had sparkled in the halogen lighting of the pool area. Back in our hotel room, as I was drying off after my shower, the loops of my terrycloth towel got caught in the metal prongs of the same ring...minus its large solitaire diamond! I was heartbroken. Aside from the material loss, the diamond ring had a sentimental value that far outweighed its actual value.

Recalling how the diamond had sparkled in the pool, I realized that it must have come loose from its setting somewhere in the pool area or along the path back to our room. We searched the pool and the hot tub. By this point, it was dark outside, and I despaired of ever being able to find the diamond in the midst of the thousands of little pieces of multi-shaded gravel that made up the path. I prayed. *I knew that God knew exactly where the diamond was and that He could somehow show me.* I had to put my despair aside and trust that the Spirit would show me where to look.

Some moments later, I noticed a beam of light emanating from a phone booth on the side of the path ahead of me. This was the only part of the path that had any light to speak of. And there it was—my diamond—sparkling brightly in the midst of the gravel *at the center of the beam of light*. Had it been daytime, I would not likely have seen it. If it had been on the unlit part of the path, I would not have found it.

Sometimes the Spirit also imparts creative ideas in our imaginations. I believe that God has spoken to countless people over the centuries, helping them to create great works of art and music, to develop amazing inventions, and to pioneer medical breakthroughs. All of us have had the experience, at one time or another, of trying to solve something...and then the proverbial light bulb has suddenly been turned on in our mind. The answer, solution, or necessary idea pops into our mind out of nowhere. When great ideas just suddenly pop into our minds like that, it may very well be the work of the Spirit. I believe that brilliant Christians like scientist Isaac Newton, classical composers Johann Sebastian Bach and George Frideric Handel, astronomer Nicholas Copernicus, Oxford scholar C.S. Lewis, poet William Wordsworth, and physicist Blaise Pascal had some divine impartation and inspiration that allowed their work to surpass what their merely human level of accomplishment would have been. We will study in more depth in a later chapter how much God wants to impart wisdom and knowledge to us.

4. Our Talents

We have all been gifted with particular talents, skills, and passions that we have hopefully developed over time. We have also received a corresponding *enjoyment* of those gifts that have augmented their development. These talents, gifts, and passions tell us something about why God has created us. He wants us to *use* those talents and to *enjoy* those passions. There is a verse I love buried deep in the Old Testament. In Exodus 35:30-33, Moses told the Israelites: "The Lord has chosen Bazelel…and he has filled him with the Spirit of God, with skill, ability and knowledge in all kinds of crafts—to make artistic designs for work in gold, silver and bronze, to cut and set stones, to work in wood and to engage in all kinds of artistic craftsmanship." First, the Spirit filled Bazelel. Then the Spirit gifted Bazelel. Bazelel was given divine assignments in accordance with those gifts. One can only assume that Bazelel took great enjoyment, fulfillment, and satisfaction from helping with the building of the sanctuary using his special talents.

If you have notable gifts in any area—music, math, art, sports, speaking, organizing, teaching, helping others, hospitality, designing, computer programming, lending a listening ear, nurturing children—whatever your gift, *this is a clue to what God wants you to do with your life*. If He has given you a gift, He surely does not want to waste it. He wants you to do what others cannot do, to go where others cannot go. He wants to tell you how you can use your talents and gifts for His glory. Do not neglect your gift unless you receive very clear guidance that it is something you must lay down.

I am fascinated by the life of George Washington Carver, the son of two black slaves, who was born in 1864. Carver became a highly talented and well-known botanist and chemist, achieving an education, career, and status that were unusual for a black man of his era. He loved to tell the story of a "conversation" he had with God. First, he had asked God to tell him why He had made the universe. God told him to ask something more in proportion to what Carver's mind could comprehend. Carver, ever the curious scientist, asked God why He had made the earth. Again, God told Carver that this was too much for his mind to grasp. Then Carver asked why God had made man. God responded that Carver still wanted to know too much. Carver, who loved botany, then asked God why He had made plants. God once again responded that Carver was asking too big a question! Finally, Carver asked God why He had made the peanut. God answered Carver by revealing to him amazing information about the humble peanut.

Carver studied the peanut in his laboratory and went on to discover *three hundred* uses for the peanut. Carver was able to speak before prominent men about his scientific discoveries relating to the peanut, including giving testimony before the Ways and Means Committee of the U.S. House of Representatives. God had led Carver to develop unique talent and knowledge pertaining to the scientific properties and myriad profitable uses of a plant that grew in his backyard.[q]

5. The Conviction of the Spirit

The Holy Spirit also works in our lives by convicting us of sin.[72] This inner conviction is also one of the ways that the Spirit can lead us or counsel us. The Holy Spirit is our Conscience. If we are allowing sin in our lives (even in the form of thoughts/emotions such as anger, jealousy, resentment, worry, or pride) then we are heading off on a wrong track. The Spirit will try to convict us so that we can deal with our sin and take whatever steps are necessary to get back on the right track. We cannot be living in some form of sin (whether in action or attitude) and be in the centre of God's will. We cannot harbor sin in our hearts or minds and expect to have unbroken communion with God. Sin will hinder or block our prayers. Sin will deceive us. Sin must be dealt with as soon as we become conscious of it or it will stop us from hearing God's counsel (other than counsel about dealing with the sin).

This takes us back to the need for us to submit and surrender to God and to obey Him, and to the requirement that we desire to be on (and stay on or get back on) the right path. Sin is essentially rebellion against God and His ways. Sin will get in the way of everything that we are discussing in this book.

The Holy Spirit will counsel us about any area of sin that has not been dealt with before He will counsel us about the issues that *we* want to be on "the front burner."

The Still Small Voice

The Holy Spirit does not usually shout at us (although there are exceptions as we will discuss below). The Holy Spirit has often been described as a gentleman. In 1 Kings 19, we are told that Elijah found himself in the midst of a powerful wind, then an earthquake, then a fire. God was not in any of these. Finally,

---

[72] John 16:8-11

God came to Elijah in "a gentle whisper" (or what has also been translated as a "still small voice").

We will only hear that gentle whisper or that still small voice if we listen for it carefully. We must want to hear it. Sometimes we must strain our ears. We must deliberately shut out all the din and babble of the world around us. We must want an intimate walk with God before we will hear that still small voice on any regular basis.

If we ignore the still small voice, sometimes God will turn up the volume. He will do so through circumstances. C.S. Lewis once said that pain is God's "megaphone" to a deaf world.[r] Sometimes God has to allow very painful circumstances in our lives to get our attention so that we can get back on track and in proper relationship with Him. King David said in Psalm 68:33, for example, that sometimes God "thunders with a mighty voice." I try to listen to the whisper so that it does not have to become a shout!

The Spirit's Help with Our Prayers

The Holy Spirit is much more than just our Counselor. One of the other roles that the Spirit plays in our lives is to help us with prayer, so that our prayer lines up with God's plans for our lives. The Holy Spirit intercedes for us in prayer. Paul wrote in Romans 8:26-27: "...the Spirit helps us in our weakness. We do not know what we ought to pray for, but the Spirit himself intercedes for us...And he who searches our hearts knows the mind of the Spirit, because the Spirit intercedes for the saints *in accordance with God's will.*" We do not always know exactly how we should pray. The Holy Spirit is there to help us and to intercede for us. *He will always pray in accordance with God's will.* I am so thankful that the Holy Spirit intercedes for me and that He prays in accordance with God's will, even when I am not yet aware of what God's will for me is.

Letting the Spirit's Voice Line Up with Other Guidance

We have to be very careful about relying *only* on being led by the Spirit, especially in the early years of our Christian walk or whenever the decision-making process involves intense emotions. This is especially true with important, highly emotional decisions like who we should date and who we should marry. Similarly, we should not rashly quit a job or back out of a commitment purely on the basis of some "impression," especially if it is emotionally loaded. Those who will *only* be led by the Spirit (and do not want to do the hard work of praying, reading the Word, and fellowshipping with other Christians who can give us wise counsel) will make mistakes. It is important, especially with major decisions, to *test* and *confirm* what we believe the Spirit is telling us. The Spirit will never speak in contradiction to God's Word. What the Spirit says will *always* line up with the Word. The Spirit can speak to significant others around us (our spouse for example) to *confirm* in them what He is telling us. The Spirit can move within our circumstances so that they eventually line up with what the Spirit is supposedly telling us.

Although one needs to be cautious when learning to listen to the Spirit, paying attention to what the Spirit is trying to tell us "in our gut" is nonetheless an invaluable dimension of God's counsel to us. This method of counsel is often overlooked and underused. As we mature in our Christian faith and become more experienced in our walk with God, we can learn how to rely on this dimension of God's counsel more and more, in conjunction with the other means of hearing from God.

Let us be encouraged to seek a deeper relationship with the Holy Spirit! He wants to be our constant companion. When the telephone rings and news arrives that shakes our world (like Anne's world, at the beginning of this chapter), we need to be in readiness for intimate dialogue with God and His indwelling Spirit.

...be filled with the Spirit...
Ephesians 5:18

...The Spirit intercedes for the saints in accordance with God's will.
Romans 8:27

Whoever believes in me ...streams of living water will flow from within him. By this, he meant the Spirit...
John 7:38-39

Since we live by the Spirit, let us keep in step with the Spirit.
Galatians 5:25

9.

The Counsel of Others

Plans fail for lack of counsel, but with many advisors they succeed.
Proverbs 15:22

…how good is a timely word!
Proverbs 15:23

A wise man listens to advice.
Proverbs 12:15b

In the spring of 2005, my mother and I had the opportunity to visit my sister, who has been an aid worker in Afghanistan for more than a decade. We had the privilege of visiting the Canadian security forces base just outside of Kabul. I was intrigued, but also sickened, to see a prominent display of all the different kinds of landmines that remain buried in Afghanistan. There are still millions of them in the countryside! Driving around Kabul, I noticed men and children who were missing limbs or wearing eye patches. They are casualties of these terrible weapons.

Needless to say, I was nervous during the day that we spent in the countryside outside of Kabul. My sister wanted to show us where she hopes to build another garden sanctuary for women and children. We walked around a large grassy field in the shadow of the snow-capped Hindu Kush Mountains. My sister assured me that there were no landmines on the side of the road that we were walking on. I was not very convinced, however, when she advised me that there likely *were* landmines on the *other* side of the road! I prayed before I gingerly took each step, trusting that God would protect me. I also had to trust the counsel of my sister. I was unfamiliar with the area. She had been there many times and had been told by people she trusted that the land where we were walking had been de-mined. There are times in life when we have to rely on the counsel of others. There are times when the judgment, knowledge, and experience of others will aid us in finding the best path.

We are not meant to live in isolation. We are not meant to be totally independent. We need one another for companionship, fellowship and support. We are also meant to seek counsel from one another. We are told in Corinthians that the Christian church is analogous to a body. The hands cannot live without the feet or the eyes or the ears.

It is wonderful to have a mentor who has traveled the road ahead. It is a rich blessing to have mature Christian friends. We are also greatly blessed if we are able to seek out the opinions and insights of wise family members. Proverbs 27:17 tells us that "As iron sharpens iron, so one man sharpens another." Proverbs 15:22 states: "Plans fail for lack of counsel, but with many advisers they succeed." God can, and does speak to us through the wise people He places around us. God can speak through human lips.

Counsel from Our Parents

As I recently re-read the book of Proverbs, I was struck by how often there was advice about listening to our parents. In Proverbs 4:1-6, Solomon wrote: "Listen, my sons, to a father's instruction; pay attention and gain understanding….When I was a boy in my father's house…he taught me and said, 'Lay hold of my words with all your heart; keep my commands and you will live. Get wisdom, get understanding; do not forget my words or swerve from them. Do not forsake wisdom, and she will protect you; love her, and she will watch over you.'"

In Proverbs 6:20, Solomon again said: "…keep your father's commands and do not forsake your mother's teaching." In Proverbs 13:1, he said "A wise son heeds his father's instruction." In Proverbs 22:6, Solomon encouraged parents: "Train a child in the way he should go, and when he is old he will not turn from it."

I have been blessed with two wise parents who have always *been there* to talk about any decision whenever I have sought their input. They have not been intrusive. They have not been overbearing. They have not been offended if, after weighing their counsel, I did not follow their advice for some reason. They have just generally *been there* for me, ready to speak out of their years of experience. As a teenager, I remember talking with them about drinking, drugs, dating, break-ups, spiritual issues, jobs, finances, travel plans, various friendships, and much more.

Even though I was coming of age in the hippie era, I never tried drugs. It was certainly not for lack of opportunity or curiosity. I remember a time in my mid-teens when I was tottering on the fence of indecision in this area. So many friends and classmates raved about their drug experiences and it all seemed so harmless. Why not smoke marijuana? Everybody else was doing it. I can still remember exactly where I was sitting the night I discussed the issue with my mom. She was busy (with four teenagers and a full-time job she was always busy in those days!). I remember that she looked tired, but she talked about the issue with me anyway. I cannot remember exactly what she said, but it was enough to convince me to avoid the drug scene.

I had a similar talk with both of my parents about drinking. I did not listen to their advice and had to learn the hard way that what they had said about the dangers of excessive drinking was right, true, and wise. Sometimes we learn to value our parents' wisdom *after* we have made the mistakes they warned us about!

One of my mother's favorite responses to any of my teen questions (that started with "what's wrong with trying....") was this: in my life, I had a choice as to whether I would be "wise" or a "fool." She said that fools eventually "shipwreck" their lives. It was very simple advice, but it impacted me. I didn't want anyone to think that I was a fool! Who in their right mind does? And I certainly didn't want to shipwreck my life! The word "shipwreck" was a very ominous word to me. I didn't need to hear about fire and brimstone. It was enough to ponder that foolish decisions might lead to the shipwreck of my life. I made a decision in my teen years that I would pay attention to how I was navigating around all of the rocks.

My mother advised all four of us teenagers that we should read the book of Proverbs. That was a good place to start if we wanted to find out how to be "wise" and how to avoid becoming a "fool." This is still effective advice for teenagers today. It is amazing that a book written millennia ago is so relevant to life issues such as work, gossip, friendship, emotional management, sexual temptation, and many other issues.

My parents are both alive, in their mid-seventies, so I am blessed to still have the availability of their wise counsel. In my adult years, they have given input on my choice of marriage partner, wedding plans, parenting, finances, travel plans, real estate decisions, and career changes. This counsel has seldom been "formal." It has arisen in the course of casual conversation. I have not always agreed with everything they said, but have always at least carefully weighed it.

There are, of course, some situations in which a person might not want to seek advice from a parent. Perhaps there has been abuse, a history of excessive criticism, or some other dysfunction. Unfortunately not all parents are wise. If you *do* have wise parents, treasure them and be deeply thankful. Wisdom is the best inheritance you will ever receive.

My husband and I both turned fifty recently. We have told our children (now young adults!) that they should listen to us, as we now have a whole century of experience between us. Talk about having been "around the block!" Because I was so blessed by the wisdom of my parents, I have always wanted to maintain a close and loving dialogue with my own children. Some of my most treasured memories with my son and daughter involve conversations after school, sitting around the kitchen table talking about what happened in class, on the recess yard, or in the backyard with their friends. As a family, we have had countless discussions over restaurant meals, while we drove in the car, and while we spent holidays together. I have always been thankful that both of my children were (most of the time) so receptive to counsel and advice (which was hopefully wise!) And yes, they have heard the "wise" person, "foolish" person, "shipwreck" speech. Who knows, they might even pass that advice on to their own kids!

Other Family

If we have invested in counseling our children, they will themselves become a *source* of great advice. My son and daughter are so much savvier than my husband and I about how to survive in the modern world. I love to hear their opinions and advice! I know who to go to if I want advice on computers, fashion, what movie is worth seeing, and how any kind of technology works. I am increasingly appreciating their counsel on a wide variety of matters.

I have also been blessed with wise siblings, who are all mature Christians. I have so deeply valued what they have had to say over the years. I have been especially close to my sister, as we are a year apart in age. I have trusted her advice more than most others in my life. I know that she will be totally honest with me, even if it hurts, even if it goes totally against my own opinion. I have not always agreed with or followed what she had to say, but I have been open to her opinions. She knows me well and has, many a time, wisely cautioned me about various situations. In my teens and twenties, she rightly advised me to break off relationships with certain men I dated. She was always quick to tell me when I was working too hard or not going to church regularly enough. We lived together for five years in our mid-twenties and her invaluable counsel (much as it sometimes upset me) helped me survive those years with fewer mistakes than I might otherwise have made! Proverbs 27:6 talks about the "wound" of a trustworthy friend—someone who cares enough to give tough advice that might hurt in the short run but bless and protect in the long run. We all need someone in our lives who is not afraid of annoying us when they give tough but appropriate counsel.

It was very important to me to ask the counsel of my parents, brothers, and sister before I married my husband Sam. (My brothers had been a valuable source of counsel in my dating life. They helped me understand how men think!) My family members were all very affirmative, supportive, and encouraging in their advice about my prospective husband. Had they been otherwise, I would certainly have carefully weighed what they had to say! I valued their insights as to what was best for me and my future. Had they been against me marrying my husband, I might not have followed their advice at the end of the day, but I certainly would have pondered their opinions and prepared myself for areas I might have to work on in my marriage.

Even my grandmother had something to say about my future husband. She had approached me, after meeting previous boyfriends of mine over the years, and had always told me, "Karen, he is not the one." I figured that I would never please her and stopped taking her advice very seriously. When she came up to me after the party celebrating my engagement, I expected to hear her usual comment. When she told me "Karen, he *is* the one," I was in a state of shock! Because of all her earlier comments, I *did* attach weight to her affirmative advice. I had fully expected her to be a "red light" on my marriage checklist! When she turned out to be an encouraging "green light," I took note. Of course, I still had to make up my own mind, but *the caution* or *the affirmation* of those close to us (who have known us during all the years of our growing up) is worth a great deal.

Our Spouse

My husband Sam has, of course, also been a constant source of counsel. He, too, knows me well after almost a quarter century of marriage—probably better than anyone else on earth. He is also not afraid to give truthful counsel, whether it accords with what I think or not. Over the years, for example, one of my greatest challenges has been maintaining the balance between a fulfilling career and spending time at home with my children. I always seemed to be second-guessing whether I was working too much or not enough and whether I was home enough for our son and daughter. My husband was always willing to talk this out with me and his counsel was always wise.

After we had our first child, our son Darrin, I had promised my law firm that I would let them know within six months whether or not I would return to work. Although I had already been offered family-friendly hours and a reduced caseload, as the six month point drew nearer, I found myself wanting to stay home full-time for the next few years. My husband strongly counseled me to accept the part-time hours and listed a number of reasons. Both he and my boss (who gave me the same reasons) told me that if it did not work out I could always change my mind and stay home. In the end, I took my husband's advice and was thankful for it. I went on to enjoy fifteen more years of my law practice, while still enjoying ample time raising my two children. My boss and my law firm generously allowed me to continue to work on a family-friendly, reduced-hours basis (while still working on awesome cases) right to the end of my practice.

I am thankful that my husband was there to coach me through the various decisions I made during all those years. At times, he seemed to know me better than I knew myself. He helped me see beyond my immediate emotions, stresses, and frustrations. I could trust that he had my best interests at heart. He was invaluable in helping me to sustain a fulfilling career while maintaining relational priorities on the "mommy track."

Women are taught in the church that they should listen to their husbands. Husbands do not get as much instruction on the worth of their wives' input. Many great men of God have learned to value their wives' contribution to the decision-making process. William and Catherine Booth started the Salvation Army. Within their own lifetimes, this denomination, with its wonderful emphasis on the "social" gospel, had spread to over fifty nations. In those same years, tens of millions of dollars had been raised for social projects that helped the poor and needy. About ten thousand men and women had joined the Salvation Army while the Booths were at the helm. Catherine was instrumental in this growth, giving her husband ideas, sermon outlines, advice, and feedback. William Booth was not too proud to accept the counsel of his wife. They were a strong partnership.

The same can be said of Billy and Nell Sunday. Billy Sunday was a professional baseball player who became a prominent American evangelist. In the days before television, he preached to over 100 million people and is credited with winning about one million souls to Christ! At pivotal times in his life, he listened to the counsel of his wife Nell. Faced with the decision of accepting a lucrative baseball contract or working for much less for the YMCA, he followed his wife's counsel to leave baseball. Billy Sunday never made an important decision without consulting Nell.

Hudson and Maria Taylor provide a similar example. Hudson Taylor was a pioneering missionary who started the China Inland Mission—he recruited over eight hundred other missionaries for the Mission by the time he died! Hudson Taylor highly valued the counsel of his wife and consulted her on all major decisions. *Together*, they had profound impact and influence on the spread of Christianity in 19th century China.

Although husbands make the major decisions in a Christian marriage, a wise husband will pay careful attention to the perspective of his wife. Wives ought to show due respect to the viewpoint of their husbands. One of the greatest blessings of marriage is the availability of the counsel that a husband and a wife can give one another. Their knowledge of one another runs deep. They become well acquainted with one another's strengths and weaknesses. They have insight into the unique personality of the other. They have awareness of the dreams, goals, hopes, and aspirations of their spouse. They know where the other person is most likely to yield to temptation. They understand the surrounding circumstances and relationships. A husband and a wife ought to highly value the counsel of one another and to never take it for granted.

Friends

Over the years, I have also had many trustworthy friends who were willing to offer counsel. Even though I am in my fifties (and should know what I am doing by now!) I find the counsel of friends more invaluable than ever. I am making more effort to surround myself with wise women and with other married couples who inspire, encourage, listen, advise, question, and even caution me when necessary.

We need to select our friends with care. They will impact and influence us. They will *sharpen us* or *dull us* spiritually.

They will keep us on track or lead us astray. They will bring us closer to God or cause us to compromise and backslide. In Psalm 1:1, the psalmist wrote: "Blessed is the man who does not walk in the counsel of the wicked..." In Psalm 16:3, King David wrote: "I want the company of the godly men and women in the land; they are the true nobility"(LB). In Matthew 15:14b, Jesus said: "If a blind man leads a blind man, both will fall into a pit." In Proverbs 14:7, King Solomon wrote: "If you are looking for advice, stay away from fools"(LB). In Luke 6:45, Jesus said: "The good man brings good things out of the good stored up in his heart, and the evil man brings evil things out of the evil stored up in his heart. For out of the overflow of his heart his mouth speaks."

Because of this Biblical advice, I have come to value church fellowship and Christian friendships more and more as the years pass. I am increasingly deliberate as to which friendships I cultivate and nourish. Find friends with good hearts and disciplined minds. They will impart wisdom, encouragement, constructive advice, hope, and support. Avoid the continual company of those who will speak out of jealousy, foolishness, pride, selfish ambition, or a critical and judgmental spirit. Be careful not to grow close to those who will dampen your faith or lead you down a wrong path.

Pastors

I have had a number of pastors over the years. A few of them have been tremendously gifted speakers. In contrast, one pastor that I knew briefly was not that easy to listen to for a whole sermon. I sometimes found myself tuning out during his sermons, thinking about where we should have lunch, what should be on my grocery list that week, what color to paint my living room, how to solve a problem at work, or whatever. One day I felt God rebuking me for this. I realized that just as God could and did speak through many other people to me, He wanted to speak through my pastor. Every week, if I was willing to pay attention, He had something to teach me through my pastor. I began to listen much more diligently and began to discover hidden nuggets of truth in even the driest of sermons—nuggets that *did* have very direct application to my life that week.

I also have a favorite TV pastor that I listen to once a week. Many times God has very clearly spoken through him. He lives a thousand miles away, but God does use him quite regularly to offer incredibly specific counsel about my life circumstances.

Once you have taken the time to be in church, there is no point in wasting that time. Keep your ears open. God can and will speak to you through your pastor if you are in a solid church. Your pastor may not say something earth-shaking every week, but he is in a special place of influence and authority in your life. God can use a single sentence in his sermon to impact your life in some way.

Prior to becoming a world-famous evangelist, Dwight L. Moody received some inspirational counsel from a pastor he met at a prayer meeting in England. That minister, Henry Varley, said to Moody: "The world has yet to see what God can do with one man wholly committed to Him." Deeply impacted by that one life-changing sentence, Moody eventually went on to preach to about 100 million people on both sides of the Atlantic.

Mentors

I came of age before it was fashionable to have a work mentor or life coach. It never occurred to me to seek out a more mature person (outside of family) to give me regular advice about my life, my career, or my relationships. As a Christian, I was developing my ability to seek counsel from the Word, to be sensitive to the Spirit, and to be watchful of my circumstances. Seeking out an older mentor was not on my radar screen at all.

Having said that, God brought various people across my path at various times who were, in fact, mentors for a season.

I did not seek them out, but *there they were,* giving advice and modeling right living. The year that Sam and I traveled across Africa, we met some older couples who taught us much about Christian marriage, parenthood, and family life. These interactions left a strong impression on both of us. I cannot imagine how wonderful it would have been to have had mentors like that consistently feeding into our lives for years! If I could have my life to live over, I would develop these kinds of relationships more.

My husband and I are mentors to some younger couples. I want to be for them what I wish I had enjoyed more for myself. It is never too late, though! I am increasingly and deliberately seeking out some older women who have great wisdom to impart to me. I am blessed, for example, to have a weekly prayer partner who is further down the road than me in marriage and parenthood. I always value Shirley's advice. Because we touch base almost every week, she knows me well.

It is a bonus that Shirley and I also pray together about ongoing life issues and decisions. The apostle Paul wrote to some of the Christians in the early church in Greece about a man named Epaphras. Paul said: "He is always *wrestling in prayer* for you, that you may stand firm *in all the will of God,* mature and fully assured."[73] Shirley and I provide companionship and counsel to one another, but we also wrestle in prayer for one another. A *praying* mentor is of special value. *We can have the path ahead paved with prayer.* We can immensely benefit from the power of a Matthew 18:19 "prayer of agreement." That verse promises that if two or more agree on anything they ask God for, He will do it.

Young people coming of age these days are fortunate indeed to have this concept of mentorship ingrained in them. They will be the wiser for it. Even seasoned leaders can benefit from mentors. I have heard and read many times that Billy Graham has been friends with several American Presidents

---

[73] Colossians 4:12

over the past half a century. The propensity of many of America's leaders to befriend and to seek spiritual counsel from godly men and women is no doubt one of the reasons that God has so richly blessed America. It is also exciting to know that about 170 Christian CEO's of multi-billion dollar Fortune 500 companies network with one another—mentoring, sharing, praying with and for one another.[s] As Christians, we need one another, whether we are at the top of our game or the end of our rope.

Counsel from Books

I love reading good books and have many favorite Christian authors. These men and women have been powerful "mentors." What a privilege to cuddle under a cozy blanket in front of a fire on a winter's night and to read a good Christian book! In Christian bookstores (and increasingly in secular bookstores) there are shelves full of amazing books on every topic imaginable. What I lacked in real-life mentors during certain seasons of my life, I made up for in books. I read at least a dozen books on marriage even before my wedding date (and realized soon after that I was going to have to re-read those books!). I have read many a book about parenting at different stages (and have re-read those, too!). I have learned much through books about dealing with anxiety, depression, resentment, forgiveness, disappointment, and hurt. Many authors have been "counselors" to me.

Watchman Nee has taught me lessons on how to deal with money as a Christian. Andrew Murray, Dutch Sheets, and others have taught me much about prayer. Corrie ten Boom was one of my first "mentors" in the area of finding courage, faith, and God's peace in the tough times. I have been challenged, inspired, motivated, and counseled by these great men and women of God. So let me encourage you to cuddle up under a blanket or find a quiet spot in the garden or in any corner of your world and spend quality time being "counseled" by these insightful authors. A mentor does not have to be someone you meet face to face!

Books can change the course of our lives. Charles Colson became a Christian after reading *Mere Christianity* by C.S. Lewis. John Newton, the author of the beloved hymn *Amazing Grace*, first turned to God after reading Thomas a Kempis's *The Imitation of Christ*. David Livingstone, the well-known African explorer, first decided to become a medical missionary after reading a book by a Chinese medical missionary. Books can be powerful influences that God brings to bear in our lives.

Many Advisors

Proverbs tells us to have *many* advisors. So seek out advisors from the various categories we have just discussed. Do not let pride stop you from asking for this help, especially if the decision is a major one. You might not find advisors in every category, but seek out at least one or two counselors.

The counsel of others is especially valuable when those others have direct interest in the matter at hand. It is more likely that they will invest some time and careful thought to it. Married couples are blessed in this regard because so many of life's decisions affect them both. Your spouse will not likely give you an off-the-cuff piece of advice about whether or not the time is right to start a family! Your spouse will not lightly counsel you about the wisdom of quitting a job before they themselves have taken a close look at the bank account and have otherwise given due consideration to the decision!

Conflicting Counsel

What about situations where you hear adverse, conflicting opinions? What about situations where you think it is best to proceed with a certain course of action and others advise you not to? How do you know when someone else's counsel is what you should listen to? Often it is just a matter of recognizing the wisdom in someone's advice.

In John 10:14, Jesus said, "My sheep know me." In John 8:47a, Jesus said: "He who belongs to God hears what God says." We must learn to recognize God's voice even when it comes through human lips. We can test advice from others by seeing if it lines up with Scripture, stirs up the good attributes of the Spirit in us, accords with circumstances, resonates with our best judgment, and seems consistent with our own life experience.

This is a further reason why we should get to know the Bible from cover to cover. When someone offers advice that is clearly consistent with Biblical principles, we need to carefully weigh that advice. If the advice flies in the face of what we believe the Bible teaches, we should disregard that advice, no matter how well-phrased, persuasive, "sensible," or "logical" it might seem to be. Just as we need to recognize our own motivations (are we acting/speaking out of love, kindness, peace, and encouragement or out of anger, pride, jealousy, a competitive spirit, or revenge), we also need to develop a keen insight into what is motivating someone else's advice to us. Sadly, the counsel of even those who are close to us might not always be pure and faultless.

Maintain Ultimate Responsibility

Although the counsel of others is important, it is not perfect. We cannot solely rely on the advice of others, no matter how wise they appear to be, before we proceed. *The counsel of others is not meant to be a substitute for careful study of the Word, prayerfully waiting and watching, paying attention to our inner spiritual impressions, and noting how circumstances are developing.* Getting advice from others and then stepping straight into action might appear to be a relatively efficient route to take, but it could turn out being costly. Prayer, Bible study, spiritual meditation, inner reflection, and patient observation all take extra time and effort. But they are worth it.

Remember that this is *your* life—it is ultimately *your* decision about career, marriage, financial investment, parenthood, or ministry. Other people will never invest the time and effort in *your* life that you should invest for yourself. While the advice of others is meant to be helpful (and might even prevail), it is not a substitute for the hard work of wisely and thoughtfully managing your own life. God places the ultimate responsibility for your life on *you*, and this can never be delegated to someone else. Keep the counsel of others in proper perspective. Query whether their counsel lines up with the other means God is using to counsel your life.

There will be times when we proceed against the counsel of others. This is not wrong, if we have received lots of other "green lights" to give us the security, safety, and confidence that we are proceeding wisely. We will need an extra measure of certainty, courage, and boldness to do this. Paul, for example, was cautioned by the brethren *not* to go to Jerusalem.[74] Paul made the decision to go, notwithstanding their counsel. He believed that this was his destiny. They turned out to be right about the danger they predicted. Paul believed, however, that he had to walk into that danger. Paul *knew* that God wanted him to go to prison and on to Rome in chains.

In modern times, a missionary named Jim Elliot went to Ecuador to work with the Auca Indians, a tribe which had not yet been reached with the gospel. Jim Elliot said that this decision was based on *God's counsel*, not on the counsel of those who suggested he should stay to work with Christians in the United States.[t] His friends quite rightly assessed that Jim was walking into grave danger, and Jim was, indeed, murdered by some of the Aucas. Like Paul, however, Jim Elliot was prepared to hear God's voice alone as he bravely faced his destiny. He felt that he had to ignore the well-meaning counsel of his friends.

---

[74]   Acts 21

Although the counsel of others is not always perfect, and in some cases needs to be put aside, we are all much richer if we are close to others on whom we can count for honest advice. Thankfully, we are not on our journey alone. Of course, God is always with us, but most of the time we also have mortal companions to share our journey with. If we surround ourselves with wise companions and mentors, they can be profoundly positive influences in our lives, helping to shape and discern our destiny. They can be a channel of God's voice to us. God can, and does speak through human lips. These counselors can keep us safe from the landmines of our lives. They can help us to determine where it is safe to walk.

The mouth of the righteous brings forth wisdom...
The lips of the righteous know what is fitting...
Proverbs 10:31-32

He who walks with the wise grows wise,
but a companion of fools suffers harm.
Proverbs 13:20

10.

Physical Signs and Circumstances

...let us be alert...
1 Thessalonians 5:6

In his early thirties, Dwight L. Moody juggled three ministries. He was a pastor. He was also very involved in the work of the YMCA in Chicago. Occasionally, he traveled as an evangelist. Although Moody felt more and more drawn to evangelism, he primarily kept occupied with his other two ministries in Chicago.

Then came the devastating Chicago fire of 1871. A large part of the city was destroyed. Moody's church and the YMCA Center were both burned to the ground. Moody tried to raise funds to rebuild the church and the YMCA, but the money did not pour in. With both of those doors slammed shut at the same time, Moody began to commit much more time to traveling as an evangelist. This was the "open door" of his life at that point.

His church was eventually rebuilt and the YMCA work in Chicago was eventually restarted. In the meantime, Moody spoke in other cities as invitation upon invitation came to him.

He ignited crowds in Britain and America, setting a faith-inspiring example for later evangelists such as Billy Graham to follow. He ultimately became one of the most famous evangelists of the nineteenth century and founder of the renowned Moody Bible Institute in Chicago. He traveled a million miles in his lifetime, preached to about 100 million people, and is credited with winning about 750,000 people to Christ. Who knows what would have happened to Moody if that fire had not occurred at such a pivotal point in his life?

Fortunately, God does not usually allow a whole city to be burned down to get our attention. But God does use our evolving circumstances to provide some clues as to what direction we should be going in.

Many times, God has guided me through physical signs and through my surrounding circumstances. Seeking God's counsel occurs mainly in the spiritual realm, but God does send signals to us through the physical world around us—sometimes subtle, other times quite obvious. We need to be always alert to what is happening all around us and to what God might be trying to communicate through our circumstances.

The Bible often refers to our journey through life as a "path." A path is *physical*—it has boundaries, crossroads, turns, and perhaps some detours. Our eyes can tell us when we are on a particular path and when we are straying from it. Paths have sign-posts or landmarks that guide our way. Our *circumstances* can be the boundaries, crossroads, turns, and sign-posts that help us to find God's ongoing direction for our lives. We can, for a season, know that we are going in the right direction (based on previous guidance), but once we come to a dead end, a sign that says "Do Not Enter," or a path that splits into two, we are compelled to once again seek direction for our lives. We can also think of our journey through life as a "road" that we travel. Roads also have signs, and all roads eventually meet intersections with other roads. We spoke in an earlier chapter about the major intersections of our lives. These intersections are usually circumstances in our lives that compel us to make a fresh decision.

In Proverbs 19:21, it is written: "Many are the plans in a man's heart, but it is the Lord's purpose that prevails." Proverbs 21:30 tells us: "There is no wisdom, no insight, no plan that can succeed against the Lord." And finally, in Isaiah 22:22b, (which is echoed in Revelation): "What he opens no one can shut, and what he shuts no one can open." God is the ultimate designer of our divinely ordained path, and therefore He must be our navigator as we journey through life.

We do not and cannot control all of the circumstances around us. Thankfully, God can. God can use our evolving circumstances, as He either wills or allows them, to show us the way that we should go. Believing that *we ourselves* can control *all* of our circumstances amounts to vanity, pride, and self-aggrandizement. These attitudes displace the sovereignty of God.

Sometimes I have followed the means of guidance that we have already discussed, such as praying, reading the Word, trying to discern what the Spirit is saying within me, and seeking the counsel of trusted advisors. And yet, having taken all these steps, sometimes the way is still not clear! It is at this point that God often provides clues and signposts in the surrounding circumstances. God does not just move *within* us through His Spirit. He is always moving in the people and the circumstances *around* us. He moves in nature. He moves in our relationships. He moves in communities. He moves in nations. He is capable of guiding us by placing specific physical signs in front of us. Let us examine these *circumstantial* and *physical* signs more closely. We will begin by looking at a few Biblical examples.

The Selection of the Twelfth Disciple

Various Bible stories demonstrate that it is legitimate to place some weight on physical signs. After the loss of Judas, notice what the eleven remaining disciples did to decide who should become the twelfth disciple. They settled the issue by drawing straws! (Some translations refer to "casting lots"). Have you ever stopped to consider that such an amazing and momentous decision as replacing the twelfth disciple was made by drawing straws? This is an example of godly men relying on a physical sign to make an important decision.

The fascinating Biblical account of this can be found in Acts 1. One hundred and twenty people, including the eleven disciples, had been holding a prayer meeting for days in an "upper room." Peter addressed the group and talked about what had happened to Judas. He then said in Acts 1:21-22: "So now we must choose someone else to take Judas' place...Let us select someone who has been with us constantly from our first association with the Lord—from the time he was baptized by John until the day he was taken from us into heaven."[75]

The assembly of one hundred and twenty then nominated two men: Barsabbas and Matthias. Like any other nomination meeting, I am sure that there was a lot of discussion! "Then they all prayed for the right man to be chosen. 'O Lord,' they said, 'you know every heart; show us which of these men *you* have chosen as an apostle to replace Judas the traitor...'"[76]

The story is concluded in Acts 1:26: "Then they drew straws, and *in this manner* Matthias was chosen and became an apostle with the other eleven." Spend a few minutes pondering that! If we have sought God's counsel in every way we can, it is actually Scriptural to draw straws or cast lots to see what God has to say about our decision! Can you imagine the selection of board members for Christian organizations or churches being determined by drawing straws? This method sounds ridiculous until you consider this Biblical account and recognize that the group of one hundred and twenty, who were trying to select a new disciple, left the ultimate decision beyond the control of men. They "let go" of the decision and "let God." It was not an

[75]　Acts 1 (LB)
[76]　Acts 1:24-25 (LB)

act of laziness. It was an act of ultimate and supreme faith that God would control the outcome.

We can ask God to intervene in our circumstances, to show His hand in them. There are times in our lives when we can prayerfully seek a physical sign, trusting that God will speak to us through the outcome. King Solomon validated this principle when he wrote in Proverbs 16:33: "The lot is cast into the lap, but its every decision is from the Lord."

Joshua Cast Lots

There are situations described in the Old Testament where great men of God also asked God to show His will by casting lots. In Joshua 18:6-10, we see that Joshua cast lots "in the presence of the Lord" to determine which of the tribes of Israel would inherit each specific portion of the Promised Land. (Another translation of the Bible refers to Joshua throwing "the sacred dice" and conducting a "sacred lottery."[77])

By casting lots *deliberately* and *consciously* "in the presence of the Lord," Joshua had faith that God would determine the outcome of the cast lots. Joshua physically threw the lots, *trusting that God would decide how they would fall* so that the land would be granted to each tribe in a manner that was fair and right. The leaders of the tribes accepted this method, so we can assume that they, too, believed that God was in sovereign control of the outcome. They were not trusting in "luck" to see who would receive which portion of land. They believed in a divinely ordained outcome.

The Urim and Thummim

Two of the most interesting physical signs used in the Old Testament were the Urim and Thummim. These are referred to in Exodus 28:30, Leviticus 8:8, Numbers 27:21, Deuteronomy 33:8, 1 Samuel 28:6, Ezra 2:63 and Nehemiah 7:65. The actual

---

[77] See Joshua 18:5-6 and Joshua 19:51 (LB)

Biblical references do not describe the Urim and Thummim in much detail. It is believed that the Urim and Thummim were precious stones placed in the breastplate that Aaron (and every high priest who came after him) was required to wear. These stones were used when a high priest inquired of the Lord, seeking God's will regarding some military, political, or spiritual decision that affected the people.

Scholars have interesting theories, based on other historical writings, as to how the Urim and Thummim worked. They conjecture that the high priest would ask God a question, seeking a "yes" or "no" answer. Some scholars believe that the stones in the priest's breastplate lit up or glowed with light in response to the priest's question (one stone representing an answer in the affirmative and the other stone an answer in the negative). Other scholars suggest that an actual ray of divine light appeared, directed toward one of the stones. The Hebrew words Urim and Thummin have been translated to mean either "Lights and Perfections" or "Revelation and Truth." In this brief paragraph, I will not attempt to substantiate any scholarly position or reach any academic conclusion. I merely wish to point out that the Bible records that the high priests, in Old Testament times, sought some divine physical sign from God, using the Urim and Thummim in some manner to receive His counsel.

Gideon's Fleece

There is also, of course, the well-known story of Gideon and the fleece. In Judges 6, we read about how Gideon *wanted to be sure* that God was going to help Israel defeat their enemy. God had told Gideon to go fight the Midianites and that He would help Israel to prevail. Gideon was having trouble believing that God had indeed spoken to him, so in verse 17, Gideon said to God: "If now I have found favor in your eyes, *give me a sign* that it is really you talking to me." God responded by setting on fire the offering that Gideon had placed on the altar.

But Gideon still wanted *a further physical sign* that God had spoken to him and had indeed promised that the Israelites would prevail in battle against the Midianites. Judges 6:36-38 records: "Gideon said to God, 'If you will save Israel by my hand as you have promised—look, I will place a wool fleece on the threshing floor. If there is dew only on the fleece and all the ground is dry, then I will know that you will save Israel by my hand, as you said.' And that is what happened. Gideon rose early the next day; he squeezed the fleece and wrung out the dew—a bowlful of water."

But still Gideon questioned whether God had indeed spoken to him! Judges 6:39-40 tells us: "Then Gideon said to God, 'Do not be angry with me. Let me make just one more request. Allow me *one more test* with the fleece. This time make the fleece dry and the ground covered with dew.' That night God did so. Only the fleece was dry; all the ground was covered with dew."

God was not angry with Gideon. Some might say that, because Gideon had to keep asking for confirming physical evidence, he was a weak, faithless, insecure person who doubted God. But I see him as a man who really cared that He was hearing from God...who really wanted to be walking in step with God...who deeply desired to be on the "right path." God honored this desire by confirming three times, through three different physical signs, that He had spoken. Gideon was than able to go out to battle, risking his life and the lives of others, because he was by that point *fully confident* and *absolutely assured* that God had spoken to him. Judges 7 tells the story of how Gideon and the Israelites did indeed defeat the Midianites.

Based on Gideon's example, we can ask God to guide us through some demonstrable means. *We are not to use this as a lazy shortcut, thinking that we can avoid the efforts of praying, reading the Word, seeking the Spirit, or enlisting the counsel of wise advisors.* We must still be diligent in seeking God by all these other means. We must not seek a fleece out of impatience or because we want "instant" resolution of our issue. But if, after pursuing those other methods of guidance, we are still not completely certain that God has indeed spoken, then we can ask for a demonstrable sign. Some might say this shows a lack of faith. On the contrary, I believe that it takes enormous faith to expect God to show up, leaving dew on a fleece one day, then keeping it dry on dewy ground the next day.

This is not usually a method of first resort, unless time is very much of the essence. It can be a final resort, however, after patiently applying the other means of seeking God's counsel.

How Isaac's Servant Found Rebecca

We described, in chapter 2, the story from Genesis 24 in which Abraham's servant was sent to find a wife for Isaac. The servant asked God to clearly show him the right girl by providing a circumstantial sign. The servant said that he would know it was the right girl if she offered to water his camels for him. The servant proposed the sign and *God responded* to that proposal as circumstances unfolded. The servant was guided by that physical sign to select Rebecca as Isaac's wife.

The Sign of the Shadow

I love the story of Hezekiah. God tenderly encouraged his faith by providing a physical sign. God had already told Hezekiah that He would heal him and lengthen his life. To strengthen Hezekiah's faith, God told him: "I will make the shadow cast by the sun go back the ten steps it has gone down on the stairway of Ahaz." Just as God promised, "the sunlight went back the ten steps it had gone down."[78] God set the clock back as a confirming sign to Hezekiah. The actual earth must have moved backwards in its revolution around the sun! God loves to strengthen our faith in what He has said.

---

[78]   Isaiah 38:7-8

Choosing a School

Some years ago my brother and sister-in-law were choosing a school for their oldest son. They had certain criteria they were looking for and they had narrowed their search down to two schools. One of the schools seemed to be the better choice, so they went to an open house at that school. On the surface, it still appeared to be the best choice, but my sister-in-law was not convinced. She prayed that God would reveal what His choice was.

Later, she came across a brochure of that school from the previous year. She compared it with the current brochure. She noticed that half of the teachers in the current brochure were different from the brochure from the previous year. For some reason, there had been a significant turnover of staff. This difference in the brochures was a clear sign to my sister-in-law that the *other* school was the better choice. A year later my brother and sister-in-law were glad that they had enrolled their son in the second school. The first school, which had been more impressive at first glance, had developed various problems and would not have been a good choice. God had used a simple brochure to confirm what His best choice was.

Out of the Ordinary Events

Still another method that God can use to guide us is by allowing very *unusual* and *noteworthy* circumstances to occur that *catch our attention*. One of the best examples from my own life occurred in my mid-twenties. I had just moved into the downtown core of Toronto, a large Canadian city. My sister and I, roommates at the time, were trying to find a church that we could attend. There were dozens of large old churches in the downtown core. So we began to attend services at one church after another, trying to discern which one God wanted us to call our new church home.

One Sunday, we attended a place called the Stone Church. By the end of the service, we had whispered to one another that this was definitely *not* the place for us. We were young and single; the majority of the congregation was older. Even the singing of the hymns seemed too slow for our tastes. The pastor had white hair, the hymnbooks contained old-fashioned music and there was not a guitar in sight on the platform. It was certainly not a place where we could expect to make many new Christian friends our own age.

We tried to scoot out of there as fast as we could, but had to shake a few hands as we left. Because of our age, we stood out. Every hand-shaker was trying to talk us into coming back the next week. (We later found out that the Board of the church, recognizing the aging of the congregation, had been diligently praying for more youthful vitality, so we were "targets" that first Sunday morning! We were later told that we had also been regarded as an answer to prayer!)

One man told us, that first morning we attended, that the church had just enlisted him to start a private bus route in the downtown core. When he found out where we lived, he said that our street corner was a designated stop on his route! He offered to wait at our intersection the following Sunday morning. We politely told him not to wait too long (hinting that we had no intention of getting on his bus!).

The next Sunday morning rolled around. As we ate our breakfast, my sister and I talked about the bus driver and about how nice and sincere he had been. We felt sorry for him as we thought of him planning to wait on our street corner. We decided to take the bus that morning, just for one Sunday.

Sure enough, the bus was waiting for us. So we got on the bus and discovered that we were the only ones on it. The bus zigzagged through the downtown streets, but no one else got on. We had a "private chauffeur service" drop us off at the church door.

Once again, the church service did not impress us. Despite the kind encouragement from all the hand-shakers on the way out, my sister and I were again quite adamant that we would not be coming back.

Yet, we got on that bus the next Sunday and many more after. The bus continued to wait on our street corner every Sunday morning. We had a lot of rain that autumn! We had to admit that the bus service was more convenient than walking elsewhere. In addition, it tugged on my heartstrings to think of that faithful driver driving that whole downtown route only to pull up to the church with an empty bus.

Over time, it also started to dawn on me that maybe, just maybe, this bus was being sent to literally deliver us to where God wanted us to be! As I look back, I believe that it was no coincidence that a bus route, which went by our home, was started up just before we first went to Stone Church and was then discontinued later that fall (because we were pretty much the only two regular customers). The bus route was in service *just long enough* for us to decide that we would attend that church. God used that bus to pick us up each Sunday until we realized that we were meant to be at Stone Church—whether or not the majority of the congregation was near our age.

Over the next months, an amazing thing started to happen! More young people began to show up. We invited a few friends and they invited friends. I ended up staying at that church *for the next fifteen years.* It brings tears to my eyes to think of the blessing (beyond description) that Stone Church brought to my life. Within a few years of the time that I began going there, *a few hundred other young adults* (mostly between their mid-twenties and mid-thirties and mostly single) also began attending the church's "College and Careers" night. One of them became my husband! Sam and I met some of the finest friends of our lives there, and we are still friends with some of them decades later. There is no doubt in my mind that a loving God reached down into my circumstances to guide me to the right church for a long season of my life.

Permit me to share another "bus story" that impacted my life. I wrote earlier about how I became a committed Christian at the age of nineteen in a little town in Greece, after losing my way on a dark night. The next day, my sister and I started to read the Bible together. We did not understand everything we were reading. As we continued to backpack across southern Europe, we went to the main cathedrals of many cities, but most of them were full of tourists (instead of worshipping congregations). What services we found were not in English, and we did not know who to ask the pressing questions that we had.

We had lively spiritual discussions between ourselves, but we increasingly craved the fellowship and guidance of more mature Christians. One day, we went to a bus station and asked where to get on the bus to Algeciras. This is a town on the southern coast of Spain, where we could catch a ferry to Morocco (a mecca for travelers our age in those days). The stationmaster pointed out a bus, and sure enough, it said "Algeciras" on the front of it.

So we boarded the bus, settling in for what we thought would be a long ride. It wasn't. After a very brief ride, we went to a nearby town called Torremolinos. Everyone on the bus got off. We stayed on, thinking this was a stop on the route. The driver did not speak very good English, but eventually communicated to us that we also *had* to get off.

It was a day that would change both of our lives. We ran into a fellow Canadian who engaged us in conversation. It turned out that he had recently become a Christian and was attending an international church in town. In fact, he was staying with a Christian community. This got both our antennae up. This was the mid-1970's, an era of hippy communes and weird religious cults. We were not sure what this "Christian community" was all about, but there was a light shining from the eyes of this Canadian. It was warm and loving (although both of us were later to say it also seemed to pierce right through us). This fellow invited us to come for dinner at a villa where some of the Christians stayed. In my spirit, I sensed that we should accept this invitation.

We did not just stay for dinner. We stayed for about five weeks! God used that community of Christians (the closest thing that I have experienced to what is described in the book of Acts) to deeply impact our lives and to profoundly disciple my sister and I. Once again, tears well up in my eyes as I think of how life-changing our experiences in Torremolinos were. *And all because of a bus that had refused (for reasons we will never know!) to carry on to its designated destination.* I can still see that bus in my mind, as we angrily got off of it. I had turned to look at the front of it—it still said Algeciras on its destination panel as the driver shooed us off in Torremolinos...I had tried to point the sign out to the bus driver, but he had waved us off with Spanish words we could not comprehend.

Looking back, I am again convinced, all of these decades later, that God intervened in our circumstances. He caused a bus to take us where we did not plan to go, or even want to go, but where I am profoundly thankful we did go. God literally had that bus drive us to, and deposit us in, the destination of *His* choosing. Our prayers for fellowship were answered there. We found the answers to the many spiritual questions we had been asking ourselves across the face of southern Europe.

Our experiences there were so amazing that my sister was later to spend a full year there. A full decade later, after our year-long trek through Africa, my husband and I also spent a few months there. Other family members and various friends were later to have significant experiences in that place. One errant bus, guided by a loving God, mightily blessed many lives.

Because of these two "bus" interventions in my life, I have learned to take note of unusual circumstances. Although there are times in life when we simply get on the *wrong* bus and wind up at the *wrong* destination (I've done that too!), I have learned that some circumstances are so compelling and so out of the ordinary that I watch them very closely. I ponder whether God has "sent the bus," so to speak (or the person...the influential book...the "open door"...the unexpected opportunity). This book is mostly about having our *spiritual eyes* wide open, but we must not forget to be alert with our *physical eyes* too!

A Recurring Theme

Sometimes God gets our attention by allowing a recurring theme to occur in our unfolding lives. We talked in an earlier chapter about George Mueller, the man who housed thousands of orphans in England. Before he took in the very first orphans, God had allowed the recurring theme of orphans to keep cropping up in Mueller's life—in books, conversations, actual orphans, and orphanages that he came across. Over time, Mueller began to realize that God was calling him to work with orphans and to build orphanages to raise them in.ᵘ

We should pay special attention when a recurring theme of some sort keeps showing up in our conversations, the material we are reading, the programs we are watching, the sermons we are hearing, and the circumstances we find ourselves in. At a certain point, we must recognize that a constantly replaying theme, coming to our attention from a variety of sources, is not likely a mere coincidence. We need to prayerfully explore what God is trying to tell us.

Nature

There are some who would question whether God speaks through nature. I believe that He often does, sometimes in quite dramatic ways. Shortly before His death on the cross, Jesus spoke to His disciples about how He would one day come back to earth. He was describing to them His future second coming. When the disciples asked Jesus when that would be, Jesus told them to watch for certain circumstances in nature so that they (and generations of Christians after them) could know when the "end times" were upon them. Jesus told them to watch for signs such as earthquakes and famines (see Matthew 24:7 and Mark 13:8). Luke 21:11 refers to these, along with "pestilences in various places, and fearful events and great signs from heaven." Luke 21:25-26 goes on to predict: "There will be signs in the sun, moon and stars. On the earth, nations will be in anguish and perplexity at the roaring and tossing of the sea. Men will faint from terror, apprehensive of what is coming in the world, for the heavenly bodies will be shaken." These signs will likely be as out of the ordinary as the terrifying tsunami wave of late 2004. God will use these physical signs in nature to speak to His people, alerting them to be on the watch for the fulfillment of other prophecies in the spiritual, political, and economic realm.

Nature is described in Scripture as having a "voice." *The sole purpose of a voice is to speak.* In Psalm 19:3-4, David refers to the glory of the heavens and the skies: "There is no speech or language where their *voice* is not heard. Their *voice* goes out into all the earth, their *words* to the end of the world." The obvious message of nature's voice is that there is indeed a God Most High. Who can meditate on a spectacular sunset, a starry sky, a shooting star, a rainbow, or the clouds on a summer day, without believing in an intelligent and wonderful Creator? Who can observe a tornado or a hurricane without noting the very force and power of God? The skies do indeed have a voice that speaks of the reality of a supreme God. Paul echoed this thought when he wrote in Romans 1:20 about the message of nature in general: "...since the creation of the world God's invisible qualities—his eternal power and divine nature—have been clearly seen, *being understood from what has been made*, so that men are without excuse." Nature speaks to us about God's reality, character and power, if we have ears to hear and eyes to see.

Sometimes in Scripture God used nature to get someone's attention. There is the well-known example of "the still small voice" that Elijah heard. Some people say that God always whispers quietly. Notice, however, that before God spoke to Elijah in a still small voice, He sent a *wind*, an *earthquake*, and a *fire*. 1 Kings 19:11 records: "...then a great and powerful wind tore the mountains apart and shattered the rocks before the Lord, but the Lord was not in the wind. After the wind there was an earthquake, but the Lord was not in the earthquake. After the earthquake came a fire, but the Lord was not in the fire. And after the fire came a gentle whisper." That got the full attention of Elijah! Similarly, before God spoke to Moses, He set a bush on fire.[79]

Countless millions in our present world have suffered through hurricanes, famines, earthquakes, and fires. God is no doubt trying to speak to each and every person who has survived these terrifying forces of nature, to whoever has ears to hear the gentle whisper of God in their lives after the winds, droughts, earthquakes, and fires have passed by.

God can also speak through nature in much more subtle ways. When my husband and I were expecting our first child, we spent weeks trying to decide on a name for both a boy and a girl. We read through a few different volumes of "name your baby" books (some containing 6,000 names!) and could not agree on names. The names were either too pompous or too cute. Some names reminded us of an old boyfriend or girlfriend that one of us had liked too much, or of an old classmate one of us had not liked. For whatever reason, I would love a particular name and my husband would hate it (or vice versa). This was becoming more difficult than the nine months of pregnancy! Finally we agreed on the name Darrin, if our baby was a boy. Then we agreed that, if it was a girl, we would name her Samantha. But we still had to find middle names and the whole process started over.

One spring day, I was sitting in a park near our home, enjoying the sunshine and praying about the imminent arrival of our first child. I noticed that a robin hopped by in front of me. It was not startled by me and, as it continued to hop by right in front of my feet, I felt sudden inspiration. I have always loved robins. They are so soft, cute, and gentle, and they herald the promise of spring. It occurred to me that Robin would be a perfect middle name. I went home, expecting my husband's negative response to this latest name suggestion. To my surprise, he loved it as much as I did.

---

[79] Exodus 3:1-4

Days later, our *son* was born and we named him Darrin. The name Robin had to wait a few years, until the beautiful summer day that our son was joined by our daughter, Samantha Robin. Looking back, I believe that God sent that robin on that long ago day, thereby ending the frustrating and somewhat stressful process of name-choosing. Once we had decided on names for both sexes, it felt like a weight had been lifted from my shoulders. *God had sent a bird to spark an idea!*

Thousands would not believe this, but the very day that I was typing these paragraphs (almost two decades after that spring day), I took a break to do some raking in my backyard...and along hopped the first robin I had seen in my yard that spring! Was God speaking to me? Sometimes God does not speak a particular message; sometimes He just smiles at us and affirms us. I had been debating whether or not I should edit out these past few paragraphs—was this story important enough to keep?—but once that robin appeared I knew that this story was meant to be told! I also felt that God was affirming to me afresh that He is very much the force and energy behind nature and that He can indeed use nature to speak to us as He pleases.

Open Doors

God can also provide guidance to us through "open doors" and "closed doors" in our circumstances. No one can open a door that God has shut or shut a door that God has opened.[80]

If we are praying about doing something and feel that we should do it (based on what we have been reading in the Word, hearing within our spirit, and what others have encouraged us to proceed with), then we are ready to watch for the "open door" of opportunity. The very existence of an open door is further confirmation that we should be proceeding in that direction. It should not necessarily be the only sign, but it is

---

[80] Isaiah 22:22b

certainly one indication that we are moving in the right direction.

The "open door" that we have been led to expect may not appear right away. If we have been otherwise guided to look for an open door to proceed, then we should patiently and prayerfully wait and watch for that open door. We might first have to face some adversity or go through some form of preparation. But if God does want us to proceed in a particular direction, we must confidently wait, knowing that an open door will appear.

Hannah Whitall Smith expressed it this way: "If a 'leading' is of God, the way will always open for it...If the Lord 'goes before' us, He will open the door for us, and we shall not need to batter down doors for ourselves."[v]

This whole concept of "open doors" comes from Scripture. In Colossians 4:3a, Paul wrote: "And pray for us...that God may *open a door* for our message." In 2 Corinthians 2:12, Paul recorded: "...I went to Troas to preach the gospel of Christ and found that the Lord had *opened a door* for me."

God can make a way where there is no way. After the Israelites left Egypt, under the leadership of Moses, they came to the Red Sea. Exodus 14 tells the story of how Pharaoh changed his mind about letting the Israelites go. He followed them with his army, trapping the Israelites by the shores of the Sea. But God parted the waters and His people passed through the Sea. God supernaturally opened a door where there had not been a door. He made a way where there had not been a way.

Brother Andrew, whose ministry is called Open Doors International, is a wonderful example of someone who is constantly alert for "open doors." He boldly walks through the open doors he finds. He has ministered over the years in Communist nations, Muslim nations, and even in the midst of Middle Eastern groups such as Hezbollah and Hamas.[w] He believes that even groups labeled as terrorists should hear about the gospel of Christ. He has been remarkably able to dialogue spiritually with men in these groups. God is capable of opening doors in very unlikely places.

We should never treat an open door lightly. There are some open doors that are open to very few. One of my brothers attended a Christian university and often heard the advice: "go where others cannot go." God wants His people to be in all nations and in all good professions and vocations. God needs many of His people to be in full-time ministry of some sort. But God also needs Christian business professionals, bankers, professors, judges, and scientists. Not everyone has the skill, personality, or opportunity to fit into many of these roles. *We should go where others cannot go.* My brother decided to pursue his MBA at Harvard Business School. One of the factors that helped him decide that he should do this was the fact that Harvard Business School was a place that only a few Christians would have the opportunity to attend. He decided to walk through an open door that most others would not have the opportunity to walk through. God will provide each one of us with certain open doors in our lives. Not everyone will have the opportunity to walk through *our* unique doors.

Corrie ten Boom once said that every Christian should find the unique place where they can be used and others cannot.[x] One of Corrie's "open doors" was Ravensbruck, a Nazi concentration camp, where God used her to reach and to comfort many despairing women. Corrie later had many exciting "open doors" as she traveled to dozens of countries around the world over three decades, speaking about God's love and about the need to forgive those who have hurt us.

One of the enemies of our ability to see our own open doors is jealousy. We will invariably miss our own open doors if we are too busy being jealous of the opportunities of others. We must get our eyes off of the open doors presented to others. It is their life, not ours. We must keep focused on our own path in life and be watchful for our own open doors. We will have our own special blessings, privileges, and opportunities if we keep focused on what God is doing in *our* life, rather than being envious or covetous of what He is doing in someone else's life. All of us experience jealousy and envy at some points in our lives, so we must consciously choose not to waste time and energy being jealous, or we risk missing the blessings and the opportunities that are waiting around the next corner on *our* path. We need to use all of our energy to press forward in our own lives, developing our own talents, seizing our own opportunities, trusting that we will indeed, have our own open doors.

Closed Doors

Sometimes God guides us by *closing* doors. We may think that we should be doing something or going somewhere, only to be met with a closed door. Sometimes the door is just temporarily shut and we must wait with faith and patience, trusting for God's timing for it to open. It is not unusual to face obstacles, trials, battles, and challenges. *But at a certain point we must face the reality of a door that is firmly shut.* A door that remains firmly shut for an extended period should make us re-evaluate the counsel that we believe we have received from God. We must continue to read the Word, pray, listen to what the Spirit is telling us, listen to the counsel of others, and keep watchful for the other doors in our lives that might be open.

The apostle Paul experienced closed doors from time to time. Acts 16:6-8, for example, tells us: "Paul and his companions traveled throughout the region of Phrygia and Galatia, *having been kept by the Holy Spirit* from preaching the word in the province of Asia. When they came to the border of Mysia, they tried to enter Bithynia, *but the Spirit of Jesus would not allow them to.* So they passed by Mysia..." Paul did not try to batter down these closed doors. He changed course.

Sometimes God allows a door to be firmly shut because we are not going in the right direction. In Numbers 22, we read about Balaam, whose donkey stubbornly refused to move forward. Balaam was frustrated until an angel spoke to him: "I have come here to oppose you *because your path is a reckless one before me.*" At this point, the angel was standing in the narrowest part of the path where there was not enough room to turn to the left or the right. Balaam was unable to proceed on that path, for his own good.

I have seen this happen in my own life, and in the lives of those around me, in the course of a romantic relationship. It is easy to get swept off of our feet by someone who is attractive. It does not matter whether we are being attracted to that person because of their physical, intellectual, or spiritual attributes. *What does matter is whether God tells us that they are the right person to be pursuing a relationship with.* When a person is attractive to us, it is only natural to want them to be "God's will" for us. It is only natural to try to seek out an affirming Scripture verse, or positive advice from a friend, or some encouraging inner impression. We might strain to prove that this attractive person is the "right one."

God cares about us and will let us know what *He* thinks, if we ask Him. He will sometimes use a "closed door" to protect us from a relationship that is not meant for us. When that attractive person decides to marry someone else, for example, this is a pretty classic "closed door" that trumps whatever other affirming "sign" or "guidance" we believe we have received.

If you are faced with a door that is clearly and firmly shut, don't beat your head against that door! Trust that a better door, an open door, will appear. Let go...let God work in your life...move on. God will show you the better door.

God is in Motion All Around Us

Another major way that God guides us through circumstances is by showing us where He is already in action. God's highest purposes never involve just us. Our lives are interwoven with those of our parents, siblings, spouses, children, friends, fellow Christians, and fellow citizens. We live in a particular family, in a particular place, in a particular time in history. God's plan for *us* will be interwoven in a complex way (that we may never fully understand in this lifetime) with many other lives and ongoing events in history. God had purposes for Abraham, Moses, David, Ruth, and Esther, but these were not plans for those individuals alone. Whole nations were affected by God's plans and purposes for those men and women. The plan for their lives fit into a much bigger plan. In the same way, each of our lives is part of a much bigger plan. Each one of us is more significant than we realize! Each one of us plays a part in our families, our communities, and the overall history of our times.

We should be constantly observing how and where God is already *in motion* in the people and circumstances around us. This can often provide some clue as to what God wants us to do. We should normally be drawn toward (and excited about!) where we see God's Spirit moving. We should question remaining in any place (whether a church, ministry, workplace, or relationship) where the Spirit never seems to show up. The Spirit works *within* us, but He is also always working *around* us and *in others*. Keep an eye on the Spirit! His movement can be like the cloud by day and the fire by night that guided the Israelites under Moses. The motion of the Spirit *around us* can be a valuable signpost. Be drawn to the Spirit!

The "Random" Generation

I have already commented a few times in this book about the tendency of many of today's youth to consider all of life "random." They like to say and do random things and find great humor in the random.

While seemingly harmless, this worldview is actually very anti-God, and it flies in the face of the Biblical perspective of life. Many youth today are the product of *a century or two* of influential secular philosophers who have believed that there is no God, and therefore, life is random and ultimately without inherent meaning. Christians, however, believe that the world was not created in random fashion. Humans are not just a random collection of atoms.

Can anyone who stops to examine the world around them honestly believe that each unique snowflake, each magnificently designed tropical fish, each desert dune, each tiny ladybug, somehow randomly came into being? God designed this world—and human beings—*perfectly, precisely, intricately and intentionally.* God has left His fingerprints on everything around us. The sheer grandeur of it all should leave us in awe. *This universe contains a trillion trillion trillion trillion tons of matter! There are one hundred million galaxies in the universe.*ʸ The most brilliant astrophysicists humbly admit that they do not know much about 96% of the universe, which is composed of dark energy and dark matter. Even the 4% they do have some insight into is subject to differing scientific theories and conjectures. Scientists understand far less than the average person supposes.

Our lives are not random! God knew us even before we were conceived in our mothers' wombs. We are described as being perfectly and wonderfully made.[81] Do you know that in the last hour alone one trillion trillion of your atoms have been replaced? That your body contains about sixty thousand miles of blood vessels? That your lungs are full of one billion trillion molecules of air? That each ear has one million moving parts? That your brain has at least ten billion neurons that form 100 trillion neurological interconnections?ᶻ Ponder for just one moment the anatomical and biological complexities behind your everyday acts of thinking, breathing, hearing, seeing, and walking. Your body is far from a random collection of atoms.

Psalm 139 also says that, even before we were born, God had *ordained* each day of our lives. As we have heard in previous chapters, God has specific plans and purposes for each one of us, and they interconnect with one another in ways we will not fully understand in this lifetime. They interconnect

---

[81] Psalm 139

with the same unfathomable complexity as those ten billion neurons in our brains. God has plans and purposes for whole generations and whole nations. Yet so many in the generation coming of age seem to believe that everything is random, which makes everything really quite *meaningless* and *valueless*. Quite the opposite is true. Nothing is random, and *therefore everything has significance,* for good or for evil.

Everything happens by intention—either God's intention, man's intention, or the intention of our adversary, who we know has plans of his own. *God says that every hair on our head is numbered. Not even a hair falls from our heads in random fashion! Not a single sparrow falls to the ground without God knowing and caring.*[82]

Because of this, Christians can believe that circumstances are not random. *Someone* has purposed for a particular event to occur—either God, we ourselves, or someone else. We need to be ever mindful of what is happening around us. We need to have some sense of who is orchestrating the circumstances we find ourselves in. Are we? Is it God, and if so, what is He trying to say or do? Is it someone else? Or is it the enemy, trying to do something destructive in our lives? In the next chapter, we will discuss cultivating wisdom, understanding, good judgment, and discernment. We need to *discern* what is happening in our circumstances and *who* is influencing them.

Joseph was the exact opposite of many of today's youth. Joseph was well aware that nothing was random. He was well aware, as a series of circumstances unfolded in his life, what God, his friends, and his enemies were doing in his evolving circumstances. He *could* have thought that it was just random that his brothers threw him into a pit and then sold him to a passing caravan. He *could* have thought it was purely random that he then served in the house of Potiphar and was falsely accused of sexual assault by Potiphar's wife. He *could* have thought it was random that he spent some years in prison and

---

[82]   Matthew 10:29-30

that he became friends of the king's cupbearer and his baker. He *could* have believed that their dreams were random fragments of subconscious thought. He *could* have believed that he randomly ended up in Pharaoh's court and that a famine happened to come along at that time. He *could* have thought it was entirely random that his brothers re-entered his life again. He could have missed the point of it all. He could have just drifted along, pulled and pushed by his circumstances, trying to survive it all.

But Joseph did not see the world as a random place. He knew God was sovereign over it all. He knew that he had enemies who tried to hurt him and friends who helped him. He knew that God was intervening in his life, through the dreams of the cupbearer, the baker, and eventually of Pharaoh himself. He knew that God had allowed the famine and that God had placed him in a position of great power at that very time so that he could save many lives, including those of his brothers and father. At the end of it all, Joseph could say to his brothers (Genesis 45:8): "It was not you who sent me here, but God." He could say to them: "You intended to harm me, but God intended it for good." Joseph was able to fulfill God's highest purposes for his life and to understand how his circumstances fit into the bigger picture. If he had viewed everything as merely (and meaninglessly) random, he would have wasted his life in bitterness, anger, confusion, and defeat. Because he saw God's purposes and God's hand in his evolving circumstances, he was able to live out tough times with strength, grace, courage, patience, productivity, and forgiveness.

Many in this generation, as they come of age, will be poorly equipped to handle some of the very difficult and painful circumstances that may come their way, if they continue to see everything as merely random. Many in this generation coming of age will be poorly equipped to lead a *deliberate* life if they continue to see everything as merely random. They will be tossed and turned in the winds and waves of change, without anchor or direction, if they continue to see everything as the product of pure chance. Many in this generation coming of age will fail to see "the signs of the times" and the gradual fulfillment of Biblical prophecy (unfolding all around us) if they continue to see everything as merely random. Those who drift in random fashion will be *easy prey* for those who know the *power and force of the deliberate.* Those who drift in random currents, refusing to search for meaning in their circumstances, will not rise up to be people like Joseph.

Be Watchful and Alert

We are exhorted many times in Scripture to be watchful and alert. It is only with our eyes and ears wide open that we will be able to hear what God is trying to tell us through the evolving circumstances of our lives. As God guides us, He will sometimes use physical signs and circumstances as guideposts. Be mindful. Be aware. Note what is out of the ordinary and give thought to it. Note when a door of opportunity opens in front of you or when a door slams shut. Note how God is already moving in the people, places, and circumstances all around you. Just as God used the Chicago fire of 1871 to speak to Dwight L. Moody, God can use our evolving circumstances (even if they seem negative!) to speak to us. Treat nothing as random. Have eyes to see the unfolding of the sovereign purposes of God in your generation and your surroundings. Watch to see how *you* meaningfully fit into the picture!

We toss the coin, but it is the Lord who controls its decision.
Proverbs 16:33 (LB)

11.

The Counsel of Collected Wisdom

[Wisdom says] "Counsel and sound judgment are mine."
Proverbs 8:14

*To God belong wisdom and power; counsel
and understanding are his.*
Job 12:13

*He will be a sure foundation for your times,
a rich store of salvation and wisdom and knowledge.*
Isaiah 33:6

Since our dating days, my husband and I have collected crocodile-themed items—mugs, letter openers, stationary, greeting cards, paperweights, and knick-knacks. This started when, on one of our first dates, my future husband gave me a little pin he used to wear on his white doctor's coat while working in a hospital for sick children. The pin was a crocodile wearing a shirt with a "little man" logo on it, intended to poke fun at the crocodile-crested shirts everyone was wearing in those days (and now again in these days!). Collecting crocodile-themed items became a romantic and sentimental symbol of our deepening relationship.

We all collect many things over our lifetimes. We collect favorite clothes. We collect furniture. We collect souvenirs from our travels. We collect photographs and memories. We may collect seashells, stamps or artwork. *If we have been a Christian for some time, we have also collected a vast storehouse full of wisdom.* This is particularly true if we have been diligent in following the disciplines and principles discussed in earlier chapters.

Merely growing older does not guarantee wisdom. If a person has been foolish throughout their lifetime, they will have accumulated a lot of mistakes and a lot of baggage, from which they may or may not have learned anything. For the person who has been actively and intimately seeking a growing relationship with God, great wisdom will have accrued each day with the same certainty that the sun rises and sets. Wisdom will come to us from the Word. Wisdom will be imparted to us by the Spirit. Wisdom will be gleaned from wise counselors and friends. Wisdom will become apparent as we ponder our responses to circumstances—as we learn from what we have done right and from what we have done wrong. Wisdom must be *acquired, collected,* and *cultivated.* It does not just magically come with age.

The Promises of Proverbs

The Book of Proverbs imparts enormous wisdom that can be stored in our hearts and minds, ready to be applied when the need arises. Solomon tells his readers at the very beginning of his book (Proverbs 1:2) that the proverbs are being written "for attaining wisdom and discipline" and "for understanding words of insight." Solomon invites the discerning to get guidance. Solomon is described in the Bible as the wisest man who ever lived. He was not, however, perfect. He also, by his own admission, learned from foolish error.

Solomon asserts in Proverbs that wisdom calls out to every one of us. In Proverbs 8:1-3, Solomon asks each one of us: "Does not wisdom call out? Does not understanding raise her voice? On the heights along the way, where the paths meet, she takes her stand; besides the gates leading into the city, at the entrances, she cries aloud." Wisdom raises her voice to all humankind.

Separate destinies await those who *receive* wisdom and those who *reject* it. In Proverbs 1:24-28, the spirit of wisdom says: "since you *rejected* me when I called,...since you *ignored* all my advice and *would not accept* my rebuke, I in turn will laugh at your disaster; I will mock when calamity overtakes you—when calamity overtakes you like a storm, when disaster sweeps over you like a whirlwind, when distress and trouble overwhelm you. Then they will call to me but I will not answer; they will look for me but will not find me."

Wisdom cannot be suddenly found in the midst of the storm. Much of the wisdom that helps us find our way in the toughest times of life must already be implanted deep into our hearts and minds. When we are in sudden pain, distress, and turmoil, it is too late to sit down and read the Bible from cover to cover. While the Spirit can certainly speak to us during the storm, or a particular Bible verse can help us to gain insight, generally we will receive a lot of inner stability, calm, and counsel from the store of wisdom *already within us*. If there is no such store of wisdom, then it will be easy to flounder in confusion, fear, anxiety, and panic when the storm suddenly hits.

A different destiny awaits those who *seek out* and *receive* wisdom, who choose to *acquire, accumulate, cultivate,* and *collect* wisdom. In Proverbs 2:1-5, wisdom says, "My son, if you *accept* my words and *store up* my commands within you, *turning your ear* to wisdom and *applying your heart* to understanding, and if you *call out* for insight and *cry aloud* for understanding, and if you *look for it* as for silver and search for it as for hidden treasure, then you will understand the fear of the Lord and find the knowledge of God." I love these verses because they show that wisdom also leads to understanding, insight and knowledge. Other proverbs show that wisdom leads to common sense, discernment, and good judgment. Who, in their right mind, does not want to walk through life with wisdom, understanding, insight, knowledge, common sense, discernment, and good judgment?

Proverbs 2:6-11 goes on to promise: "For the Lord gives wisdom and from His mouth come knowledge and understanding....you will understand what is right and just and fair—every good path. For wisdom will enter your heart and knowledge will be pleasant to your soul. Discretion will protect you and understanding will guard you." This verse meant much to me during my twenty years of legal practice. I prayed over every file that crossed my desk and asked for wisdom. I asked that I would understand what was "*right* and *just* and *fair*."

Litigation was, in essence, conflict between various parties over various issues. I wanted to know the right, just, and fair way to resolve that conflict...how to weigh and to interpret the facts, law, issues, and expert opinions... whether to pursue settlement, mediation, trial, or appeal.

In Proverbs we are further told that wisdom will save us from specific persons and situations, such as the adulterer or seductress (Proverbs 2:16-22), who will take us on a path that leads to spiritual death. Other proverbs warn us how we can wisely avoid poverty, poor health, ruin, disaster, and destruction of all kinds.

Proverbs 3:13-15 confers blessing on those who seek wisdom: "Blessed is the man who finds wisdom, the man who gains understanding, for she is more profitable than silver and yields better returns than gold. She is more precious than rubies; nothing you desire can compare with her." A little further in that chapter, in verses 21-23, Solomon wrote: "My son, preserve sound judgment and discernment, do not let them out of your sight...Then you will go on your way in safety and your feet will not stumble."

Proverbs 4:7-8 counsels us: "Wisdom is supreme; therefore get wisdom. Though it cost all you have, get understanding. Esteem her and she will exalt you; embrace her and she will honor you." A few sentences later, in Proverbs 4:11-13, God promises: "I guide you in the way of wisdom and lead you along straight paths...Hold on to instruction, do not let it go; guard it well, for it is your life."

Jesus: Comparing the Wise Man and the Fool

Jesus also talked about accumulating wisdom and about the consequences of being wise. In Matthew 7:24-27, He compared the destinies of the wise man and the foolish man. Jesus said: "...everyone who *hears these words of mine* and puts them into practice is like a *wise man* who built his house on the rock. The rain came down, the streams rose, and the winds blew and beat against that house; yet it did not fall, because it had its foundation on the rock. But everyone who hears these words of mine and does not put them into practice is like a *foolish man* who built his house on sand. The rain came down, the streams rose, and the winds blew and beat against that house, and it fell with a great crash." Is this not a strong incentive to *start* your "five and five" if you have not already done so, or to *build* even more upon that daily discipline of praying and reading the Word? The storms of life will come to all of us. Who wants their life to fall apart in the storm?

In Matthew 13:11, Jesus said: "The knowledge of the secrets of the kingdom of heaven has been given to you..." Jesus imparted enormous wisdom and knowledge to all those then (and now) who have ears to hear. Why should we ignore such a precious gift? Solomon said that "wise men store up knowledge."[83] Read the words of Jesus. Read them over and over until you know them. Store them up. Have them written

---

[83] Proverbs 10:14

on your heart and in your mind so that you will hear those words whispering within you when the storm becomes fierce.

God's Wisdom Versus the World's Wisdom

The wisdom, knowledge, and understanding described in the Bible are not necessarily the same as "IQ" or "education." A person can earn a PhD and still lead a very foolish life. I have known many people with impressive degrees who have made total messes of their lives. Their intelligence and their education have not helped them when it came to managing their health, sustaining their marriage, raising their children, controlling their emotions, or finding true happiness in life. In some cases, their stellar education has not even been enough to keep their business afloat.

I consider myself to be intelligent and have a law degree on my résumé, but quite frankly, this "intelligence" and "education" have been quite useless with respect to many of the most important decisions in my life (or even with respect to the smaller everyday decisions that help or hurt the people around me). We need God's wisdom if we are to live our lives well. An uneducated man who is pursuing God understands the universe around him far better than the world's most educated men and women who refuse to acknowledge God or to seek His wisdom.

The Bible talks about God's wisdom as being different from earthly wisdom or mere human wisdom. The Bible says that the "foolishness" of God confounds the wise of this world. Paul wrote: "For the message of the cross is foolishness to those who are perishing, but to us who are being saved it is the power of God. For it is written: 'I will destroy the wisdom of the wise; the intelligence of the intelligent I will frustrate.' Where is the wise man? Where is the scholar? Where is the philosopher of this age? Has not God made foolish the wisdom of the world? For since in the wisdom of God the world through its wisdom did not know him, God was pleased through the foolishness of what was preached to save those who believe....For the foolishness of God is wiser than man's wisdom...Brothers, think of what you were when you were called. Not many of you were wise by human standards; not many were influential; not many were of noble birth. But God chose the foolish things of the world to shame the wise; God chose the weak things of the world to shame the strong...It is because of him that you are in Christ Jesus, who has become for us wisdom from God..."[84]

In 1 Corinthians 2:13 Paul goes on to talk about how God imparts His thoughts to us through the Spirit. "This is what we speak," Paul wrote, "not in words taught us by human wisdom but in words taught by the Spirit, expressing spiritual truths in spiritual words." He concludes in 1 Corinthians 2:16 that, because of this spiritual impartation of godly wisdom, "we have the mind of Christ."

James also made a distinction between worldly wisdom and godly wisdom. He wrote: "Who is wise and understanding among you? Let him show it by his good life, by deeds done in the humility that comes from wisdom. But if you harbor bitter envy and selfish ambition in your hearts, do not boast about it or deny the truth. Such "wisdom" does not come down from heaven but is earthly, unspiritual, of the devil...But the wisdom that comes from heaven is first of all pure; then peace-loving, considerate, submissive, full of mercy and good fruit, impartial and sincere."[85]

In my teen years, I was fascinated by many of the world's great philosophers. I found that the great works of the world's most prominent thinkers initially led to intellectual vanity and pride in my life. These writings ultimately led to depression, confusion, and meaninglessness. They did not give me direction, passion, energy, meaning, purpose, clarity, or any light for my next footsteps. I went on to reject the vanity,

[84] 1 Corinthians 1:18-21, 25-27, 30
[85] James 3:13-17

futility, and despair of many supposedly great thinkers when I eventually realized how empty the world's wisdom was.

The words of Solomon, the apostle Paul, and even more importantly, the words of Jesus have encouraged me over the past decades to store up *God's* wisdom and to diligently apply it. Immersing ourselves in God's Word will build our store of godly wisdom and help us to discern where that differs from this world's "wisdom." Seeking the Spirit will further increase our godly wisdom, as the Spirit helps us to spiritually discern truth.

Wisdom from Experience

As we *apply* godly wisdom to our lives, we learn even more from our *ongoing life experiences.* Jesus said in Matthew 11:19b that "wisdom is proved right by her actions." We learn what works well in our lives and what does not. We learn what helps us and what harms us. We learn what leads to "life" and what leads to "death." We learn great lessons from our successes and from our failures…from our right decisions and from our mistakes…from the cost and the consequences of our actions.

We must examine our lives. It is not enough just to *read* about being wise or foolish. We must all *experientially learn*, as we *live out* our lives, what is, *in fact*, wise or foolish. In Deuteronomy 4:9, Moses told the Israelites: "Only be careful, and watch yourselves closely so that you do not forget the things your eyes have seen or let them slip from your heart as long as you live." What we learn from the experiences we go through is meant to be treasured, remembered, and drawn upon. God is able to use our experiences as "teachable moments." As I raised my two children, I tried to be aware of "teachable moments" when I could instill some lesson in my children. One day it occurred to me that God does the same thing with His children! He shows us how our experiences in life can teach us great lessons about what is wise and foolish, right and wrong. What we learn in the experiential realm affirms the truth of what is in the Word.

Dozens of Daily Decisions

We make countless decisions every day. We do not have time to ponder each one. Not all decisions can be deferred until some later time. Of course, the major decisions, such as choosing a career or a marriage partner, require a lot of time and reflection, and these decisions should be based on multiple sources of divine guidance. But many of our daily decisions can be made quite quickly, based on the wisdom stored within. Our acquired wisdom and good judgment probably applies to about 90% of the daily decisions we make.

Take, for example, the many decisions a person makes going into a grocery store. The shopper has to decide on many items. A wise shopper will apply *the wisdom stored within* regarding nutrition, disease prevention, favorite foods that will delight a spouse or a child, special items that will show honor to a dinner guest, and what fits within a sensible budget for groceries. Even in a grocery store, one can be wise or foolish. Unwanted pounds, clogged arteries, complaints at the dinner table, and stretched budgets can often be traced back to wrong decisions made in a grocery aisle. Similarly, a fit and healthy body, family clamoring for second helpings, and guests raving about the appetizers can be traced back to wise decisions made in that very same aisle.

We make wise or foolish decisions about whether or not we eat breakfast, how fast we drive on the expressway, how we treat a co-worker in a moment of stress, whether we impart some juicy gossip at the water fountain, how much we exercise our credit cards on our lunch break, how much television we watch in the evening, whether or not we set aside a few moments to read our Bible and pray, and whether we say something positive or negative to our family members. We do not have the luxury of time to give a lot of thought to each of these unfolding and often spontaneous decisions. They will be made based on the acquired and cultivated wisdom (or lack of it) that we bring to bear *in the pressure of the passing moment.*

We are busy. Modern life moves at a fast pace. The modern technology of e-mails, text messaging on our phones, beepers, and Blackberries often requires very quick decisions. So, my friend, I urge you to have much stored wisdom (and its fruits—knowledge, insight, understanding, discernment, good judgment, and common sense) available to draw upon, moment by moment, in the crunch of your busy day. *Just as stored calories provide ongoing energy as required, stored wisdom provides God's ongoing counsel as required.*

The Wise Person

If we become wise people, our counsel will in turn be sought out by others. In 1 Kings 10:24, it states: "The whole world sought audience with Solomon to hear the wisdom God had put in his heart." It has been said that the world beats a path to the door of the person who knows how to pray. The world also beats a path to the door of the person who has acquired godly wisdom and can offer wise counsel. I pray that each one of us becomes a wise counselor in a world that so desperately needs the wisdom and counsel of the Most High. It is fun to collect crocodile memorabilia, travel souvenirs, photographs, and seashells. It is *life-changing* to collect wisdom!

Wisdom makes one wise man more powerful than ten rulers in a city.
Ecclesiastes 7:19

...we have not stopped praying for you and asking God to fill you with the knowledge of his will through all spiritual wisdom and understanding.
Colossians 1:9

Therefore do not be foolish, but understand what the Lord's will is.
Ephesians 5:17

But where can wisdom be found? Where does understanding dwell?

...God understands the way to it and he alone knows where it dwells.
Job 28:12, 23

Oh, the depth of the riches of the wisdom and knowledge of God!
Romans 11:33

12.

What Would

Jesus Do?

Your attitude should be the same as that of Christ Jesus …
Philippians 2:5

This is my Son, whom I love; with him I am well pleased.
Listen to him!
Matthew 17:5b

Do you remember, back in the 1990's, the leather bracelets that many Christian youth wore that bore the letters WWJD? The acronym was short for "what would Jesus do?" It was actually a wonderful question for teenagers to ask themselves. In trying to discern what decision we should make in a given situation, it remains a good question for all of us. When we take a moment to ask WWJD, often the answer is clear, and we do not need to spend additional time praying, searching the Word, or seeking advice.

The WWJD question is particularly useful when it comes to moral decisions. We make moral decisions every day. Should we see the movie our friends are planning to see? Should we linger on a website we have come across? Should we get in the habit of watching a particular TV program? Should we hang out with friends whose language usually offends us? Should we have that second drink (should we have had the first drink)? It is easy to rationalize and compromise. It is more difficult to tolerate immorality when we imagine Jesus by our side. The WWJD question is often quick to pierce our conscience. What do you think Jesus would say to you about your situation if you could chat with Him at Starbucks and ask His opinion?

We should not waste time wondering whether or not to enter into a dubious or dishonest business transaction. We should not agonize over whether or not to rent a questionable video that several Christian friends have warned us about. We should not waste a lot of time considering whether or not to keep dating someone who does not share our beliefs, hoping we can change them. We do not need to mull over whether to rob a bank or tell a lie. We do not need to seek advice about whether to live with someone before we marry them. We do not have to ponder whether or not to seek revenge. We only need to ask ourselves WWJD and it should become quite clear that Jesus would not do, nor encourage others to do, these things. In other words, we do not need to laboriously exercise other steps in seeking God's counsel when the issue is a moral one and the answer is quite clear.

The WWJD question is also useful when it comes to doing something that puts others ahead of ourselves. Should we help our neighbor when it is within our power to do so? Should we visit someone who is sick, even if it is not convenient? Should we lend (or give) to someone in need? Should we "walk the extra mile" in a particular situation? Should we accept an opportunity for ministry of some kind? Should we spend time with someone who crosses our path who is hurting? Most of the time, the answer will be "yes," but not always.

We cannot help every single person around us or give money to every single person in need. Our time, resources, and energy have limits. In trying to decide what to do in a specific situation, we should ask WWJD? Jesus helped many in need but He also sometimes retreated from the crowds to spend restorative time alone or with those close to Him. Jesus understood the danger of burn-out and knew that He could not minister 24/7. In Mark 6:31, for example, we read about an encounter between Jesus and His disciples: "...because so many people were coming and going that they did not even have a chance to eat, he said to them, 'Come with me by yourselves to a quiet place and get some rest.'" We need to become acquainted with the *whole* picture of the life of Jesus. We will learn that it is okay to say "no" to ministry opportunities sometimes, and to instead seek needed rest, refreshment, recharging, and renewal.

The WWJD question is sometimes useful when we are asked to do something in connection with our faith. Should we speak about our faith when asked to, either publicly or with a seeking individual? Should we pray with someone who has asked us to come pray with them? Jesus spoke often, but you will note that when confronted by his accusers just before His death, He did not always respond.[86] He knew when to speak and when to be silent. Reflect on when Jesus spoke and when He didn't.

The WWJD question is useful when we have only a few moments to respond or react to a situation. A friend of ours once spent a week preparing an elaborate festive dinner for his large extended family. On the day of the dinner, he had to go out on a quick errand just as the finishing touches were being made to the feast. He expected that his family would not sit down at the table until his return, as he was not driving very far. When he returned, however, he walked in on a meal already underway. He had missed the traditional opportunity to welcome everyone, to make a few comments, and to say grace. As the host of the event, he was understandably upset. He had to decide *in that passing moment* whether to express his

---

[86]   See, for example, Matthew 26:63

disappointment or to even show it by his facial expression. He ultimately chose to wisely ask himself: WWJD? It then became clear to him that he should graciously and forgivingly carry on with the meal. He entered into the feast and the fellowship, choosing to enjoy (not destroy) the results of the loving preparation that had gone into the meal.

This WWJD question can only be properly answered by those who have invested time in studying the life and ministry of Jesus. The more we know about what He did and said, the easier it is to speak and act like Him. The more we mature in our Christian walk, the more "second nature" it is to imitate Jesus. We are to grow more and more into His likeness as we grow in our faith. The more we do so, the more we just *know* what we should do or say (or *not* do or say) in a particular situation. Paul told us that we are to have the mind of Christ. The more we have His mind in us, the easier it will be to know whether or not to help a particular person...or whether it is time to rest...or time to retreat to a solitary place to pray.

God speaks to us as we meditate on the life and words of His son Jesus. In Hebrews 1:1-3, we are told "In the past God spoke to our forefathers through the prophets at many times and in various ways, but in these last days he has spoken to us by his Son...The Son is the radiance of God's glory and the exact representation of his being, sustaining all things by his powerful word." Do you want to hear from God? Listen to His Son. Become intimately acquainted with every word He spoke. This is the counsel of God the Father. The Father dearly wants us to know His Son.

This is in keeping with what we have discussed in previous chapters. The process of getting to know Jesus is inseparable from the other dimensions of our faith. If we spend a lifetime getting to know the Word, if we have a rich prayer life, if we are keenly sensitive to what the Spirit is saying to us, if we surround ourselves with mature Christian friends, if we build a strong inner foundation of wisdom, knowledge and discernment, then we will usually intuitively know what Jesus would say or do in a particular situation.

Jesus walked in love. Jesus forgave. He cared for the sick, the poor, and the oppressed. He fed the hungry. Jesus was honest. Jesus was patient. Jesus was compassionate. He seized opportunities to advance the Kingdom of God. He was deliberate and intentional and did not just "go with the flow" of the world around Him. Jesus taught and lived by clear standards.

If we want to imitate Jesus, we must desire to be on the path God has designed for our life. Jesus desired to know and to follow the will of His Father. Even when it cost Him his very life, Jesus was willing to say: "not as I will, but as you will...may your will be done."[87] As He neared His death, Jesus also said: "...the world must also learn that I love the Father and that I do exactly what my Father has commanded me."[88]

The very fact that you are reading this book and seeking the counsel of the Most High shows that you also desire to know and to fulfill the Father's will for your life. In this, you are imitating Jesus. This pleases the Father immensely.

If we want to imitate Jesus, we need to get to know Scripture. If we study the life of Jesus, we will see how often He quoted Scripture. For example, in Matthew 4, when Jesus was being tempted in the wilderness, He responded by saying three separate times: "It is written..." One of His three responses was: "It is written: 'Man does not live on bread alone, but *on every word that comes from the mouth of God.'*"[89] Jesus revered Scripture and knew it well. Asking WWJD is a quick prompt to draw out the stored Biblical wisdom and knowledge we have accumulated and cultivated. It is like a "quick-link" or a "hot key" on a computer program. Often a particular verse will come into our mind.

---

[87] Matthew 26:39-42
[88] John 14:31
[89] Matthew 4:4

If we want to imitate Jesus, we need to be led by the Spirit. Jesus was, for example, "led by the Spirit" into the desert.[90] Even Jesus, the Son of God, followed the leading of the Spirit. If we want to imitate Jesus, we must also value communion with the Father. We must prioritize time in prayer.

If I had my life to live over, I would ask the WWJD question far more often. There are movies I would not see, books I would not read, relationships I would not pursue, company I would not keep, jokes I would not laugh at, words I would not say, and opportunities I would not miss…that is, if I could re-live my days. I would particularly ask myself that question when I am put on the spot and have to give a spontaneous answer to invitations like: "Would you like to go out for dinner with me?", "Do you want to come to this movie with us tonight?", "Do you want another glass of wine?", "Can we count you in?", "Will you help me?", "Can you come to my party?", "Will you support my cause?", "Can you take on this client/this file?" I do not have a WWJD leather bracelet on my arm. But I carry this question in my heart and mind, ready to ask it when suitable occasions arise.

…fix your thoughts on Jesus…
Hebrews 3:1

…and he will be called Wonderful Counselor…
Isaiah 9:6

---

90   Matthew 4:1

13.

Extraordinary Counsel

I will pour out my Spirit on all people.
Your sons and daughters will prophesy,
your old men will dream dreams,
your young men will see visions.
Even on my servants, both men and women,
I will pour out my Spirit in those days.
Joel 2:28-29

All of the ways in which God counsels and guides us are extraordinary. They are worthy of our awe, gratitude and praise. The dialogue and the intimacy *between God* (the Divine, the Most High, the Creator of the universe) and *mere mortals* is something worthy of our continual amazement and wonder. By making a distinction between the "ordinary" and the more "extraordinary" ways in which God leads us, I do not wish to trivialize, marginalize, or minimize how absolutely incredible it is that God bothers to speak to us at all! The fact that God loves us enough to communicate with us is marvelous and incredible. All counsel from Him is extraordinary.

Having said that, there are some ways in which God guides us that are more commonplace, more "normal," and more widely experienced by all Christians the majority of the time. These are the methods which we have already discussed in previous chapters. God speaks to Christians in free nations through His Word, the Bible. From the moment a person chooses to become a Christian, the Holy Spirit comes to reside within that person and the inner voice is available to all who would quieten their hearts to listen. Anyone can pray for a greater measure of the indwelling Spirit. All of us should look for wise counselors in our lives. All of us should train ourselves to look at our circumstances with spiritual discernment as they unfold day by day. All of us should be developing wisdom, knowledge, insight, understanding, and good judgment as we live out our lives, following the above means of right living, continually learning from our experience as we grow. This is all so unspeakably wonderful, amazing, marvelous, and incredible that I hesitate to call any of it "ordinary" or "normal," and yet these means of hearing from God should become part of the normal course of our lives. Study the biography of any great Christian, past or present, and you will see that these means of hearing from God have been part of the *everyday* courses of their lives.

In this chapter, I will deal with more "extraordinary" forms of guidance—those means of hearing from God that are less common, less frequent, less everyday. These include dreams, visions, angelic visitations, and prophecies. Many of us may not experience any of these means of guidance in our lifetimes. Others will. It is not that one person is more "spiritual" than another. We do not control these means of guidance. God chooses to reveal Himself in these more extraordinary ways. We *receive* dreams, visions, angelic visitations, and prophecies. We do not earn them, conjure them up, or control them. We cannot make them happen!

These various means of guidance were used on various occasions in both the Old and New Testaments. There are so many recorded stories of dreams, visions, angelic visitations, and prophecies that a whole book could be written on this topic. I will give a few examples of each to demonstrate that these are all Scripturally sound means of guidance that God has used in history. We will also look at some modern examples of God using these forms of guidance.

Some would say that, although these "extraordinary" means of guidance have been used in the past, they are not meant for today. I beg to differ. I have known too many sincere and mature Christians who have experienced these kinds of divine guidance that I am fully convinced of their reality and modern day application. Powerful Christian leaders of the past century or two have experienced them. God is the same yesterday, today, and tomorrow. He stills operates in the realm of the natural and in the realm of the supernatural.

Dreams

There are many examples of significant men and women in the Bible having dreams that guided them.

Joseph in the Old Testament had dreams that changed his life and the destiny of an entire nation. In Genesis 37, we are told about the dreams that Joseph had while still a youth, dreams about how one day his father and brothers would bow down to him. Such dreams were taken seriously by God's people in those days. After Joseph told his father about his dreams, "his father kept the matter in mind."[91] These prophetic dreams did, in fact, come to pass in Joseph's life.

While in prison, Joseph interpreted the dreams of two fellow prisoners.[92] Joseph took these dreams seriously and believed that they came from God. The content of these dreams came to pass just as Joseph had interpreted them. Pharaoh heard about Joseph being able to interpret dreams and asked Joseph to interpret two of his own dreams. These dreams

---

[91]　Genesis 37:11
[92]　Genesis 40:8

forecast the years of plenty to be followed by the years of famine.[93] Pharaoh and Joseph were able to prepare the land of Egypt for the long years of famine because they believed that those dreams had come from God.

King Solomon had a dream in which God appeared to him. God asked Solomon what he wanted most. Solomon asked for wisdom. God granted him this.[94] Solomon received much wisdom, (although he did not always act in accordance with the wise guidance he gave others!)

The prophet Joel predicted that the Holy Spirit would come upon all of God's people (instead of just a special few on special occasions, as was the case in the Old Testament). Joel said that in those days "your old men will dream dreams."[95]

In the New Testament, Joseph (husband of Mary, the mother of Jesus) had several dreams, both before and after the birth of Jesus. Matthew 2:13 tells us that, after the birth of Jesus, "an angel of the Lord appeared to Joseph in a dream. 'Get up', he said, 'take the child and his mother and escape to Egypt. Stay there until I tell you…'" Joseph believed that this dream was from God and acted upon its counsel.

The Magi (the three wise men) visited Jesus just after He was born. Matthew 2:12 tells us that: "having been warned in a dream not to go back to Herod, they returned to their country by another route." They followed the counsel received in the dream.

Over the next few years, Joseph continued to be guided by dreams. "After Herod died, an angel of the Lord appeared in a dream to Joseph in Egypt and said 'Get up, take the child and his mother and go to the land of Israel, for those who were trying to take the child's life are dead.' "[96] Shortly thereafter, Joseph was directed in a dream to go to Nazareth, in Galilee,

---

93   Genesis 41
94   1 Kings 3
95   Joel 2:28
96   Matthew 2:19-20

where Jesus then spent most of his lifetime.[97] Once again, we see that Joseph considered these dreams to be communications from God and he acted upon them.

Just before the crucifixion of Jesus, Pilate's wife had a dream in which she was told that Jesus was an innocent man. She pled with her husband Pilate: "Don't have anything to do with that innocent man, for I have suffered a great deal today in a dream because of him."[98] It sounds like it was a very vivid and disturbing dream.

I have never personally had a dream that I believe was meant to be a message to me inspired by God. I have known others who have. Of course, we all dream every night, whether we are aware of it or not. Although God can speak to us through a dream, we should not *lightly* believe that a particular dream is guiding us to do something. Remember that this is an extraordinary, not ordinary, means of guidance.

When I was a teenager, I read some books about interpreting dreams. One book said that we should keep a notepad and pen by the bedside and, the very moment we wake up, we should scribble down notes about our dream before the memory of it vanishes. I trained myself to do this. I journalled about my dreams for several months. I discovered that I rode a bicycle in my dreams a lot, although I did not cycle much in real life. I frequented a place called "The Blue Lobster Café," although I was not a lobster fan in those days and have never in my life been to, or heard of, such a place. People would show up in my dreams that I had not seen in a long time and I would have passionate arguments with them that made no sense to my wakened mind or had no apparent connection with real events. My subconscious mind intrigued me, but quite frankly, I learned absolutely nothing from that whole experience. I certainly did not feel led to get on a bicycle and set out to find The Blue Lobster Café! Who knows? Maybe one day I will find myself on a bicycle and I will pass by such a

---

[97] Matthew 2:22
[98] Matthew 27:19

café and something life-altering will happen that day, but for now, I say with a chuckle that the mind does whatever it does in our dream world and we do not really understand much of it. *We need to exercise much caution and discernment in this area.* We will be led astray if we try to attach great significance to every dream we have.

Having said that, I know of others who have had dreams that were of significance. I do not laugh at them. I believe that when a person has a God-inspired dream, it is so vivid, so powerful and so capable of both interpretation and application that the dreamer knows that it is clearly from God.

I have met a few Afghans, born and raised Muslims, who have had dreams that have brought them to Christian faith. One of them, a woman, was developing interest in the Christian faith prior to her dream. She decided to see if Jesus was real and alive by telling Him that she was cold at night and needed a blanket. It was not long before she ended up receiving a blanket. Soon after, she saw Jesus in a dream. He was asking her if she was warm now. This dream showed her how much God cared about her. She became a Christian soon after, at great risk to her personal life.

Other Afghans have had dreams in which Peter, John, and Jesus have appeared to them. I believe that God used dreams to speak to these Muslims because they did not have much opportunity to speak with Christians or read the Bible.

I have no doubt that God uses dreams in many places to reach the otherwise unreachable. I have heard similar stories from missionaries in various countries. This is an awesome manifestation of God. Governments can close borders to Christians, Bibles, and missionaries, but they cannot close the border to the supernatural work of the Holy Spirit.

These stories provide an interesting answer to those seeking hearts and minds who won't accept the Christian faith until all their questions are answered, one of which often includes: "What about all the people in the deserts or the jungles of remote places who have not had the chance to read the Bible or hear about Jesus?" What about them? God is capable of reaching them, speaking to them and guiding them with all the extraordinary and supernatural means at His disposal.

If God could speak to Moses from a burning bush or to Paul from a blinding light, then God can speak to those in the "desert" places of this world by whatever means He chooses, however extraordinary. Let us stop asking such feeble questions about the Creator of the universe. God is capable of circumventing mere human means of reaching and speaking to people. Romans 1 tells us that God already speaks to all people through the splendor and majesty of nature and the complexity of the created world. God chooses to display His majesty through the natural world, but God can also speak through the supernatural. The more that governments work at closing the door to the gospel, the more it seems that God uses supernatural means in these "closed" countries. Men in power cannot beat, chain, silence, imprison, or kill the Holy Spirit.

Visions

God gave visions to many Biblical characters. In Genesis 13-15, God gave Abraham a vision of what God was going to do for him. In Genesis 13:14-15, God told Abraham to *look* and *see* the land that God was going to give to him. (God can tell us in this same way to "look" and "see" the home we should buy, the business or ministry we should start, the people we should help, or the book we should write). Genesis 15:1 further records how the Lord came to Abraham in a vision. Abraham was told to look at the stars, for his offspring would be as numerous as the stars. This must have been an encouraging vision for Abraham, who at that time had no children and was growing old.

God spoke to the father of Joseph, in the Old Testament, through a vision. Genesis 46:2-3 records: "And God spoke to Israel [Joseph's father] in a vision at night and said...I am

God...Do not be afraid to go down to Egypt" (where Joseph would eventually provide him and his other sons with grain during the famine). Israel obeyed the counsel received in this vision.

Others in the Old Testament, such as Isaiah, Ezekiel, and Daniel, also received visions.

In the New Testament, Paul and Ananias were separately given visions in which they were told to meet one another.[99] This was just after Paul (formerly Saul, the great persecutor of the Christian church) had been blinded by a great light on the road to Damascus and had heard the voice of Jesus. Ananias was understandably afraid to meet Paul until, in the vision, God told Ananias that Paul was going to become God's chosen instrument. Both men acted on the visions received.

Peter and Cornelius also both had visions of such powerful impact that Peter was thereafter not afraid to preach the Christian faith to both Jews and Gentiles.[100] Up until that time, the gospel was only being preached to the Jews. After his vision, Peter was able to say: "I now realize how true it is that God does not show favoritism but accepts men from every nation who fear Him and do what is right." The vision described in Acts 10 guided Peter's subsequent ministry.

John, on the island of Patmos, had the visions that form the Book of Revelation. These were powerful visions that told him what would occur in the future. John fully recorded these visions, so that we are all able to read about them.

Are there men and women *today* who claim to have had visions that have guided them? Let me share a few stories.

I wrote earlier about an incredible church and Christian community in Spain that I experienced for several weeks when I was nineteen (and then again for a few months with my husband, a decade later). The church and community had been started by an American pastor. He had previously been the pastor of a church in Cuba, but had to leave after Castro came

---

[99] Acts 9
[100] Acts 10

to power. After leaving Cuba, he had asked God what he should do. One door had firmly closed. He was praying for, and waiting for, an open door to go elsewhere.

It was during this period that he had a vision of a vessel of oil being poured out over Spain. Oil is one symbol of the Holy Spirit. The vision was so clear to him that he moved his family to Spain. He encountered many serious setbacks as he tried to start a church in Spain. His guidance from God had been so clear to him that he persisted through the many difficulties he faced.

Over a few decades, his work increased from one small church, which had initially grown slowly, to dozens of national churches and other ministries. Many in my family have been deeply impacted by this man and his ministry. Over the years, I have met many others who have been influenced and ignited by this man of vision.

Another man of vision is a well-known present day evangelist named Reinhard Bonnke. He began working in Africa many years ago. He was prepared to speak on street corners to whoever would stop to listen, whether one person or five. While his ministry was still relatively small, God gave him a vision of a "blood-washed Africa"—a continent totally covered with the blood of Jesus. When I heard of his vision, I noted its stark contrast to a continent awash in the violently spilled blood of men, women, and children...victims of human conflict in many nations...victims of colonial arrogance, government corruption, greed, tribal hatred, and genocide. The blood of Jesus, in contrast, was shed to bring love, forgiveness, mercy, grace, and peace. Better a continent covered with the blood of Jesus than the blood flowing from the senseless slaughter of millions of African people.

Like the pastor in Spain, Bonnke was able to persevere through many difficult years because his vision was so real to him. In recent years, Bonnke has led huge crusades where more than one million Africans will gather on a single evening to hear him speak. Video footage of these gatherings is astounding! About 34 million Africans have made documented decisions for Christ as a result of this man's ministry in the past three or four years. Stories abound of miraculous healings and dramatically changed lives.[aa]

In earlier chapters, we talked about Corrie ten Boom, who spent time in a Nazi concentration camp during World War II because she had allowed Jewish refugees to hide in her Dutch home. Corrie's sister Betsie was incarcerated in that same camp for that same reason. While the war still raged on, Betsie had some powerful visions about what would happen after the war. In her visions, Betsie could see a home in Holland that would minister to released prisoners of concentration camps. Betsie could specifically see a large and beautiful home, full of polished wood, surrounded with gardens full of flowers. Betsie had a second vision of traveling the world, speaking about the love of God, which sustained the two sisters through their darkest hours, and which compelled them to forgive those who had hurt them. Betsie had a third vision of taking over one of the concentration camps after the war, renovating it and using it to house those needing emotional healing and restoration. One day, however, still in the midst of the war, Corrie found Betsie's body slumped in the corner of a washroom in the concentration camp, surrounded by other corpses. Betsie did not live to see the fulfillment of the visions. Corrie, however, lived to fulfill all three visions, exactly as her sister had "seen" them while the war was still in progress.[bb]

My own sister has had a vision that has changed her life and work. She has been working as an international aid worker in Afghanistan for a number of years. In the early years, she used her skills in various aspects of media.

Some years ago, she was traveling by train in Pakistan, on her way to a retreat. She became weary of looking out the window at miles of dusty scenery full of debris, poverty, and camel carcasses. In the midst of that bleak scenery, she saw a lovely green garden. While later reflecting on that garden at the retreat, she believed that God was telling her that she would be "a well-watered garden" in the midst of the Afghan women and children when she returned there. During her years in Afghanistan, she had developed a love for the Afghan women (especially the widows) and the Afghan children (especially the orphans and street kids).

In the next months, she developed a strong vision of creating actual garden sanctuaries for the women and children of Afghanistan. This was a whole new direction for her. She knew from her years of living in Kabul that the city was partly in ruins from a few decades of turmoil (ten years of Soviet occupation, the subsequent battles between the mujahadeen warlords, the years of Taliban rule, and a brief period of bombing by the American military just after 9/11).

Women had been forced for some years to primarily stay behind the high walls surrounding their homes. They were allowed to venture in public to go to the markets—busy, dusty, noisy places, with no place to leisurely socialize with women friends. My sister's vision of planting gardens involved seeing, in her imagination, beautiful green parks abounding with trees, rosebushes, grass and flowers, fountains and teahouses, shady grape arbors and benches, and play equipment for children. She could visualize places of refreshment, serenity, rest, conversation, and play—literal oases for the healing of women and children who had been through so much.

My sister did not personally have much horticultural experience, knowledge, or skills. But the vision was so clear to her that she surrounded herself with men and women (some Afghans, some Westerners) who had such experience, knowledge, and skills. She then found donors for the necessary funds to bring the vision to life.

She was granted permission to work on restoring part of a former women's gardens in Kabul that had fallen into ruin. Not only did this become a place for women and children to gather, talk, play, and picnic, it became a place where Afghan women could be trained in gardening and agricultural skills. On some weekends, about ten thousand women and children have come to enjoy these gardens. My sister is now designing an even grander garden sanctuary to be located on a beautiful piece of property just outside of Kabul. That was the property we were walking on the day that I was nervous about stepping on possible landmines.

How does a person know if they have had a vision, as opposed to just an idea or some image in their imagination? I believe, from talking to or reading about those who claim to have had clear visions from God, that these visions are ideas and images in their minds that are so powerful that they shape the course of their lives. They are willing to pay any cost, expend any energy, and endure any hardship to see the fulfillment of their vision. They are willing to risk their very lives. The vision remains, no matter what obstacles or difficulties beset them. Others around them are able to get a glimpse of the vision, to "catch" the vision, too, and are themselves willing to give time, money, energy, and even their lives to see the vision fulfilled.

The vision is usually also *confirmed* and *affirmed* by the various other means of guidance we have been discussing. These visionaries usually receive verses from the Bible that confirm the vision. They receive affirmation from the Spirit working within them; they are led forth by love, faith, joy, inner peace, wisdom, compassion for others, courage, and other clear fruits of the Spirit. The vision usually meets the test of affirmation by wise counselors. The visionary receives the knowledge, understanding, discernment, and good judgment necessary to proceed forward with whatever they have envisioned. God ultimately provides the circumstances for the vision to be fulfilled.

I suppose it could be said that all of us have "visions" whenever we, too, receive inspiration to do something good that we sense is God-inspired. We see in our imaginations, by faith, what it is that we believe God wants us to do. I envisioned this book in my mind before I wrote the first sentence. If our vision is from God, He will provide the ongoing motivation, inspiration, strength, energy, and all necessary resources for the vision to come to pass. The vision will survive all difficulties and obstacles. If the vision is from God, it *will* be confirmed by other means of guidance such as Scripture, the wise counsel of others, and unfolding circumstances.

Angels

There are numerous stories of angelic visitation in both the Old and New Testaments. Sometimes the angels appeared in a dream, other times in bodily form, and on one occasion in a burning bush. Angels can be divine "messengers."

In the Old Testament, angels appeared and spoke to Hagar, Abraham, Jacob, Moses, Samson's father and many others.[101] My favorite angel stories are in the Book of Daniel. Daniel 3:21-28 tells the story of three men who were thrown into a fiery furnace because they would not worship a god of gold. They were not touched by the flames. A fourth "person" was seen walking in the fire with them. When Daniel was thrown into a lion's den because he refused to stop praying to God, in defiance of a royal edict, he also was not harmed. Daniel later told the King: "My God sent His angel, and he shut the mouths of the lions."[102]

In the New Testament, angels appeared to Joseph (husband of Mary, the mother of Jesus), Zechariah (regarding his son John the Baptist), and to those gathered at the empty tomb of Jesus, telling them various messages. These latter angels told the history-changing news about Jesus: "He is risen." They also foretold that Jesus would appear to the disciples, after His death, in Galilee. Angels later appeared to Philip (telling him to go speak with someone), and to Paul

---

[101] Genesis 16:7-9 and 21:17; Genesis 22:11; Genesis 31:11-13; Exodus 3:2; Judges 13:9
[102] Daniel 6:22

(telling him not to be afraid to stand before Caesar). An angel led Peter out of prison.[103]

I have never seen an angel. I have known others who have, however, and I have no reason to doubt their stories.

My own grandmother claimed to have encountered angels in the last months of her life. She was a godly woman who had lived in Eastern Europe through the First World War and the Russian Revolution. To escape Communism, my grandparents fled to Germany just as the Nazis were coming on the scene. As Hitler continued his rise to power, and his intentions became clearer, my grandparents were wise enough to leave Germany before the Second World War. They arrived in Saskatchewan, a western province of Canada, in time for the hardships of the Great Depression! My grandfather took me to church as a young child and my grandmother gave me my first Bible at the age of seven, which I still have to this day.

My grandmother lived until her early nineties and was quite lucid and communicative to the end. In the last months of her life, she was in a nursing home. She told me that most mornings, angels would come and speak with her, telling her the end was getting very near and that they had been assigned to her. My grandmother was not at all frightened by them. She was just excited. She had no fear of death or dying. She was a bright, loving, lively, and wise woman. Having lived through so many of the historic upheavals of the last century, she had learned to be a practical and hard-working woman, grounded in both natural and spiritual realities. I marvel to this day at her stories of angelic visitation. I would love to some day have the same experience! My grandmother died peacefully, with a smile on her face. Who knows what she was seeing and who she was greeting as she passed from this life into the next?

I have always been intrigued by the verse in Hebrews 13:2, where Paul tells us that sometimes we have "entertained angels without knowing it." If we expect gossamer wings and halos,

---

[103] Matthew 1:20; Luke 1:11; Mark 16:5-6; Luke 24:4-6; Acts 8:26 and 27:23-24; Acts 12

we may miss them. In Hebrews 1:14, Paul wrote: "Are not all angels ministering spirits sent to serve those who will inherit salvation?" I have a desire to learn more about these "ministering spirits."

Billy Graham has written a whole book about angels.^{cc} It is full of Scripture and amazing modern day stories. Billy Graham discusses the role that angels have played as messengers. It is worth reading by anyone interested in learning more about this topic.

I do not believe that we are meant to fully understand all there is to know about angels. In Judges 13:17-18, when Samson's father asked the angel his name, the angel answered: "Why do you ask my name? It is beyond understanding." While we will not in this lifetime fully understand the angelic realm, we ought not to discount or disparage its existence.

Prophecies

Prophecy, which quite simply means the proclamation of a divine message, can be found frequently in the Old Testament. The early New Testament church also regularly practiced prophecy. Paul wrote much about prophets and prophecy in his various letters. Prophecy is described by Paul as a "gift" of the Spirit and as a calling. Prophetic messages might (but do not necessarily) speak of future events. Prophecy communicates what is on God's mind and heart regarding the present or the future.

There are a few dozen Old Testament prophecies that predated but specifically predicted the birth, life and death of Jesus. These are called the "Messianic prophecies." For example, the Jews believed that the Messiah would be born in Bethlehem, where Jesus was, in fact, born.[104] The Jews believed that the Messiah would come from the tribe of Judah, the family of Jesse and the house of David. This ancestry

---

[104] Micah 5:2; Matthew 2:1, also Luke 2:4-7, John 7:42

corresponds with the recorded genealogy of Jesus.[105] The Jews believed that the Messiah would receive the Spirit, which Jesus did.[106] The Jews believed that the Messiah would be preceded by a special messenger. Jesus was preceded by John the Baptist.[107] There are numerous other prophecies in the Old Testament regarding Jesus' life, death, and resurrection.[dd]

Biblical prophets also foretold events that would happen to various nations and civilizations. Many such events have, in fact, historically come to pass. The Old Testament prophets such as Daniel, Ezekiel, Isaiah, Jeremiah, and others foretold what would happen to ancient civilizations such as Tyre, Sidon, Petra-Edom, Thebes-Memphis, Babylon, Jerusalem and Palestine. These prophecies were later fulfilled.[ee] God has used prophecy to foretell what would happen to many nations over the course of history. Some of these prophetic words have yet to be fulfilled.

Jesus foretold much about his own future while He was still on earth. He told His disciples that He would be betrayed by Judas, that He would soon die, that Peter would deny that he knew Jesus three times before the cock crowed, that He would rise again, and that He would appear to them again, after His death, in Galilee.[108]

The Book of Acts and the letters of Paul provide a wealth of information about prophecy and how it is meant to be practiced in the Christian church. I encourage you to become familiar with all that Paul had to say on this fascinating subject.

In 2 Peter 1:21, Peter wrote: "For prophecy never had its origin in the will of man, but men spoke from God as they were carried along by the Holy Spirit." Prophecy is one manifestation of the Holy Spirit. We cannot create or conjure up true prophetic words. These words do not flow from our

---

[105] See Genesis 49:10, Isaiah 11:1, Jeremiah 23:5 for prophecies; Matthew 1 and Luke 3 for genealogies

[106] Isaiah 11:2; Matthew 3:16-17, also Mark 1:10-11, Luke 4:15-21, John 1:32

[107] Isaiah 40:3 and Matthew 3:1-2, also Luke 1:17, John 1:23

[108] Matthew 26

intelligence, wisdom or knowledge. They flow from the Holy Spirit working within us.

The Book of Revelation is full of prophecies which foretell the events that will unfold at the end of the world. Some of these correspond to what was already foretold by prophets such as Daniel. We can receive much counsel about where this world is headed if we study these books of the Bible. This subject is too vast to be dealt with in this book!

Prophecy is practiced in this day and age in many churches. On a personal level, I have been present for general prophecies where, for example, a church congregation has been told that God has heard their prayers and will respond to them, or that God wants to heal or help the people present. These kinds of general prophecies are awesome and have ministered to me in circumstances where I have been hurting or needing help or encouragement of some kind.

I have known people who have been the recipients of very specific prophecies about their lives. My own sister has had various prophecies about the gardens I wrote about earlier. Specific prophetic messages seem to be given to those who are doing something that is very difficult or which requires such vast faith that these messages are almost necessary to enable them to pass through the very deep waters of their journey.

False Prophets

The Bible warns us about false prophets. How do we know if a prophet is a true prophet or a false prophet? In Deuteronomy 18:21-22, God gave the following test: "You may say to yourselves, 'How can we know when a message has not been spoken by the Lord?' If what a prophet proclaims in the name of the Lord does not take place or come true, that is a message the Lord has not spoken. That prophet has spoken presumptuously."

Isaiah 44:25 talks about how God "foils the signs of false prophets." God does not allow all of their predictions to come true.

1 Kings 22:20-22 tells about how God allowed lying spirits to be in the mouths of Ahab's prophets to entice Ahab into a losing battle. (Ahab was a King who disregarded God's ways). Jeremiah 14:14 also refers to lying prophets: "The Lord said to [Jeremiah], 'The prophets are prophesying lies in my name. I have not sent them or appointed them or spoken to them. They are prophesying to you false visions, divinations, idolatries and the delusions of their own minds.'" Prophecy must always be tested.

Jesus warned about false prophets who would appear and deceive many. In Matthew 7:15, He said: "They come to you in sheep's clothing, but inwardly they are ferocious wolves." Jesus said, in Matthew 7:20, that it is by their fruit that we will recognize a false prophet or a true prophet. Prophets who seek to generate hatred, fear (other than an appropriate fear of God), strife, confusion, panic, malice, division, and other negative fruit are not true prophets. Those who deny the deity of Jesus Christ are also false prophets.[109] On the other hand, prophets whose words bring forth awareness of sin and its consequences, repentance, obedience to God, godly deeds, a spirit of love, faith, clarity, generosity, kindness, compassion, and courage are more likely speaking the words of God. Paul tells us in 1 Corinthians 14:1 -5: "Follow the way of love and eagerly desire spiritual gifts, especially the gift of prophecy....everyone who prophesies speaks to men for their strengthening, encouragement and comfort....he who prophesies edifies the church."

Counterfeit Forms of Guidance

We have talked about supernatural guidance in the form of dreams, visions, angelic messages, and prophecies. While these forms of guidance can be real, and from God, *this whole area*

---

[109] 1 John 2:22

needs to be approached with great caution. There is a lot of room for being deceived or misled. Wisdom, Biblical knowledge, understanding, mature judgment, and deep spiritual discernment are required to test these forms of guidance.

One cannot write about the subject of the supernatural without strongly warning that there are counterfeit forms of supernatural guidance. These are occult forms of guidance such as astrology, contacting spirits of the dead, fortune-telling, psychic visions, and crystal ball reading.

There are warnings and prohibitions regarding the occult in the Old Testament. Deuteronomy 18:10, for example, instructed: "Let no one be found among you...who practices divination or sorcery, interprets omens, engages in witchcraft, or casts spells, or who is a medium or spiritist or who consults the dead." Leviticus 19:26b and 19:31 gave the Israelites similar prohibitions about sorcerers, spiritists, and mediums.

Practitioners of the occult may on some occasions demonstrate real powers. Examples of this can be found in the story of Moses. On many of the occasions that Moses performed miraculous signs for Pharaoh, Pharaoh's sorcerers could duplicate the supernatural feats. Just as a false prophet is not accurate all of the time, however, the sorcerers of Pharaoh could not duplicate *all* of the miracles of Moses. In Exodus 8:18 we are told, for example, that "when the magicians tried to produce gnats by their secret arts, they could not."

1 Samuel 28 tells the story of how Saul went to a medium and had her successfully contact the spirit of Samuel (who had previously died). God was so displeased that this cost Saul his life, less than twenty-four hours later. In 1 Chronicles 10:13-14, we are told: "Saul died because he was unfaithful to the Lord; he did not keep the word of the Lord and even consulted a medium for guidance...[He] did not inquire of the Lord."

Isaiah 8:19-20 appropriately challenges anyone curious about the occult: "When men tell you to consult mediums and spiritists, who whisper and mutter, should not a people *inquire of their God*? Why consult the dead on behalf of the living?"

In the New Testament, Paul spoke with bold authority against practitioners of the occult. In Acts 13, a sorcerer (also a false prophet) was trying to interfere with Paul's spiritual discussion with the governor of Cyprus. Note how Paul responded: "Then Paul, filled with the Holy Spirit, glared angrily at the sorcerer and said, 'You son of the devil, full of every sort of trickery and villainy, enemy of all that is good, will you never end your opposition to the Lord?'"[110]

In our modern age, the occult is thriving. I have met prominent professional and business people who regularly consult psychics and mediums. I was once at a dinner party with a number of medical specialists and was quite shocked to hear of the frequency of their consultations with the occult world. They sought the guidance of psychics regarding personal, relational, health, and financial decisions. I recently heard about a social gathering of CEOs—they were told upon arriving that the night's entertainment would be a "psychic" that could be consulted by them. There has also been a fresh outpouring of the occult from Hollywood.

I had a few brief experiences in the realm of the occult in my teen years. I learned enough to know firsthand that there is some supernatural form of power in the occult that is real. It is not reliable, however, and not without consequences. After some particularly strange experiences, I battled nightmares and fears until I experienced Scriptural teaching in this area along with appropriate prayer.

Teenagers in each generation need to be freshly warned about the dangers of the occult. Reading horoscopes, having their palms read, having tarot cards or tea leaves read, and attending séances can be regarded by teenagers as innocent fun or entertainment, but these forms of guidance open the door to misleading supernatural power. Christians ought never to flirt with this realm. These are not methods of seeking God's counsel, but potentially the counsel of other powers.

---

[110]   Acts 13:9-10 (LB)

Conclusion

God does provide counsel through supernatural means such as dreams, visions, angels, and prophecies. I must repeat, however, that this realm of guidance needs to be approached with great caution and due respect. It requires mature wisdom and Scriptural knowledge to rightly discern if God is speaking in such ways. The supernatural realm is not to be lightly dabbled in.

As I stated at the outset, these forms of guidance are not very usual or frequent. These kinds of guidance may never happen to you in your lifetime. Any "message" supposedly received from God through any of these supernatural means ought never to go against the Word, the peace of the indwelling Spirit, the clear counsel of wise advisors, or our inner store of wisdom, good judgment, discernment, and common sense. Although we need to be careful, we should not dismiss the notion that God uses these means to speak to His people in this present age. God is sovereign over all and can do whatever He pleases. There are too many credible stories of how God continues to visit Christians in the supernatural realm for these forms of guidance to be disregarded.

Do not interpretations belong to God? Tell me your dreams...
Joseph, in Genesis 40:8

And God spoke to Israel in a vision at night...
Genesis 46:2

Are not all angels ministering spirits sent to serve
those who will inherit salvation?
Hebrews 1:14

For prophecy never had its origin in the will of man, but men spoke
from God as they were carried along by the Holy Spirit.
2 Peter 1:21

14.

Waiting for Counsel

I wait for You, O Lord; you will answer, O Lord my God.
Psalm 38:15

I wait for the Lord, my soul waits...
My soul waits for the Lord
more than watchmen wait for the morning.
Psalm 130:5-6

During my years as a trial lawyer, there were many occasions when I poured my heart and soul into a complex legal argument before a judge or gave an impassioned address to a jury...and then I had to wait for their response! Judges often "reserve" their decisions and can take weeks or even months to render a written decision. Juries can take hours or days to deliberate before coming to a decision. It was always agonizing and nerve-wracking to *wait* for the response of the judge or jury. In the meantime, I had to carry on with the rest of my work.

One of the first things that all of us learn, as we seek God's counsel, is that He often does not answer us right away. I can think of so many instances where I have prayed for months, or even years, about whether or not I should leave a job, end a relationship, move, or make some other major change in my life. These seasons can be filled with impatience, doubts, and frustration. Occasionally, these seasons can be excruciating. In these times, I have identified with David when he cried out to God: "My soul is in anguish. How long, O Lord, how long?"[111] I have learned, however, that there is nothing we can do to speed up God's timetable! We cannot demand an immediate answer from Him any more than I could demand an immediate decision from a judge or jury.

When we seek God's counsel, *more often than not* we have to wait for His response. *Seldom* do we receive immediate answers to our questions. The wait is often especially long when we are praying about a major issue such as the right person to marry or whether to leave one career or ministry for another. King David understood this concept of waiting on God. He wrote many Psalms about waiting, such as Psalm 38:15: "I wait for you, O Lord; you will answer, O Lord my God." David clearly believed that God would *eventually* respond.

During these "waiting seasons," we need to keep reminding ourselves that God has our best interests at heart. He loves us. He knows what is best for us. He is not wasting the time that is passing. He is using it to accomplish certain things, whether in ourselves or others or circumstances, that are often invisible to us. We need to trust Him. We all need to cultivate more patience!

I have heard from many wise Christians in my life that God is never a moment late. This is very Scriptural. The Bible tells us that there is an *"appointed time"* and a *"due season"* for all matters, including the timing of when God speaks to us. In Genesis 18:14, for example, Abraham and Sarah were told that Isaac would be born the following year, at "the appointed time." In Habukkuk 2:3, the prophet wrote that "the revelation awaits an appointed time." As He drew nearer to His time of death, Jesus said: "My appointed time is near."[112] In Psalm 75:2, God says "I choose the appointed time." God has already

---

[111] Psalm 6:3
[112] Matthew 26:18

appointed the times when He will *speak* and when He will *act*. God will tell us what we need to know when we need to know it. God will also bring His purposes to pass at their appointed times. King David understood this when he wrote: "My times are in your hands."[113] His son Solomon wrote: "There is a *proper time* and procedure for every matter."[114]

Nature provides ample evidence of God's appointed times for all things. The prophet Jeremiah said: "Even the stork in the sky knows her appointed seasons, and the dove, the swift and the thrush observe the time of their migration."[115] Tulips and hyacinths know to bloom in the spring. Daisies and daylilies know that their time to bloom is in the summer. Chrysanthemums wait until the autumn to flower. Snow does not fall in the summer. Many animals hibernate in the winter. These appointed times come and go with nature's cooperation. Only mankind dares question the timing of God. Only mankind impatiently falls out of step with God.

In the waiting season, I have learned to carry on with the light that I already have, even if it is just for the next step or two. I have learned to keep moving forward even in a small amount of light, trusting that more light will come. We must stay on the path we are on until we are clearly told to turn to the right or the left. Occasionally, when there appears to be no light at all, we must stop and rest until some light comes. Whether we are "resting" or "moving," we must keep following God's *general* will as revealed to us in His Word and in our hearts. For example, we must move forward loving one another, doing our present jobs to the best of our abilities, investing richly in right relationships, and avoiding all known sin. If we remain deep in the Word, we will have enough *general* guidance as to how to live the right kind of life, day by day, until more *specific* guidance is given about a change we

---

113 Psalm 31:15a
114 Ecclesiastes 8:6a
115 Jeremiah 8:7a

should make. If we are doing what is right, we *are* on the right path (until we are directed to another right path).

The Israelites, under Moses, waited as long as they had to for God to lead them. You will recall that as they left Egypt, heading for the Promised Land, God guided them forward by a cloud during the day and a pillar of fire by night. If the cloud or pillar of fire moved, they moved with it. If the cloud or the pillar of fire remained stationary, they camped until the cloud and the pillar of fire started to move. *They wanted to be in step with God.* In Numbers 9:22, we read: "Whether the cloud stayed over the tabernacle for two days or a month or a year, the Israelites would remain in camp and not set out; but when it lifted, they would set out." They were prepared to wait so that they remained in step with God.

I have learned that if I run ahead of God, I run into trouble! King Solomon wrote: "It is not good to have zeal without knowledge, *nor to be hasty and miss the way.*"[116] Trying to run ahead of God is like running onward into darkness or fog without a flashlight, compass, or map. What is the point? I have learned the hard way that it is better to rest (maybe God knew I needed a rest!) than to rush ahead and have to later retrace my steps to get back on track. Resting until clarity comes is a lot less tiring than running around without directions! I want to be *in step* with God, not ahead of Him or behind Him. Paul advised us to live this way when he said in Galatians 5:25: "Since we live by the Spirit, *let us keep in step with the Spirit.*" My prayer for you and for me is that we learn to keep in step with God, even if that means waiting!

Clearing Sin from Our Lives

If God seems to be silent for a long time, we need to examine our hearts to see if something has offended God. Maybe He is waiting for us to recognize some sin in our lives. God will not necessarily speak to us in one area of our lives if we are

[116] Proverbs 19:2

harboring sin in another area. He may be trying to get our attention focused on an area *He* wants to deal with. We may not be hearing Him because we are so stubbornly trying to talk to Him about the issue *we* want to address. Once we do recognize that area of sin and seek to correct that area, God will often be ready to talk about our pressing issue. I have learned that *His* pressing issue is more important and necessary than *our* pressing issue.

The psalmist expressed this truth when he wrote: "I cried out to him with my mouth...*If I had cherished sin in my heart, the Lord would not have listened...*"[117] We must deal with the sin in our lives before God will fully reveal His counsel to us.

Practicing Patience

If, however, our conscience is clear, we must trust that God has other reasons for His timing. We must be patient as we wait.

Job has often been described as a model of patience. He suffered much. He cried out to God in his anguish and posed many questions. *For a long time, God did not speak back.* In the meantime, Job had to endure the endless comments of his friends, who thought they understood what God was up to. During the painful period that God was still silent, Job said: "...he knows the way that I take; when he has tested me, I will come forth as gold. My feet have closely followed his steps; I have kept to his way without turning aside. I have not departed from the commands of his lips; I have treasured the words of his mouth more than my daily bread."[118] This is a wonderful model of the attitude that we are to have while we are waiting for God to answer our questions and to reveal Himself in the midst of our circumstances. We are to keep doing what we believe to be right and keep generally following the truths in God's Word.

---

[117] Psalm 66:17-18
[118] Job 23:10-12

After further waiting, Job asked, "Does he not see my ways and count my every step?"[119] God had still not spoken to Job, but Job was confident that God had not forgotten about him. It is not until Job 38:1 that we are told: *"Then* the Lord answered Job out of the storm." *Finally,* God did speak. God told Job all that was on His mind in response to Job's impassioned prayers, petitions, and questions. After He spoke, God also blessed Job twice as much as He had before. Job's patient waiting for God during his painful trials was richly rewarded.

Florence Nightingale is another example of someone who faithfully and patiently waited. For *more than a decade,* Florence prayed intensely for God to show her what she should do with her life. She grew up in a wealthy British home, spending her time socializing in high aristocratic circles. She found this life to be empty, frivolous, and self-centered. She was convinced that God had higher and more fruitful purposes for her life—so she prayed and sought God's will and *waited* as one year passed into the next. Her letters and diaries reveal her anguish, confusion, and restlessness during this long waiting season of her life.

Over those years, God *eventually* spoke to her in various ways, slowly showing her that her calling was to care for the sick and the suffering. God brought many people into her life who influenced her to consider the vocation of nursing. God brought opportunities to care for the sick and the suffering in her immediate surroundings. The Spirit impressed this calling upon her as she began to realize that she had great passion, inclination and energy for this kind of work. Although her family did not mind her caring for sick elderly relatives, they actively discouraged the pursuit of the calling of nursing as a vocation, as they thought it was "beneath" someone of her social rank. *Sixteen years* passed between the time that Florence clearly felt God *generally* calling her to give her life in unspecified service to Him and the year in which she was

---

[119] Job 31:4

asked to be the director of the Institute for the Care of Sick Gentlewomen.

Florence Nightingale later became famous for her work with the war-wounded in the Crimea (where the British were fighting the Russians). Although she had to deal with filth, lack of food and supplies, lack of medicine and proper bedding, she persevered in her horrible surroundings, believing that she was finally fulfilling the purpose for which she had come into the world. She was more than a nurse. She supervised over one hundred other nurses in the Crimea. She personally attended to over two thousand soldiers on their deathbeds. In later years, she became a political activist and a pioneer in the areas of hospital administration and nursing standards. After the Crimean war, Queen Victoria was more nervous meeting Florence than Florence was meeting the legendary Queen. Florence Nightingale became a great legend in her own right. None of this would have transpired if she had not been willing to intensely pray, *year after year*, patiently and persistently *waiting* for God to reveal what He wanted her to do with her life.ᶠᶠ

Perhaps, my friend, you think that God has forgotten you. Perhaps you think that He will never answer you or that He will never give you directions. I encourage you to be patient. God sees every step that you take. He sees your faithfulness in the midst of your circumstances. During your trials, resolve to "come forth as gold" like Job. God is at work in you and around you, whether you are aware of Him or not. He will reward your hours or days or even years of waiting for Him to counsel and guide you.

Building Character

God sometimes uses the time that we are waiting to *build character*. I wrote earlier about how I left the practice of law after enjoying it for twenty years. As I ended my practice, I did not know what I was supposed to do next. I sought God's guidance. I waited. I prayed. I immersed myself in the Word. I found good, useful, and fruitful work to do to keep myself occupied while I waited. I invested in the relationships around me. As I look back, I see that this was a season of preparation for things to come. It was a season of character-building. Over a period of a few years, it has become increasingly clearer what God wants me to do. I have much greater clarity now and know that I am much better prepared for what lies ahead. Waiting was not always fun. I sometimes grew weary. I sometimes felt frustrated. I sometimes felt confused. I sometimes battled doubts. To be honest, I sometimes felt bored!

It was during that season of waiting that much of the Scriptural material and other notes and research for this book were amassed, as I tried to understand what God's highest and best onward purposes for my life are. This book would never have been written but for that season of waiting and seeking, growing, and learning. As I struggled to hear God's counsel and guidance for my mid-life change in direction, I learned lessons that will hopefully bless others. God also used the season of waiting to get my attention regarding character issues that needed to be addressed. During this time, I attended a Henry Blackaby luncheon address. He said that God always gives us assignments that match our character. Sometimes God has to work on our character before we are ready for the *next level* of assignment.

An excellent example of how God used a long season of waiting *to build character* can be found in the life of John Newton. Newton was a notorious slave trader who lived in the 1700's. He initially lived a life of sexual immorality, drunkenness, and profanity. He mocked the Christian faith. After a series of events, however, he became a Christian in 1748, while still in his early twenties. He was not immediately ready to fulfill God's high purposes for his life. God had much work to do in changing Newton's character. Sanctification and spiritual maturity do not take place overnight in any of our lives.

Newton began to realize that he could no longer participate in the black African slave trade. But he did not initially know what else he should do or even *could* do. God enabled him to leave the slave trade and to become a tide surveyor back in England. In one of his letters, Newton wrote that the offer of this job had been "unsought and unexpected...The good hand of the Lord was in this event." But God did not intend for Newton to live out the rest of his days as a tide surveyor.

Years passed. John Newton *eventually* realized that God was calling him into the ministry. He was not ordained into the Church of England until 1764, however, *sixteen years* after becoming a Christian and *five years* after deciding that he should become a minister. He was almost forty years old by the time he first stepped into a pulpit of his own.

The many years of waiting were not wasted. During those long years, Newton became an avid student of prayer. He enjoyed hours of "divine communion" alone with God, sometimes on board a ship, other times while hiking around the countryside. He found a wise mentor in the company of another ship captain who was a mature Christian. Newton later wrote in a letter: "I was all ears; he not only increased my understanding, but his teaching warmed my heart. He encouraged me to open my mouth in social prayer; he taught me the advantage of Christian conversation; he put upon me an attempt to make my profession more public, and to venture to speak for God." Newton developed many Christian friendships and immersed himself in reading the best authors of theology. God slowly guided his life, using all the methods we have been exploring in this book. In the meantime, God worked on Newton's character.

Newton said that God's timing is like the timing of the tide, which no human being can speed up or slow down. We must wait for God's timing to take effect in the unfolding of our lives and destinies. Listen to these incredible words that Newton wrote, during his years of waiting to become an ordained minister: "It is sufficient that He knows how to dispose of me, and that He both can and will do what is best. To Him I commend myself. I trust that His will and my true interest are inseparable."

Newton went on to write the beloved hymn *Amazing Grace* and to preach until he was more than eighty years old. The sixteen years of waiting, spiritual growth, character change, and seeking God's counsel were to bear much fruit. Even today, centuries later, Newton's life impacts our own as we sing his marvelous hymns.[gg]

Waiting on God is also illustrated in the fascinating life of George Mueller. I have already told some stories pertaining to his well-known ministry to thousands of orphans in England. As a young man and a new Christian, Mueller initially felt that God was calling him to be a missionary. In his early twenties, he left Germany, his country of birth, to briefly work as a missionary to Jewish communities in England. Then, for several decades, he became occupied with his ministry to orphans. His call to be a missionary had to sit on the "back-burner" for about five decades. Talk about waiting! Starting at the age of seventy-one, Mueller finally received God's marching orders regarding his missionary calling. Between the ages of seventy-one and eighty-eight years old, Mueller traveled to forty two countries on three continents, preaching and ministering as an itinerant missionary.[hh] Even at seventy years of age, a person can find new beginnings!

So do not despair! You have probably heard some variation of the modern day proverb: if God wanted to grow a cucumber He could do it in a summer. It takes years to grow a mighty oak! It may take years (or even decades) for us to fully understand God's highest purposes for our lives, and perhaps further decades of waiting until those purposes come to pass. In the meantime, God continues to mature our character as we yield to Him.

I am quite excited to think that some of God's highest purposes for my own life might be revealed and fulfilled in my fifties, sixties, seventies, or even eighties! That might be true for you too. God did not send Moses to confront Pharaoh and to lead His people out of Egypt until Moses was eighty. All that you have been through up until this point of your life (*especially* the difficult times) are the preparation of your character *for what is yet to come.* Many of the great characters of the Bible (Joseph, David, and Ruth) had to go through some years of trial, tragedy, struggle, and difficulty (probably mixed with some confusion and a lot of uncertainty) before God revealed their highest destiny. So take heart! Move forward with hope and anticipation! At any age, God can still use you to do mighty things!

Building Skills, Knowledge, Relationships, and Finances

God also uses the time of waiting to help us prepare our *abilities* and our *circumstances* for the next steps, even if we do not recognize how these are being prepared. Perhaps we are learning a *new skill.* Perhaps we are *increasing our knowledge.* Perhaps we are *forming relationships* that will become critical to God's purposes for our lives. Perhaps we are *building our finances.* We must exercise faith and trust as we yield to what God is doing in our lives. He knows *what* and *who* we are going to need when His next purposes for our lives are ultimately revealed.

God may be using the time to get other people ready who will be part of our evolving circumstances. For example, we might pray for years regarding who we should marry. We might wonder why God is taking so long to answer our prayers for guidance. It might very well be that God needs that time to work in the life of that future spouse. Perhaps they are not yet a Christian when we first begin to pray. Perhaps there are areas of their life that need to be worked on and we are being spared the grief of living with them while certain sin, wrong attitudes, or old emotional baggage are being dealt with. Perhaps they are spending years in intensive education.

Perhaps they are battling an illness. Perhaps they are in another relationship and need time to recognize why that other person is not the best partner for them. God knows what He is doing and He will bring them into our life when the time is right.

Perhaps God needs that time to work in our lives, too! My husband and I met in our late twenties. We often joke that, if we had met in our early twenties, we would not even have dated one another! God needed those extra years to mold and shape us so that we became reasonably ready to get along!

Spiritual Warfare

After we have prayed about something, we do not always see all that is happening in response to our prayer. It may look like *nothing* is happening. *Much* might, in fact, be happening that is *invisible* to us, not just in the circumstances and the people around us, but in the supernatural realm. A good example of this is found in Daniel 10. Daniel had prayed. He did not receive a response for twenty one days. On the twenty-first day, an angel spoke with Daniel and said this: "Do not be afraid, Daniel. Since the *first day* that you set your mind to gain understanding and to humble yourself before your God, *your words were heard*, and I have come in response to them. But the prince of the Persian kingdom resisted me *twenty-one days*. Then Michael…came to help me, because I was detained there with the king of Persia."[120]

The topic of spiritual warfare is beyond the scope of this book. I mention it because we need to remember that God is never asleep. He hears us the very moment we pray. He is not distracted, disinterested or too busy for us. There are reasons for a delayed response. We do not always know what is happening behind the scenes, in either the natural or the supernatural realm. We may never find out. We must *trust* that God is, *in fact*, at work behind the scenes, and that He will answer us in due season.

---

[120]　Daniel 10:12-13

Retreats

During a season of waiting it is sometimes useful to go on a "retreat" if that is possible—to find a place of silence and solitude where we can pray, meditate, and seek God. I love my family cottage for that reason. I love to sit on the deck overlooking the lake. I love to watch the birds, the squirrels, and the sunset. Even if I still do not hear God's voice on a particular issue, I at least feel refreshed, recharged and ready for another period of waiting.

If I cannot go away for a while, I find ways at home to do the same thing. I love to go for a long walk, or to putter in my garden, or to "retreat" to a warm bathtub, or to sip on a hot cup of tea in a quiet corner away from the family fray. Waiting on God can be restful and restorative if we let it be. In these moments of retreat, God may not speak to me about the issue that I am waiting to hear from Him on… but I can still just soak in His love and presence, trusting that *the hour will come* when He will speak. My only task is to be ready to listen.

God is Never Actually Silent

I do not believe that God is ever truly silent. Why do I say that? His Word is readily available to most of us on this earth and we can hear from Him the very moment we dust it off and open its pages. God has a lot to say to all of us. It may not be what *we* want to hear in our immediate circumstances (or to hear at all). What we read in our daily devotions might not seem as relevant as what *we* think God should be speaking to us about. But as long as we have a Bible, we cannot accuse God of being silent. We have sixty six books within the Bible that we can keep ourselves occupied reading while we are waiting to hear God's specific guidance and counsel on a particular issue. As we read the Bible day by day, God will speak to us. The day will come that He will address the specific question that we have asked. He will one day speak to us through His Word, but also through some or all of the other ways that we have been talking about in this book. In the meantime, He is not silent. He has a lot of other matters that He wants to talk to us about! Perhaps those other matters need to come first!

Further Waiting

Even after God does speak and does reveal His counsel and guidance, we may still have to wait for God's purposes to come to pass. God may, for example, *tell us* that we should go back to university. We may not be able to *do* this right away. We might have to finish a work commitment. We might have to save up more money. We might have to wait to be accepted into a particular program. We might have to wait for the right timing and the right circumstances. Even after God *speaks*, there might be a further season of waiting for God to *act* in our circumstances or to *provide* something we need. We might as well learn to enjoy the wait.

The Waiting Will End

The season of waiting will end. In all my legal cases, the judge or jury always *eventually* responded to me. Behind the scenes, while I had waited, they had been busy, carefully and diligently preparing their response to all that I had articulated. In the same way, we can trust that the counsel and guidance of God *will come.* God will do more than speak to us. God will fulfill His purposes in our lives, in due season. He loves us. He will be our Shepherd. He will also provide what we need. He will equip us and help us to *fulfill* all that He *reveals* to us. He can be trusted. Wait for Him!

...walking in the way of your laws, we wait for you...
Isaiah 26:8

Wait for the Lord; be strong and take heart and wait for the Lord.
Psalm 27:14

We wait in hope for the Lord...May your unfailing love rest upon us,
O Lord, even as we put our hope in you.
Psalm 33:20, 22

15.

Correcting Counsel: Being Restored to the Right Path

...whoever heeds correction shows prudence...
Proverbs 15:5

...he who hates correction is stupid.
Proverbs 12:1

*I thought about the wrong direction in which I was headed,
and turned around and came running back to you.*
Psalm 119:59-60 (LB)

One of my favorite cases that I handled in my years of practicing law involved a well-educated professional couple. They had both been senior employees at a large bank. In the early period of the bank computerizing its records, they had devised a way to defraud the bank of a large sum of money.

Before the fraud was discovered, they had taken the money and skipped the country.

For the next few years, they enjoyed themselves, traveling in luxury around the world. They eventually started new lives overseas, settling down and finding new careers in a foreign country. Over the course of time, seeking pleasure became boring. They felt empty and directionless. They started to search spiritually. As a result, both of them became Christians and started on a fresh path in their lives. It was not long, however, before they started to feel uneasy about the money that they had dishonestly taken. They sought the counsel of other Christians. They prayed. God impressed upon them that they had to confess to their past crime and pay whatever penalty came their way.

So there they were, in my office one day, having recently returned to Canada. They wanted to confess to what they had done. They were ready to face whatever consequences ensued. I admired their courage! They strongly believed that getting off the wrong path and finding the right path for their new lives meant resolving this outstanding issue from their past.

Discussions began with the police, the bank, and the prosecutor assigned to the case. Initially, all three of those entities wanted a stiff prison sentence to deter others from this kind of sophisticated electronic "white collar" crime. The authorities were finally convinced, however, that such a sentence would deter people like my clients from voluntarily admitting their crime and trying to make matters right. My clients still had a sum of money that they were willing to give back. If allowed to return to their new careers overseas, they were prepared to make further restitution out of their future paycheques. A deal was struck and they were allowed to return to their new roots overseas without ever serving a day in prison. God blessed their honesty, integrity, and bravery—their desire to pursue a right path no matter what the cost. Although they did not escape all the consequences of the wrong path that they had pursued, God lovingly helped them to leave that path behind and to move forward, without having to look over their shoulders for their past to catch up with them.

Straying from the Right Path

All of us will, at one time or another, find ourselves lost and on a wrong path. Sometimes we will have deliberately and rebelliously strayed. We will have purposely done something wrong. Other times, we will have just drifted. We all "fall asleep at the wheel" sometimes, or go through periods where we become lukewarm about spiritual matters. We wake up one day and realize that we have lost our way.

Psalm 106:13 records what happened to the Israelites after God so miraculously brought them out of Egypt. After God supernaturally brought them through the parted waters of the Red Sea and so dramatically saved them from their enemies, they initially sang His praise. "But," the psalmist tells us, "they soon forgot what he had done and did not wait for his counsel."

Have you ever had this happen? God delivers you from difficult circumstances; perhaps He heals some sickness or provides for some great need you have. He helps you through a tough time. He defeats your enemies. He guides you along a treacherous path. But once you are "safe" and life is good again, how easy it is to grow spiritually lukewarm and to stop daily, intimate communion with God. How easy it is to *drift* away from God and His counsel. Other times, we *consciously* rebel or *deliberately* turn our backs on God because the pleasures of this world are too distracting and enticing.

There are consequences to either *drifting* from the counsel of God or *rebelling* against it. Psalm 107:10-12 warns: "Some sat in darkness and the deepest gloom, prisoners suffering in iron chains, for they had rebelled against the words of God and despised the counsel of the Most High. So he subjected them to bitter labor; they stumbled and there was no one to help."

There is further warning in Psalm 81: "Hear, O my people, and I will warn you—if you would but listen to me....But my people would not listen to me; Israel would not submit to me. So I gave them over to their stubborn hearts to follow their own devices."[121]

Proverbs gives us even more dire warnings about ignoring the wisdom and counsel of God. Proverbs 1:24-32 states: "...since you rejected me when I called and no one gave heed when I stretched out my hand, since you ignored all my advice and would not accept my rebuke, I in turn will laugh at your disaster; I will mock when calamity overtakes you—when calamity overtakes you like a storm, when disaster sweeps over you like a whirlwind, when distress and trouble overwhelm you. Then they will call to me but I will not answer; they will look for me but will not find me. Since they hated knowledge and did not choose to fear the Lord, since they would not accept my advice and spurned my rebuke, they will eat the fruit of their ways and be filled with the fruit of their schemes. For the waywardness of the simple will kill them and the complacency of fools will destroy them..." These are harsh words that show the consequences of ignoring the counsel of God and of refusing His knowledge and wisdom. It is no light matter to stray off of the right path in life.

Perhaps the greatest consequence of rejecting God's words and His ways is that He no longer hears our prayers when we sin. Isaiah 59:2 states that "your iniquities have separated you from your God; your sins have hidden his face from you, so that he will not hear." Isaiah 59:10 reveals the further consequences of being separated from communion with God: "Like the blind we grope along the wall, feeling our way like men without eyes. At midday we stumble as if it were twilight; among the strong, we are like the dead." Isaiah also warned: "'Woe to those who go to great depths to hide their plans from

---

the Lord[122]...Woe to the obstinate children, ' declares the Lord, 'to those who carry out plans that are not mine. [123]'"

In the New Testament, these truths are affirmed. In John 9:31, it is written: "We know that God does not listen to sinners. He listens to the godly man who does his will." In John 12:35b, Jesus said: "The man who walks in the dark does not know where he is going."

Hope for the Wayward

But there is *hope* for those who are prepared to truly repent of their waywardness. It is never too late. The message of both the Old and the New Testaments is that God wants to redeem us, heal us, restore us, forgive us, wash away our sins, and give us another chance. Jesus died for sinners. That includes you and it includes me. In 1 John 1:9, John wrote to his fellow Christians: "If we confess our sins, he is faithful and just and will forgive us our sins and purify us from all unrighteousness." John asserted that all Christians sin from time to time. In the very next verse, John wrote: "If we claim we have not sinned, we make him out to be a liar and his word has no place in our lives." In 1 John 2:1-2, John then continued: "My dear children, I write this to you so that you will not sin. But if anybody does sin, we have one who speaks to the Father in our defense—Jesus Christ, the Righteous One. He is the atoning sacrifice for our sins, and not only for ours but also for the sins of the whole world."

If we repent of our sins and confess them to God, then God forgives us and restores us. We are then back in an intimate relationship with Him. We can come boldly to His throne of grace. God can then guide us towards the right and best path for our lives. *There is room at the Cross for all of us, no matter what we have done!*

---

[122] Isaiah 29:15
[123] Isaiah 30:1

Psalm 107:10-12 speaks about the darkness and deepest gloom that envelopes those who rebel against God and despise His counsel. But note the very next verses, in Psalm 107:13-15: "Then they cried to the Lord in their trouble, and he saved them from their distress. He brought them out of darkness and the deepest gloom and broke away their chains. Let them give thanks to the Lord for his unfailing love and his wonderful deeds for men."

We also quoted earlier from Isaiah about the consequences of following our own wayward plans. Isaiah goes on to affirm that there is yet hope, forgiveness, healing, and restoration for those who repent. Isaiah spoke these words from God: "I live in a high and holy place, but also with him who is contrite and lowly in spirit, to revive the spirit of the lowly and to revive the heart of the contrite....I have seen his ways, but I will heal him; *I will guide him* and restore comfort to him."[124]

David knew all too well what these words were about. Although King David is described as being a man close to God's heart, he rebelled against God. At the lowest point of his life, he committed adultery and then murder.[125] David is an example of a man who confessed his wrongdoing and truly repented. David deeply grieved that He had offended God and had broken fellowship with Him. God lovingly restored David. King David was a man who well understood the dangers of the wrong paths in life and the wondrous blessing of the right path.

Other great men of the Bible made mistakes, rebelled, or ignored God. From Moses to Jacob to Jonah, we read of men who lost their way but whom God lovingly restored. The key is always genuine repentance, which can simply be defined as making a 180-degree turn from our wrongdoing. Instead of heading towards sin, we must flee the other way.

I have already shared the story of how I became a committed Christian at the age of nineteen. I had found myself

---

[124] Isaiah 57:15, 18
[125] 2 Samuel 11

literally lost, late at night, in a small town in Greece, after a night of drinking. Prior to that night, I had spent a year or two drinking, partying, and pursuing many empty pleasures in life. Almost all of my friends at that time were not Christians. I had been backpacking around Europe for a number of months, searching for meaning and purpose in life. I had traveled down some wrong paths. That dark night in Greece, God heard my prayer of confession and repentance. He heard my cry for help. He helped me find my way back to my hotel that night. He also helped me find a much better path for my life.

Over the years, even after becoming a committed Christian, I have wandered onto other wrong paths. Some of those wrong paths have been in my *interior world*. I have walked down paths of unforgiveness, bitterness, resentment, anger, jealousy, greed, worry, and selfishness. I have learned that the wrong paths of the *interior* world of our souls can be more treacherous than the wrong paths of the *exterior* world of our life circumstances. The wrong paths in the inner world usually lead to wrong paths in the outer world, if we do not get off of those paths soon enough. Over and over, I have experienced God's forgiveness, mercy, grace, healing, and restoration. When I have cried out to Him, in confession and repentance, He has always helped me find my way back to the right path for my life.

You might relate to this. Perhaps you have drifted—whether through fatigue, distraction, confusion or complacency. Perhaps you have deliberately rebelled and consciously disobeyed God. Perhaps you have been enticed by sexual immorality or the pleasures of seeking riches in this world above all else. Perhaps you have chosen dishonest gain. Perhaps you have lied to spare yourself the consequences of your actions. Perhaps you have chosen to be motivated by hatred, anger, bitterness, malice, revenge, jealousy, or selfish ambition. However you have strayed, there is always a way back. There is always another chance. God places no limit on the number of times He will forgive us. We are never beyond the reach of God's mercy, forgiveness, and grace. On the cross, Jesus died for *all* of our sins, past, present, and future. I joyfully repeat that most wonderful truth: there is room at the Cross *for all of us* to unload our weary burdens of sin.

Taking Our Footsteps Seriously

We should not, however, seek "cheap grace" by getting into a habitual sin/habitual confession pattern. We will sow what we reap even if God forgives—He does not always spare us the logical consequences of our sin. After David committed adultery and murder, God allowed certain negative consequences to come into David's life. Even after David confessed his sin, God took the life of the child that had resulted from David's adultery. God allowed later troubles into David's family life.[126] God forgave David and went on to bring further blessing in David's life, but He did not spare David all of the consequences of his wrongdoing. This is one of the reasons why we should never lightly stray onto a wrong path.

How Do We Know We are on a Wrong Path?

Sometimes it is obvious to us that we have strayed onto a wrong path, especially if we deliberately rebel and disobey. Other times, it is not so obvious. We can know we are on the wrong path by the same means we can discern the right path. Think back to what we have been discussing in previous chapters. Ask yourself: what does the *Word* say about what you are doing and where you are heading? If you are doing something contrary to the Word, then you are on the wrong path (no matter how much you try to rationalize). If you are troubled in your *spirit*, full of turmoil or confusion, anger or fear, hatred or discontent, boredom or bitterness, then you are straying off of the right path. As soon as you lose your peace,

---

[126] 2 Samuel 12, and following

your joy, your contentment, or your hope, you have lost your way, even if it is still just in your inner world.

If it is still unclear to you whether or not you are on the right path or the wrong path, get the *counsel of others*. Seek out someone more mature in their Christian walk who can give you some sound advice.

Sometimes *circumstances* tell us that we are on the wrong path. We have already said that the right path is sometimes dark and difficult. Just because our way becomes difficult (full of opposition or obstacles) does not necessarily mean that we are on the wrong path. But if we take a certain path for quite some time and it brings us nothing but trouble and grief—if it brings destruction, hurt, conflict, moral compromise, or "static" in our relationship with God or others, then it is time to take a closer look at where we are going. The right path might be difficult, but it is never destructive. The right path will not lead us to deliberately hurt others. The right path might cause us to face opposition, but it should never cause us to initiate strife. The right path might shake us to the very core of our being in the darkest hours of the night, but it will not lead us to moral compromise.

Sometimes, if we persist in our waywardness, God sends one or more people across our path to point out our wrongdoing. This can be painful. It is one of the ways that God disciplines us. If we are wise, we will pay attention to those who try to rebuke or correct us. Proverbs 15:31-32 tells us that "he who listens to a life-giving rebuke will be at home among the wise...whoever heeds correction gains understanding." Proverbs 17:10 observes that "a rebuke impresses a man of discernment more than a hundred lashes a fool." My prayer for you and for me is that we become more attentive to those who try to correct us. No one likes to be criticized, judged, corrected, or rebuked, but if the rebuke is warranted we are wise to pay heed to it! The next time someone criticizes you, instead of getting angry and upset, pause to consider if there is even a kernel of truth in what they are saying.

God Himself will help you to discern if you are on the wrong path. Remember that He is your Shepherd. A shepherd uses the curved end of his staff to wrap gently (or, sometimes, as forcefully as need be) around the neck of a sheep who has headed towards danger. God will always pursue a sheep that has strayed off the path. His staff brings that sheep back towards the Shepherd and back towards the safe path, if the sheep is willing to be led. God cares about every single sheep![127]

Encouragement to Correct Your Course

I encourage you, my friend, if you are walking down a wrong road, to seek God and His help. It does not matter what road you are presently on. Whether you are an alcoholic, an inmate serving time for a crime you committed, an adulterer, a person who has grown weary of living for "self," a person who has become bored with the paths of your own creation, a liar, a cheater, or a thief—God can and will forgive you if you ask Him to. God sent His beloved Son to die for your sins and to provide the means of being reconciled to God. *It is not too late to find your way back to a good path for your life.* No matter what you have done or where you have been, God loves you. He is waiting to forgive, heal, help, and restore you. *He can help you change the course of your life.* Although you might not escape all of the consequences of your wrong ways, God will, in His mercy, help you deal with any consequences that He allows. He will help you to make things right. Like the clients I told you about, who made peace with the bank they had defrauded, God will help you to deal with your past so that you can forever leave it behind. A fresh and new chapter of your life is waiting to be written. A much better path beckons. There is *exquisite hope* for your future!

---

[127] See, for example, Luke 15:3-7 (the parable of the lost sheep)

Then they cried to the Lord in their trouble,
and he saved them from their distress.
He brought them out of darkness and the deepest gloom
and broke away their chains.
Psalm 107:13-14

If we confess our sins, he is faithful and just
and will forgive us our sins…
1 John 1:9

Jesus said: "I have come into the world as a light,
so that no one who believes in me should stay in darkness.
John 12:46

For you were like sheep going astray, but now you have returned
to the Shepherd and Overseer of your souls.
1 Peter 2:25

16.

Acting on the Counsel of God

Love the Lord and follow his plan for your lives.
Cling to him and serve him enthusiastically.
Joshua 22:5b (LB)

In the years leading up to World War II, Adolf Hitler began to disseminate his views on the Jewish race in an autobiography called *Mein Kampf*. He provided advance notice in his book, and later in his speeches, about his plans to erase the Jewish race. Some people, in Germany and abroad *knew* what Hitler planned to do, yet they failed to *act* on it. Knowledge without action was futile. About six million Jews died because this *knowledge* was not translated into *action* soon enough.

In 2005, the media was saturated with images of the devastating flood in New Orleans after Hurricane Katrina. Experts had predicted for years that the levees surrounding the city would not hold if a Category 4 or 5 hurricane hit the city. Experts had predicted that the extent of the potential damage would be huge because the city was built below sea level and would rapidly fill up with deep water if the levees gave way. The predictions came to pass. It is estimated that it will take over 100 billion dollars to repair the damage. Numerous lives have been lost and hundreds of thousands displaced. *Knowledge* was not turned into *action*.

In previous chapters, we have been discussing how to seek and to receive God's counsel, on matters large or small, major or minor. God wants to speak to us and He will speak to us if we listen. It is not enough, however, to receive *knowledge* of what God wants us to do. We must *act* on the counsel He gives us. We must *step out* in faith and *fulfill* the plans and purposes He has revealed to us. This is important, whether God has spoken to us about some minor everyday matter or about the highest, most significant purposes of our lives.

In Luke 6:46-49, Jesus spoke these powerful words to His followers: "Why do you call me 'Lord, Lord,' and do not do what I say? I will show you what he is like who comes to me and *hears* my words and *puts them into practice*. He is like a man building a house, who dug down deep and laid the foundation on rock. When a flood came, the torrent struck that house but could not shake it, because it was well built. But the one who *hears* my words and *does not put them into practice* is like a man who built a house on the ground without a foundation. The moment the torrent struck that house, it collapsed and its destruction was complete."

In Luke 8:21, Jesus again talked about *hearing* God's word and then *putting it into practice*. This was just after He told the parable about the farmer who went out to sow his seed. Some of the seed fell off the path, some fell on rock, some fell among thorns and some fell on good soil. The seed represents the word of God. The soil represents the hearts of those who receive the word. In each case, the person *hears* the word of God. For various reasons, the first three categories of people do not go on to *act* on the word as time passes. Only the fourth kind of person is fruitful and faithful over time. Jesus explained, in Luke 8:15, "the seed on good soil stands for those with a noble and good heart, who *hear* the word, *retain it*, and by persevering *produce* a crop." The hearing is translated into action.

This echoes what God had spoken to the prophet Ezekiel many years before. He said: "My people come to you, as they usually do, and sit before you to *listen* to your words, but *they do not put them into practice.*"[128] This had been the failing of the Israelites under Moses who *heard* what God commanded and promised, but did not *act* in accordance with what God had said. Psalm 78:57b tells us that "like a crooked arrow, they missed the target of God's will"(LB).

In Psalm 95:7-8, the psalmist exhorted: "Today, if you *hear his voice*, do not harden your hearts..." After God speaks to us, He wants us to respond. He wants us to act. It may be something we do in our interior world: confessing a sin He has shown us, forgiving someone, changing a negative attitude, uprooting bitterness, or controlling our temper. Or it might mean action in the physical world: going somewhere, saying something, giving to someone, performing some task, or setting off on a new path.

We established earlier that God is not some cosmic fortune cookie, bearing a message that we can accept or reject on a whim. We cannot come to Him with idle curiosity, "checking out" His will, and then casually cast that revelation aside if it does not appeal to us. If we *hear* God's voice, we must *obey* Him, especially if we want to hear from Him again. God *tells* us His plans and purposes so that we can *fulfill* them. God gives us detailed guidance so we can act on it.

The apostle Paul understood this. In Philippians 2:13, he said that "it is God who works in you to will and to *act* according to his good purpose." Once God has revealed His "good purpose" for a season of our lives, we must set our wills to act according to that knowledge. Paul wrote similar words in Ephesians 2:10: "For we are God's workmanship, created in Christ Jesus, to *do* good works, which God prepared in advance

---

128 Ezekiel 33:31

for us to do." We are not meant to just accumulate knowledge about God, His ways and His plans. We are meant to *hear His voice* and then to *do* those good works that He created us for.

God will help us, if we are willing to act on what He has told us. Paul tells us in Hebrews 13:20-21: "May the God of peace...*equip you* with everything good for *doing* His will." God will give us the energy, faith, finances, resources, and all the help that we need to carry out His revealed will. Our part is to *hear His voice* and then to *step out in obedient faith* to follow His revealed counsel.

It is also important not to dither or delay. Hannah Whitall Smith advised: "The first moment that we clearly see a thing to be right is always the moment when it is easy to do it—If we don't act once the door opens and the way is clear, we may lose the golden opportunity...and obedience becomes more and more difficult with every moment's delay."[ii]

And so I urge you, my friends, as you learn to listen to God's voice, also learn to trust and obey Him. My prayer for each of you is that you find God's highest purposes for your life—that you understand His plan for you, that you discover His will in all its fullness, that you see which is the best path to follow. But I am also praying for you that you achieve those highest purposes, fit into that divine plan, embrace His will, and set your feet to follow that best path with energy, excitement, and enthusiasm. Let none of us be crooked arrows, missing the target of God's will!

So be strong and...observe what the Lord requires:
Walk in his ways, and keep his...laws and requirements...
so that you may prosper in all that you do and wherever you go...
1 Kings 2:2-3

...the man who does the will of God lives forever.
1 John 2:17

May the God of peace...equip you with everything good
for doing his will.
Hebrews 13:20-21

17.

A Life of Highest Purposes

*For we are God's workmanship, created in Christ Jesus to do
good works, which God prepared in advance for us to do.*
Ephesians 2:10

*All the days ordained for me were written in your book
before one of them came to be.*
Psalm 139:16

*...he who began a good work in you will carry it on
to completion until the day of Christ Jesus.*
Philippians 1:6

One day, in the spring of 2005, a man named Brian Nichols
was in an Atlanta court room, facing a rape charge. Witnesses
allege that the following events occurred. Nichols suddenly
overpowered the deputy guarding him, stole her gun and shot
the judge. He then shot the court reporter and the sheriff's
deputy who pursued him. After killing these three people,
Nichols carjacked a series of vehicles as he made his getaway.

A city-wide manhunt ensued. Within hours, Nichols was believed to have killed a fourth person.

During the night, Nichols followed a woman named Ashley Smith to her apartment door. He forced her into her apartment at gunpoint. He then held her hostage in her own home, a home she had only been living in for two days! Smith was held captive by Nichols for more than seven hours.

Ashley Smith had seen this man on the news earlier in the day and was well aware of who he was and what he had done. Yet she managed to remain calm. Smith talked with her captor about her own difficult past, her Christian faith and her family. She also talked with him about how God has a purpose for each person. Smith had been reading a best-selling Christian book that talked about some of God's general purposes for all of our lives. She read a part of that book to her captor and also a passage from the Bible.

Despite the fact that this man had an alleged history of violence and crime, Smith gave him hope that his life might yet have a good purpose in God's eyes. She told him that God could use him, even in prison. After talking for several hours, Smith asked her captor if she could go to pick up her young daughter. He undoubtedly knew that she would call the police the moment she was free, but he let her go anyway. Smith did, in fact, call the police, who were able to take Nichols into custody without further harm to anyone.

One aspect of the story that has struck me is this: Ashley Smith, at one point, apparently asked her captor why he had chosen *her* home. He said that it was a *random* choice. Do you believe that it was random? Smith did not believe these events were random. She told her captor that she believed that God had led him to her place and that there was purpose in their meeting. God allowed this man to choose Smith's home because this was the setting in which this man could be convinced to put down his weapons, stop his killing spree, and permit himself to be captured peacefully, without harm to himself or further victims. Nichols' long conversation with

Smith provided hope and potential redemption for this man. I absolutely agree with Ashley Smith that God *can* use a man like Nichols, if he is willing to let God work in his life. God may yet have good purposes for this man. It is not too late for this man to find a better path for his life. His life still has potential opportunity for meaning and significance.

Ashley Smith has written her own book, telling her story in more detail. This event (and its consequent widespread publicity in the media) was surely one of the significant purposes of *her* life.

The pastor who had baptized Smith in 1992 agrees with the perspective that this episode was a divine appointment. This was not some meaningless, random event. The encounter between Smith and Nichols was surely a divine encounter, with God's fingerprints all over it. How awesome that God *could speak* to Smith even in the midst of such a frightening hostage situation. How awesome that Smith could calmly respond to the inner prompting to show compassion to this man, to speak with him, to listen to him and to offer him hope.[ii]

God is at work throughout our world. In the process of writing this book, I read many books and articles. I came across some fascinating Christian websites. I read the profiles and biographies of dozens of interesting Christians, many from past centuries, and just as many who are currently impacting our world. I became so enthralled by the stories I was reading that hours passed night after night. When I looked at my watch some nights, it was midnight all too soon!

I read about an American athlete who had wandered from her Christian faith. When she made the decision to come back to God and to seek His forgiveness and restoration, she overcame various obstacles to win an Olympic gold medal. She is a wonderful example of a woman who realized she was on the wrong path and purposed to find the right path for her life. In another article, a well-known tennis star told the story of how God led him down a path that pinnacled in a Grand Slam title. I read about a former Playboy centerfold model who committed her life to Christ and now works with orphans and other needy children in the Third World.

In yet further articles, I found more awesome biographies. A Hollywood animator, who worked on such beloved movies as *Toy Story* and *Finding Nemo*, shared about all that God has done in his life. I came across an update on the life of Nicky Cruz, former New York City teen gang leader. He had once been heavily involved in a world of violent gang warfare, narcotics, stealing, and heavy drinking. After stabbing several teenagers and being in jail a dozen times, he became a Christian at a David Wilkerson youth rally for teenage gangs. God has used Nicky Cruz to reach countless others for Christ over the past four decades.[kk] I read about how God had guided astronauts, politicians, actresses, and business executives.

Each of these individuals has discovered God's unique plans and purposes for their lives. And God has not finished with them yet! God is *calling* and *leading* such an amazing variety of people in our generation—people from such diverse backgrounds. God is at work amongst the poorest of the poor in the Third World. God is also at work among the brilliant men and women of the Ivy League. The Veritas Forum at Harvard, and other stellar universities, has brought together some of the brightest Christian minds of this generation.[ll]

There are also so many books written about great men and women of years gone by who came into personal relationship with God and found high purposes for their lives: the explorer Christopher Columbus, the artist Michelangelo, the brilliant philosopher and physicist Blaise Pascal, 18th century British anti-slavery activist William Wilberforce, medical missionary and explorer David Livingstone, classical composers George Frideric Handel and J.S. Bach, prison reformer Elizabeth Fry, poets William Wordsworth and T.S. Eliot, novelists Leo Tolstoy and Fyodor Dostoevsky, Mother Teresa, the Nobel prize-winning nun who worked tirelessly for the poor in Calcutta, and so many others—artists, scientists, royalty, street beggars, and criminals—people who became extraordinary men and women of their times after seeking God and His counsel.

I encourage you to spend time reading the profiles and biographies of Christians, past and present, who have *found God* and *then found God's unique purposes* for their lives. Great men and women, past and present, have also received God's intimate counsel regarding the more minor *everyday* details of their lives. If you want inspiration for your life...if you want to better understand how various Christians have found and followed the best path for their lives...if you want more examples of how others have had daily dialogue with a personal God...then surf the internet, visit the library, and browse the bookstore.

Read the full life stories of men and women like Corrie ten Boom, George Mueller, Eric Lidell, Dwight L. Moody, George Washington Carver, David Wilkerson, Brother Andrew, former President Jimmy Carter, Chuck Colson, and others that I have referred to in this book. I have mentioned only one or two examples of how each of them sought and received God's guidance. Their life stories are rich with many more examples. Their life stories show how they *integrated* prayer, Bible study, advice from wise counselors, keen observation of developing circumstances, and in some cases, even prophetic words and visions, into their ongoing understanding of God's will for their remarkable lives.

As I enjoyed article after article, book after book, I thought about what I had written at the start of this book. It does not matter whether you are black or white, Asian or Hispanic, living in the West or in the Third World—God has a wonderful purpose for you. It does not matter if you are rich or poor, starting life in the ghetto, or working in the White House. God has a role for you to play that matters in His Kingdom. It does not matter what your gift or your talent or your interest is. It does not matter if *you* think you have no talent. God can show you hidden talents you are not even aware of! God's power working through a humble but yielded human life can change history. God's power is incomparably greater than mere human talent, intellect or physical assets.

God can use you to accomplish His purposes. *It does not matter if you are at the end of your rope or at the top of your game.* God can take your life and instill great significance in it, if you are willing to let Him. Not all of us will become famous. Not all of us will be superstars. *But all of us can matter. All of us can count.* Every one of us was born for a reason. Every one of us is very precious to God. God has plans and purposes for every individual. May each one of us learn the divine details of these unique plans and purposes—that is my daily prayer for myself and for each reader of this book!

Do not be discouraged by thinking that this process of seeking God's counsel seems too complicated, too time-consuming, or too hard. In fact, it is not. Most of all it requires a particular attitude, an attitude of submission and surrender to God, of desiring God's plan for your life, not your own plan. Then it requires an investment of time that can be as little as five minutes a day of prayer and five minutes a day of reading God's Word. After spending that ten minutes a day, you can try to be consciously aware of what the Spirit is saying within you throughout the day and of how God is working in and through the people and circumstances around you. This does not take time. It just takes spiritual alertness as you go about the business of your day. You will acquire wisdom and discernment as you pass your days in this fashion.

It is not too complicated. It is not too time-consuming. It is not too hard. In fact, as I have said many times throughout this book, it is easier and ultimately less time-consuming than trying to figure your life out all on your own. To the extent that seeking God's counsel takes some measure of time, effort, and discipline, it is always worth it!

Let us submit and surrender to our God Most High! Let us desire the right and best path for our lives. Let us cultivate a deeper prayer life and treasure the dialogue we have with God.

Let us never take for granted the privilege that we have of coming boldly to the throne of the Creator and Sustainer of this amazing universe! Let us cherish the Word, seek the Spirit, value the counsel of the wise among us, watch our circumstances with anticipation and alertness, and accumulate our own precious store of godly wisdom and knowledge. Let us not fear or belittle the extraordinary and more unusual ways that God shows up around us.

Let us listen for His voice. Let us wait for Him. Let us become all that God intended for us to become, one day at a time, as we gratefully treasure the counsel of the Most High.

We can never know the full joy and privileges of the life hid with Christ in God until we have learned the lesson of daily and hourly guidance...Above everything else, trust Him. Nowhere is faith more needed than here. He has promised to guide. You have asked Him to do it. And now you must believe that He does, and must take what comes as being His guidance...
Hannah Whitall Smith[mm]

... let us run with perseverance the race marked out for us.
Hebrews 12:1b

...we confidently and joyfully look forward to actually becoming all that God has had in mind for us to be...
Romans 5:2 (LB)

...the Lord Almighty, wonderful in counsel and magnificent in wisdom...
Isaiah 28:29

...your Kingdom come, your will be done...
Matthew 6:10

Appendix A

A Prayer to Accept Christ

If you would like to become a Christian, you can pray this prayer today:

Father, I believe that You exist and that You are God Most High. I believe that Jesus Christ is Your Son, as He claimed to be. I believe that He walked this earth and that He died on the Cross to pay the penalty for the sins of all men and women. I believe that He has risen and is now seated at Your right hand.

I confess that I am a sinner. I confess all known sins and desire to turn from them. I confess that my greatest sin has been ignoring You and rebelling against Your sovereignty in my life. I ask that You would forgive all of my sins, on the basis of what Jesus did on the cross for me. Please wash me so that I am white as snow. Create in me a clean heart! Please remove my sins as far as the east is from the west, as You promised You would. Please give me a fresh, new start in my life.

I ask that You would now live in me by Your Spirit, empowering me to live as I should. I ask that You would show me the best path for my life and help me to walk on it. I give my life to You. I submit and surrender to You and to Your unfailing love. May I be aware of Your loving Presence every day. Thank You!

I pray in faith, in the name of Jesus Christ, Amen.

My friend, if you have prayed this prayer, you have made a new beginning in your life! The Enemy of your soul will start to attack you with doubts and discouraging thoughts over the coming days. Do not listen to him! I encourage you to begin to do what I describe in my book. Get yourself a Bible and begin to read it every day, especially the New Testament. Commit even just five minutes to your reading each day. Pray each day, talking to God as you would talk to a friend. Start by spending even just five minutes a day in prayer. Ask each day to become more and more aware of the Holy Spirit who now lives within you. Find a Bible-believing church and start to make Christian friends.

You are beginning a journey that will bring you life, light, joy, peace, love, strength, great adventure, direction, high purpose, and God's wonderful counsel. Welcome to the family of God and to the fellowship of His people. I am praying for you!

Appendix B

Checklist of Questions that Help to Discern God's Will

As you think through the answers to these questions with respect to any decision you are trying to make, consider whether each answer is a *green light* to proceed forward, a *red light* to not proceed or a *yellow light*, warning you to either proceed with great caution or wait until the guidance is clearer. You can make a chart with three columns if that is helpful, labeled Green, Red, and Yellow. Note which column receives the most checkmarks.

1. Is the proposed action consistent with *general* Biblical principles? Or does the proposed action violate any Biblical principle?

2. Have you received any *specific* Biblical guidance (verses that seem directly applicable to your situation)? Have any of those verses surfaced in your ongoing daily Bible reading? Have they jumped off of the page as you read them? Have any of these verses crossed your path in some interesting manner recently?

3. What was your initial impression in the matter? What were your first thoughts and feelings about the proposed step? Has that initial impression changed? Why?

4. Do you have definite peace about proceeding? Can you act with a clear conscience? Are your sleep and appetite patterns being affected by this decision?

5. Can you step forward with bold faith? Are you confident that God is in this?

6. Does the thought of proceeding bring joy and gratitude into your spirit? Does this proposed action accord with your God-given dreams and desires?

7. Is the proposed action consistent with love? Have you thought about how other people will be impacted?

8. Does the thought of proceeding fill you with energy, excitement, enthusiasm, passion, purpose, inclination, and motivation?

9. Does the thought of proceeding fill you with stress, turmoil, confusion, dread, guilt, fatigue, or a sense of overload? What are you feeling at gut level?

10. Are you being motivated by any wrong thoughts/emotions/ desires, such as revenge, anger, resentment, jealousy, fear, selfish ambition, greed, or pride?

11. Do you feel an inner prompting to proceed or an inner warning to not proceed? Has the inner prompting or the inner warning been persistent over time?

12. Will the proposed action use your best talents? Are you suitably educated, experienced and equipped? Has God gifted you and empowered you in this area?

13. What counsel have you received from your pastor, other spiritual mentor or a Christian professional that you have consulted?

14. What counsel have you received from wise people close to you such as parents, a husband or wife, siblings, adult children, and friends who know you well?

15. Have you received counsel from some applicable book or speaker?

16. How are the circumstances lining up? Do you have the time, money, energy, and opportunity to proceed? Is the "door" open or closed? If it is closed, what obstacles are you facing? Can they be overcome?

17. Can you see God's hand in your evolving circumstances? Are the evolving circumstances an answer to earlier prayers? What does God seem to be doing in the people and events surrounding you? Is something out of the ordinary happening?

18. Does the proposed action seem wise? Would you be acting with common sense, good judgment, mature understanding, and sound knowledge? Do you need to acquire more knowledge before coming to a decision?

19. Will the proposed action honor God and advance His Kingdom? Or are you trying to promote self? If you ask yourself WWJD, what is your honest answer?

20. Has God spoken to you in any "extraordinary" way, e.g. through an unusual dream or an idea that you cannot get out of your mind? (Exercise caution in this area.)

21. Is the proposed action consistent with any earlier guidance that you have received? Or is there a conflict? Is this a radical departure from past direction?

22. Can you proceed right now or is it best to wait? What would be the benefit of waiting?

As you assess your answers, try to discern if, *overall*, the light is green, red, or a cautionary yellow. If you are not sure, wait until the guidance seems clearer! If you want further guidance, pray and ask God to speak to you through His Word, the Spirit, the counsel of others, evolving circumstances, and your inner sense of wisdom and good judgment. God will answer you in due course!

Appendix C

A Prayer to Receive More of the Holy Spirit

If you would like to receive more of the Holy Spirit, you can pray this prayer:

Father, thank You for giving me the Holy Spirit when I became a Christian. Thank You for the indwelling presence of the Holy Spirit in my life. I ask that the Holy Spirit would be my constant Conscience, Counselor, Comforter, and Companion, guiding me into all truth as Jesus promised He would, and guiding me onto the best path for my life. I ask for more of the Holy Spirit. I create room in my heart, mind, and spirit. I confess all known sin, casting off all pride, anger, unforgiveness, bitterness, resentment, envy, selfish ambition, greed, and other wrong thoughts, feelings, and desires. I want nothing to hinder my prayer for more of Your Spirit.

Come Holy Spirit! Come and fill me afresh! Come as a mighty river of living water, flowing deep within me—cleansing, purifying, energizing, refreshing, and empowering me. Come in the fullness of Your power!

Come Holy Spirit! I want an intimate relationship with You. I want You to guide me and counsel me. Show me the Father's highest purposes for my life. Help me to fully submit and surrender to those purposes. Equip and empower me to fulfill those purposes. Help me to always desire the right path for my life.

Please help me to pray. Help me to read the Word faithfully each day. Help me to find wise Christian friends and mentors. Help me to see how You are working in the people and circumstances around me. Help me to see the open doors in my life. Fill me with Your wisdom and with knowledge, discernment, insight, good judgment, and understanding. Fill me until I am overflowing, so that all around me can also be blessed by Your presence and power in my life.

Holy Spirit, I wait for You!

Father, thank You for hearing my prayer and thank You in advance for answering it. Jesus promised that, if we ask for anything in accordance with Your will, You will do it for us. I know that it is Your will for me to be filled and overflowing with Your Spirit. I can therefore be confident that You will answer this prayer.

In Jesus' name I pray, Amen.

Contacting the Author

If you have enjoyed this book and have been blessed by it in some way, the author would love to hear from you. The author can be contacted by e-mail at khenein@rogers.com.

The author is available for speaking engagements on the topic of receiving God's counsel and on other topics of interest to Christians.

Due to the volume of correspondence the author receives, she regrets that she is not able to counsel readers on an individual basis. She apologizes in advance for not responding to mail or e-mail requests for personal counsel.

The author wishes to thank you for reading her book and hopes that she has been a blessing to you. She prays regularly that each reader will receive God's clear counsel for their lives.

Purchasing Further Copies

If you wish to obtain further copies of this book, and you are not able to acquire or order copies at your local bookstore, please note that this book is available on-line as an Adobe e-book. This book can also be purchased on-line at Amazon.com and barnes&noble.com.

Bibliography

Bailey, Faith Coxe. *D.L. Moody*. Chicago, Illinois: Moody Press, 1959.

Bailey, Faith Coxe. *George Mueller*. Chicago, Illinois: Moody Press, 1958.

Bonnke, Reinhard. *Even Greater*. Orlando, Florida: Full Flame, 2004.

Brother Andrew. *For the Love of My Brothers*. Minnesota: Bethany House, 1998.

Brother Andrew. *Light Force*. Michigan: Revell, 2004.

Brother Lawrence. *The Practice of the Presence of God*. (1692 original version, public domain).

Carlson, Carole. *Corrie ten Boom: Her Life, Her Faith*. New York: Jove, 1984.

Caughey, Ellen. *Eric Liddell*. Ohio: Barbour, 2000.

Colson, Charles. *Born Again*. New Jersey: Fleming H. Revell, 1977.

Elliot, Elisabeth. *Through Gates of Splendour*. London, England: Hodder & Stoughton, 1968.

Ellis, William T. *Billy Sunday: The Man and His Message*. Philadelphia, Pennsylvania: John C. Winston, 1936.

Gonzalez-Balado and Playfoot (ed.). *Mother Teresa of Calcutta*. New York: Ballantine, 1985.

Graham, Billy. *Angels*. Nashville, Tennessee: W Publishing Group, 1995.

Hawkins, B. Denise. *Condoleezza Rice's Secret Weapon*. Today's Christian magazine, September/October 2002 issue, Vol. 40, No. 5.

Holt, Rackham. *George Washington Carver: An American Autobiography*. New York: Doubleday and Co., 1943.

Huggett, Joyce. *Listening to God*. Intervarsity Press, 1986.

Lewis, C. S. *Mere Christianity*. Glasgow, Scotland: William Collins Sons & Co., 36ᵗʰ ed., 1982.

Lewis, C. S. *The Problem of Pain*. New York: MacMillan Publishing Company, 1962.

McDowell, Josh. *Evidence That Demands A Verdict*. Volume 1. Nashville, Tennessee: Nelson, 1979.

Michell, Dr. David J. *I Remember Eric Liddell*. Scotland: Archives of the Eric Liddell Centre.

Monroe, Kelly (ed.). *Finding God at Harvard*. Michigan: Zondervan, 1996.

Newton, John. *John Newton: His Autobiography*. Chicago, Illinois: Moody Press.

Norton and Slosser. *The Miracle of Jimmy Carter*. New Jersey: Logos, 1976.

Petersen, William J. *25 Surprising Marriages: Faith-Building Stories from the Lives of Famous Christians*. Michigan: Baker Books, 1997.

Smith, Ashley. *Unlikely Angel*. Michigan: Zondervan, 2005.

Smith, Hannah Whitall. *The Christian's Secret of a Happy Life*. (public domain)

Swenson, Dr. Richard. *More Than Meets the Eye*. Colorado Springs: Navpress, 2000.

Ten Boom, Corrie (with John and Elizabeth Sherill). *The Hiding Place*. New Jersey: Fleming H. Revell Co., 1971.

Ten Boom, Corrie. *Tramp for the Lord*. New Jersey: Fleming H. Revell, 1974.

Wellman, Sam. *Florence Nightingale*. Ohio: Barbour, 1999.

Wilkerson, David. *The Cross and the Switchblade*. New York: Jove, 1978.

Endnotes

Chapter One

[a] From Dr. Henry Blackaby's talk at a Board of Trade luncheon on February 10, 2005 in Toronto, Ontario, Canada.
[b] See, for example, Andrew Morton's biography about the life of Princess Diana, which refers several times to her relationship with New Age practitioner Simone Simmonds.

Chapter Two

[c] This is a fascinating area for further study. Scientific research exploring the origins of the universe continues to be done regarding the microwaves and radio waves that occupy the lower frequencies of the electromagnetic spectrum. Scientists have discovered that space has a cosmic microwave background. Scientists continue to develop theories regarding how sound waves were related to the interaction of matter and light in the gravity field of high density regions of the early universe. Some scientists are trying to connect those early sound waves with the constant low-level noise that is still present in the universe.
[d] If you want to study C.S. Lewis's full argument regarding "the great trilemma," it is presented in more detail in his book *Mere Christianity*, pp. 52.
[e] From Hannah Whitall Smith's *The Christian's Secret of a Happy Life* (public domain).

Chapter Four

[f] Facts from a public talk John Grisham gave at the "Art and Soul" Conference at Baylor University (Waco, Texas) in February, 2000, and from the official Random House website.

Chapter Five

g The 1692 original version of Brother Lawrence's *The Practice of the Presence of God* is in the public domain. For more modernized language, I recommend Frank Laubach's book *Practicing His Presence* (Texas: The Seed Sowers, 1973).

h Howard Norton & Bob Slosser, *The Miracle of Jimmy Carter*, pg. 109.

Chapter Seven

i Chuck Colson's full story is told in his book *Born Again*.

j These facts, and many further fascinating facts about the Bible, can be found in Josh McDowell's *Evidence that Demands a Verdict*, Volume 1, Chapter 1. My legal mind loves the factual evidence presented in this book about many aspects of Christian faith.

k From Dr. David J. Michell's article, *I Remember Eric Liddell*, in the Archives of the Eric Liddell Centre in Scotland.

Chapter Eight

l See Joyce Huggett, *Listening to God*, pg. 39.

m Quote from Hannah Whitall Smith's *The Christian's Secret of a Happy Life* (public domain).

n David Wilkerson, *The Cross and the Switchblade*.

o Brother Andrew, *For the Love of My Brothers*, see especially pages 8, 11 and 12, and chapters 6 and 7.

p Gonzalez-Balado and Playfoot (ed.), *Mother Teresa of Calcutta*.

q Rackham Holt, *George Washington Carver: An American Biography*.

r C.S. Lewis, *The Problem of Pain*.

Chapter Nine

s Information re: CEO network comes from Dr. Henry Blackaby's luncheon address at the Board of Trade in Toronto, Canada on February 10, 2005, and his breakfast address at the Toronto Stock Exchange on October 21, 2005.

t Elisabeth Elliot, *Through Gates of Splendour*, pg. 14.

Chapter Ten

u Faith Coxe Bailey, *George Mueller.*
v From Hannah Whitall Smith's *The Christian's Secret of a Happy Life* (public domain).
w Brother Andrew, *Light Force.*
x Carole Carlson, *Corrie ten Boom: Her Life, Her Faith,* pg. 160.
y Dr. Swenson, *More Than Meets the Eye.*
z Dr. Swenson, *More Than Meets the Eye.*

Chapter Thirteen

aa Reinhard Bonnke, *Even Greater.*
bb Carole Carlson, *Corrie ten Boom: Her Life, Her Faith.*
cc Billy Graham, *Angels.*
dd See, for example, Josh McDowell, *Evidence that Demands a Verdict,* Volume 1.
ee See, for example, Ezekiel 26, 28, 30, 36; Isaiah 13, 14, 34; Jeremiah 31, 51; also see Josh McDowell, *Evidence that Demands a Verdict,* Volume 1.

Chapter Fourteen

ff Sam Wellman, *Florence Nightingale.*
gg John Newton, *John Newton: His Autobiography;* letters and writings of John Newton (public domain).
hh Faith Coxe Bailey, *George Mueller.*

Chapter Sixteen

ii Hannah Whitall Smith, *The Christian's Secret of a Happy Life* (public domain).

Chapter Seventeen

jj Jennifer Schuchmann, *My Life Is a Testimony,* article in *Today's Christian* (July/August 2005 issue); Ashley Smith, *Unlikely Angel; People* magazine, March 28, 2005 issue; details pertaining to what Nichols supposedly said or did are from the allegations of fact provided by witnesses as reported in the above sources.

ᵏᵏ Articles referred to in this and previous paragraph can be found at "Profiles" at www.christianitytoday.com/tc; also see David Wilkerson, *The Cross and the Switchblade* for further background regarding Nicky Cruz.

ˡˡ To read some amazing stories about how God has been moving in Harvard, may I recommend this book: Kelly Monroe (ed.), *Finding God at Harvard*.

ᵐᵐ Hannah Whitall Smith, *The Christian's Secret of a Happy Life* (public domain).